Assessment to Support Learning and Teaching

This book outlines the key problems associated with the intersections of assessment, learning and teaching, and presents guiding principles to effective assessment that schools can follow in order to optimise student outcomes.

Addressing challenges such as competing conceptualisations of assessment, the burden of responsibility on teachers and conflicting views of what effective assessment actually is, this book provides an in-depth analysis of these problems, how they are explored, what factors influence them and their implications for learning and teaching. It proposes practical solutions to address these challenges, supported by 29 case studies that capture examples of practice from Asia, Europe, the USA and Australia. The book concludes with the key features of the effective implementation of assessment reform, based on findings from a variety of scenarios, across different contexts and levels of education.

Providing critical insights and practical guidance, this book is an essential reference for teachers, school leaders and postgraduate students of education.

Dennis Alonzo uses mixed methods in his research on the intersections of curriculum, assessment, equity, evaluation of educational programs and teacher education and development. He works with educational systems and schools to lead their assessment reforms focused on articulating policies, developing assessment resources, implementing professional development and changing teachers' beliefs and practices.

"A powerful overview of the key messages about Assessment to support learning and teaching. Alonzo captures the fundamental purposes – to inform the next steps for teachers and students, with a focus on the interpretations and not stopping with the numbers. The best one-stop-book on the market."

John Hattie, *Laureate Professor Emeritus,*
The University of Melbourne, Australia

"This book on assessment to support learning and teaching is a unique and powerful contribution to assessment research, policy, and practice internationally – outlining the key steps towards system-wide and context-sensitive assessment reform through a range of case studies illustrating the key problems and pitfalls and proposed solutions. A valuable contribution for teachers, researchers and policy-makers everywhere."

Chris Davison, *Emeritus Professor, The University of*
New South Wales, Australia

"This book is a digest version of theories and research on educational assessment for learning and teaching. It answers major questions stakeholders ask and proposes solutions to problems related to the conceptualisation, implementation, and evaluation of assessment. Classroom teachers, school leaders, and policymakers will find the book a treasure-trove full of timely resources in guiding their decision-making at all levels."

Peter Yongqi Gu, *Associate Professor, Victoria University of*
Wellington, New Zealand

Assessment to Support Learning and Teaching

Problems and Solutions

Dennis Alonzo

LONDON AND NEW YORK

Designed cover image: © Andriy Onufriyenko/Getty Images

First published 2024
by Routledge
4 Park Square, Milton Park, Abingdon, Oxon OX14 4RN

and by Routledge
605 Third Avenue, New York, NY 10158

Routledge is an imprint of the Taylor & Francis Group, an informa business

© 2024 Dennis Alonzo

The right of Dennis Alonzo to be identified as author of this work has been asserted in accordance with sections 77 and 78 of the Copyright, Designs and Patents Act 1988.

All rights reserved. No part of this book may be reprinted or reproduced or utilised in any form or by any electronic, mechanical, or other means, now known or hereafter invented, including photocopying and recording, or in any information storage or retrieval system, without permission in writing from the publishers.

Trademark notice: Product or corporate names may be trademarks or registered trademarks, and are used only for identification and explanation without intent to infringe.

British Library Cataloguing-in-Publication Data
A catalogue record for this book is available from the British Library

ISBN: 9781032499697 (hbk)
ISBN: 9781032499680 (pbk)
ISBN: 9781003396277 (ebk)

DOI: 10.4324/9781003396277

Typeset in Galliard
by KnowledgeWorks Global Ltd.

To my wife, Celeste, and children, Adriel and Driego,
this book is a testimony where our faith could lead us.
Your prayer and support are reflected in every text
found in this book.

Contents

Acknowledgements	*viii*
1 Overview of Assessment and Teacher Assessment Literacy	1
2 The Historical and Conceptual Development of Assessment	24
3 Isn't Assessment to Support Learning Just Good Teaching?	42
4 Are Formative and Summative Assessments Different?	61
5 Beyond One Size Fits All?	79
6 When Do We Engage Students in Assessment?	98
7 Are Teacher Assessment Practices Reliable and Valid?	118
8 Are Teachers and Students the Only Key Players in Assessment?	135
9 How Do We Decide If Students Are Improving?	152
10 How Do We Know When Teachers Are Doing It Right?	169
11 How Do We Know When Schools Are Doing It Right?	188
12 The Key Elements of Implementing Effective Assessment Reform	206
Index	*226*

Acknowledgements

I am grateful to be surrounded by wonderful colleagues in the School of Education, University of New South Wales Sydney. Their support and encouragement are overwhelming. I would like to mention Prof. Kim Beswick for supporting me with my application for the Special Studies Program grant, which gave me seven months for writing this book. I would like also to acknowledge Associate Professor Sally Baker, Prof. Andy Gao, Associate Professor Hoa Nguyen, Dr. Meghan Stacey, and Caitlin Hannigan for reviewing this book. Their feedback provided me critical insights to evaluate my arguments and consider other perspectives. Most importantly, I would like to shout my biggest gratitude to Emeritus Professor Chris Davison who has been extremely helpful from conceptualising to the final editing of this book. They say, "you only need to believe in one person to succeed, and that person is you." However, in a very daunting process of writing this book, I needed her as my sounding board – another person who believes that I will succeed. She never sees my inadequacies and always points me to the right direction.

Moreover, I would like to acknowledge the teaching relief and financial support provided by the Faculty of Arts, Design and Architecture through the Special Studies Program. Special thanks to my editors, Vilija Stephens and Georgia Oman, who have been really patient in supporting me throughout the process of completing this book.

Chapter 1

Overview of Assessment and Teacher Assessment Literacy

Introduction

Ensuring effective learning and teaching requires implementing interventions that have the highest impact on increasing student outcomes. Schools are obligated to develop a learning environment that uses theoretically and empirically supported learning and teaching practices to optimise student learning. Studies show that teaching competence is significantly associated with student outcomes (Ferguson & Brown, 2000). The contribution of teachers to student learning explains roughly 30% of the variance observed in student performance (Hattie, 2003). This means that teacher competence is the next most important determinant of student achievement after student factors, which account for 50% of the variance in their learning. However, not everything that teachers do in the classroom brings about desired learning improvement. Hattie (2008) emphasises that about 95% of what teachers do in the classroom influences student achievement, but not all of these teacher activities positively impact student learning. Thus, it is imperative that teachers, school leaders, policy makers, parents and the school community should have a shared understanding of what really works inside the classroom to support individual students in their learning. Among many teaching practices, the use of assessment to support learning and teaching is one of the most effective interventions that has the highest impact on increasing student outcomes. Understanding the theoretical and empirical support for using assessment to support learning and teaching is critically important to develop positive dispositions about assessment.

Empirical Support for Using Assessment to Support Learning and Teaching

Effective assessment calls for a shift in teachers' assessment practices from recording and evaluating student achievement to helping and encouraging students' active engagement in learning through assessment (Adie et al., 2021; Black & Wiliam, 1999; Hattie, 2008). Some core assessment strategies include the detailed elaboration of learning outcomes, sharing success criteria and performance standards (Jones et al., 2017); implementing assessment tasks

DOI: 10.4324/9781003396277-1

2 Assessment and Teacher Assessment Literacy

designed for learning (Davison, 2007; Thompson & Wiliam, 2007); eliciting and giving feedback (Hattie & Timperley, 2007; Sadler, 1989); and using of self and peer assessment in teaching (Patri, 2002; Yan et al., 2020).

The significant effects of assessment practices on various aspects of learning and teaching are strongly supported by research evidence. Among these studies, the works of Black and Wiliam (1999) and Hattie (2008) provide strong empirical evidence that assessment practices are the most effective interventions in improving student learning. Both studies have achieved an unmatched level of status and credibility, with more recent studies (Cowie & Khoo, 2018; Hendry et al., 2012; Zhang, 2021) validating the results of the earlier studies and supporting the role of assessment in improving student learning. In both studies, the authors compared a large number of educational interventions and used effect size measures to establish and interpret the impact of these interventions on student achievement, with Black and Wiliam (1999) finding a range of effect sizes from $d = 0.4$ to $d = 0.7$, while Hattie (2008) reported a range between $d = 0.41$ and $d = 1.44$.

Mathematically, the effect size of an intervention is obtained by dividing the difference between the mean scores of students who have received the intervention and the mean scores of those who have not received the intervention by the square root of the average of the squared standard deviations (Cohen, 1988). To interpret the magnitude of effect size, Hattie (2008) developed a scale where the effects of interventions on student achievement are seen as a continuum ranging from reverse effects, developmental effects and teacher effects to a zone of desired effects. He called this continuum the 'barometers of influence', with an effect size of $d = 0.4$ and higher as the zone of desired effects where interventions at or above this cut-off point are believed to advance students' learning far more than could typically occur in a year of teaching. An intervention with an effect size of $d = 1.0$ can advance the learning of students by two to three years or improve learning by 50%, or in the case of experiments, those students who received the intervention could exceed the performance of those who did not receive the treatment by 84% (Hattie, 2008). Hattie interprets effect size through the use of average percentile gain. Since an effect size is equivalent to a point in normal distribution, it can be equated on the same scale as the percentile gain. To highlight the desired effect of an intervention, $d = 0.40$ would mean that students who received this treatment would add 16 percentile points from their original standing, which means that they can perform better (by 66%) than those students who did not receive the intervention. Generally, for every increase in effect size, there is a corresponding increase in the percentile gain. Hence, the higher the effect size observed in an intervention, the higher the gain in student achievement.

Using the concept of effect size, Hattie's (2008) work shows that teacher assessment practices are among the top interventions: self-report grades being the highest with an effect size of $d = 1.44$, formative evaluation being the third ranked ($d = 0.90$), teacher clarity (e.g. explicitly stating and communicating learning outcomes, using criteria and standards and informing students of the assessment approach) ranked eighth (d = 0.75), reciprocal teaching (actively involving students in learning and teaching activities by letting students take the role of a teacher and lead their classmates in summarising, questioning, clarifying and predicting) being the ninth ranked (d = 0.74) and eliciting and giving feedback being tenth (d = 0.73). Other teacher assessment skills with effect sizes greater than the threshold value of 0.4 include using prior achievement in teaching (d = 0.67), effective teacher-student relationships (d = 0.72) and engaging students in self-questioning (d = 0.64). Based on these results, key assessment strategies associated with teacher AfL literacy are arguably the most important components of effective learning and teaching. Also, highlighted in this study is the benefit of teacher engagement in professional development, which is among those interventions with a higher effect size (d = 0.62). Thus, it can be argued that teachers' use of assessment in the classroom can be fully optimised if they continuously engage in professional development related to assessment.

However, despite the prominence and status of the work of Black and Wiliam (1998) and Hattie (2008), both studies have not escaped criticism. For example, Black and Wiliam's study has been challenged for its claimed lack of theoretical pedagogic context (Perrenoud, 1998), concerns about the reliability of some included studies and discrepancies in results (Smith & Gorard, 2005), methodological limitations (Dunn & Mulvenon, 2009) and inconsistencies in the use of terminologies (Taras, 2007). Similarly, Hattie's study has been criticised for its exclusion of some factors that might have changed the results of his meta-analysis, his supposedly unrealistic conceptions of teaching and effective teachers (Terhart, 2011), problems with the dependency of Provided.effect size to sample size, social, background and context effects not being considered when discussing the results, concerns about the inclusion of some low-quality studies and some not being assessed for validity, achievement defined only by quantitative measures, inapplicability of some studies to the real classroom (Snook et al., 2009) and inappropriateness of inferences drawn from the results to inform policy due to the weakness of methodology used when studies included in the meta-analysis have different social and cultural contexts (Evers & Mason, 2011). However, despite these issues, the work of these researchers has been used to justify the introduction of assessment to support learning and teaching as a key component of government educational policy around the world (e.g. Ministry of Education of Brunei, 2008, 2011; Queensland Department of Education and the Arts, 2005; Hong Kong Curriculum Development Council, 2001; Learning and Teaching Scotland, 2006; Singapore Ministry of Education, 2008).

Theoretical Support for Using Assessment to Support Learning and Teaching

Although teachers' assessment practices can be viewed through a behaviourist lens [with a focus on outcomes (Nuthal, 1999)], through a humanist lens [with a focus on learning progress, prior learning (Friedman & MacDonald, 2006)

4 Assessment and Teacher Assessment Literacy

and the role of motivation (Martin & Dowson, 2009)] or through a constructivist lens [with a focus on learning tasks as assessment tasks (Keppel & Carless, 2006), learning autonomy and the active construction of knowledge (Marshall & Drummond, 2006)], the emphases of behaviourism and constructivism in the interactions of thinking processes and learning and teaching are confined to individual learners, ignoring the role of social, political, economic and cultural processes in the learning process. Recent research suggests that teachers can only fully understand and implement assessment when they recognise the social, political, economic and cultural contribution and impact of their assessment practices and how these factors shape their assessment practices (Alonzo et al., 2021; Arsyad Arrafii, 2023). Through a socio-cultural lens, teachers should view assessment as a tool that can be used to create a learning community (Lave & Wenger, 1991) of students and teachers, which then shapes teachers' classroom practices and students' learning behaviour. Also, from this perspective, learning is defined as more than just individual cognitive processes; in addition, it takes into account the social processes, political and economic contexts, and cultural settings that influence learning. Research in assessment (Boistrup, 2017; Clark, 2014; Herzog-Punzenberger et al., 2020; Klenowski, 2014) highlights the importance of social interactions, cultural contexts and the belief systems of both students and teachers and how these factors shape students' identity (Cowie, 2005), and the nature of power and control in the classroom (Black & Wiliam, 2006). Although one of the aims of using assessment in the classroom is to guide students to become self-regulated and independent learners (Chen & Bonner, 2020; Guo & Wei, 2019), the process of self-regulation is critically dependent on interactions with their teachers and their peers to activate and support their learning. Thus, teachers' assessment knowledge and skills, referred to as teacher assessment literacy (Alonzo, 2016; Stiggins, 1991; Xu & Brown, 2016), are critically important in ensuring the effectiveness of assessment.

The conceptualisation of teacher assessment literacy from a socio-cultural perspective is seen in the roles and beliefs of teachers required to activate student learning. The seven key points explained below summarise the conceptualisation of teacher assessment literacy from a socio-cultural perspective.

Teachers' Beliefs about Learning

Effective teaching starts with teachers being clear about learning outcomes (Hattie, 2008), determining students' existing knowledge and skills and bridging the gap to help them achieve the desired learning outcomes. This view is consistent with the belief in a socio-cultural perspective that teachers need to view learning as a process of moving students from novice to expert status while supporting them to negotiate their identity in the classroom constantly (James, 2006). The belief of teachers that learning occurs in a social environment and is influenced by the cultural setting of the classroom and the school, in general, enables them to develop socially and culturally relevant learning and teaching activities that facilitate interaction. Teachers' belief about learning and teaching is a critical factor in helping students engage in their learning. As Willis (2009) argues:

> In order for teachers to engage students in [assessment to support learning and teaching] practices and create a community of practice that enables all students to develop an identity as an autonomous learner, teachers need to work beyond the curriculum, pedagogy and assessment of a purely behaviourist paradigm.
>
> (p. 4)

A critical aspect of the role of teachers in supporting students to learn from a socio-cultural perspective is to help them acquire autonomy in their learning. This outcome cannot be achieved through cognitive processes alone but rather must be facilitated by social processes in the classroom. Through students' interactions in the classroom, they develop and shape a community of practice (CoP), which eventually shapes their identity as autonomous learners (James, 2006). Willis (2009), drawing from the definition of Lave and Wenger (1991), defines learner autonomy in the context of socio-cultural perspective as the "socially constructed identity of a self-monitoring student who participates in culturally accepted ways within a community of practice" (p. 3). The challenge for teachers is providing opportunities for student interactions in the class to support the negotiation and formation of student identity. To facilitate these interactions, teachers need to view students not as mere passive receivers of external knowledge but rather as socially active individuals who see knowledge as a dynamic output of interactions (Gipps, 1999).

Teachers' Beliefs about Assessment to Support Learning and Teaching

Consistent with a socio-cultural perspective, assessment strategies, tasks and processes are seen as tools to help students identify their strengths and weaknesses. The same assessment processes can be used to further enhance their learning (Adie et al., 2021; Gipps, 1999). Teachers need to strongly believe that assessment is only useful (and should be used) if it helps students learn more effectively (Alonzo, 2020; Sadler, 2012). To ensure that assessment is aligned with the socio-cultural perspective, teachers should develop authentic tasks, within the level of student ability, and facilitate interactions among students and between teacher and students (Alshakhi, 2021; Beck et al., 2020; Villarroel et al., 2018).

The work of Keppel and Carless (2006) demonstrates the use of assessment tasks to fulfil both learning and measurement functions. Using a learning-oriented assessment framework, students were highly involved in the assessment

6 Assessment and Teacher Assessment Literacy

process through clear communication during the assessment process, providing students with the opportunity for collaboration to complete the assessment tasks and requiring them to assess and provide feedback on their peers' work. Students' learning experiences in completing assessment tasks through active collaboration, interaction and feedback negotiation facilitate the construction of knowledge. In a more detailed study by Marshall and Drummond (2006), apart from explicitly using assessment tasks as learning tasks, they required teachers to consider the scope of the tasks and ensure that the learning processes students undertake to promote learning autonomy. They showed that explicitly sharing learning outcomes and criteria is not enough to develop student learning autonomy, but rather it requires that students are highly involved in the development of criteria. Also, teachers use of models or exemplar materials to demonstrate what quality performance could challenge students to produce the same high-level performance in various ways. Using exemplars gives students the idea that quality is not a fixed and finite concept.

Another important assessment approach that embodies the principles of a socio-cultural theory of learning is differentiated assessment to support students (Alonzo & Loughland, 2022) and give them opportunities to best demonstrate their learning. Teachers' effort in broadening their assessment approach helps students to offer alternative evidence of their learning (Linn, 1992), which avoids the conception of assessment as a 'one-size-fits-all' activity. The use of differentiated assessment tasks, apart from ensuring fairness and accessibility, also develops student motivation and engagement (Koshy, 2013). According to Reeves (2013), three overlapping concepts are essential to initiate and sustain the motivation and engagement of students. These are student choice, power and competence. Reeves argues that

> Empowered students who exercise choice, doing what they want to do, may be temporarily engaged. But if they never become competent, they will become frustrated and distracted. Conversely, competent students who master a skill but never have the opportunity to enjoy a degree of choice or exercise power over the content and nature of their assessments, will dully go through the motions but never achieve a high level of engagement.
>
> (para 4)

Teachers' View of Student Roles in Assessment

The Assessment Reform Group (2002) used the term 'assessment *for* learning' (A*f*L) instead of 'formative assessment' to emphasise the key role of students in assessment as primary participants and not just passive recipients of assessment processes and outcomes. The responsibilisation of students in assessment highlights the socio-cultural belief of teachers about students' role in learning as partners in constructing their knowledge and skills within the context of learning (Lave & Wenger, 1991). This notion is supported by several studies demonstrating that students who assume active roles in all aspects of learning, teaching and assessment have higher achievement levels (Ahmadi, 2022; Yan et al., 2020). Apart from the positive effect of student engagement on their achievement level, the social environment and processes created by teachers and students promote self-esteem, encourage engagement and increase motivation (Clark, 2011). The active involvement of students in the learning process and the ability of the teachers to develop a culture of trust and respect inside the classroom are important practices that consequently increase student motivation (Pereira et al., 2017).

The role of students in assessment is demonstrated in teachers' use of peer assessment to promote student engagement and interaction. The work of Marshall and Drummond (2006) highlights the role of students as active assessors of their peers' output and as important resources who can provide feedback to each other. The use of peer assessment initiates the engagement process between students, while dialogue between students and teachers to reinforce the peer feedback further enhances engagement and interaction. The nature of a learning environment where every student is valued and seen as active contributor to knowledge construction empowers students "to contribute in a positive and productive way both inside and outside the school" (Clark, 2011, p. 9).

Teacher and Student Relationships in Assessment

The interpersonal relationship between teachers and students affects motivation and achievement (Martin & Dowson, 2009). As argued by Willis (2009), the nature of the teacher-student relationship in the classroom determines students' level of participation in both learning and assessment. Teachers' classroom assessment practices and the power and control between teachers and students can promote student autonomy (Pedder, 2006), depending on how teachers establish relationships in the classroom to develop students' active participation. In a social learning environment, the multiple identities of teachers and students are recognised. The nature of learning is seen as a product of social interactions, influenced by power and control (Pryor & Crossouard, 2005). One could ask, if students are considered to be independent learners, are they the ones controlling the social environment of learning? What power do teachers have in the social environment? These issues of power and control can be addressed if negotiation between students and teachers is open. These identity issues are important considerations in the meta-contextual reflection of students and teachers as they engage in assessment processes (Pryor & Crossouard, 2005). The identities formed by students and teachers enable them to relate to their social environment, and they use these identities when they are faced with a new context for learning.

One indicator of a good teacher-student relationship is that success and failure in learning are a shared responsibility between teachers and students (Alonzo & Loughland, 2022; Hannigan et al., 2022). This shared

8 Assessment and Teacher Assessment Literacy

responsibility reinforces teachers' roles as activators of learning (Hattie, 2008) and the role of students as independent learners. Both teachers and students constantly monitor learning progress and identify learning needs, and they collaboratively work together toward meeting the desired learning outcomes. If failures occur, teachers and students work together to change the learning context or use new learning and assessment tools to find better ways to achieve the desired learning outcomes (James, 2006).

Teachers' Roles as Assessors

Teachers are seen as the more able individuals who assist students. This is consistent with the ideas of Lave and Wenger (1991) that teachers, together with students, monitor student progress and help develop students' learning autonomy. One way to support students in their learning is for teachers to identify individual students' zone of proximal development (ZPD), defined as the difference between what the students can independently do and what they can do with assistance (Vygotsky, 1978). The ZPD has a wide application in assessment as it not only provides information to teachers about the current level of ability of individual students, but it also enables teachers to identify appropriate learning interventions and support to address students' individual learning needs. The information related to students' ZPD leads teachers to develop a differentiated assessment approach to provide opportunities for students to demonstrate their learning regardless of their ability level.

Ash and Levitt (2003) argue that working with the construct of the ZPD facilitates the transformation of teachers' practices and enhances professional development. As teachers assess the work or performance of students, they develop a further understanding of the assessment task and define quality work using the success criteria. This is further enhanced when they work collaboratively with other teachers as their collaboration initiates the development of a shared understanding of the quality of performance. In addition, as teachers assess students' performance, they can identify if there is a mismatch between their expectations and student output. The identified mismatch can facilitate teachers' reflective thinking to evaluate their practices and other components of learning and teaching activities and use the results of their reflection to adjust their teaching, success criteria and expectations to appropriately meet the needs of students. Teachers' regular reflection and adaptation enhance their skills in using assessment information to inform learning and teaching.

Teachers as Part of a Community of Practice

In a socio-cultural paradigm, teachers' involvement in a CoP helps them put knowledge into practice (Schlager & Fusco, 2004), validates their ideas and beliefs, gains access to and evaluates the application of new information from colleagues (Rhodes & Beneike, 2002) and co-constructs new knowledge and skills together (Flagg & Ayling, 2011). According to Harrison (2005), teachers' engagement in discussions related to their practices deepens their understanding of their profession and serves as agents of change for others to establish shared common goals in enhancing their capabilities. The effects of these teacher interactions on student learning are shown by the study of Goddard et al. (2007), in which they found that the teacher's collaboration level influences student achievement. This is because teachers who actively engage in discussions around curriculum, instruction and assessment use context-based learning and teaching practices.

The Influence of Cultural Setting and Policy on Assessment

Cultural, political and economic factors affect how assessment is implemented (Davison, 2013). Inside the classroom, the different backgrounds of the students need to be considered by teachers to develop and implement effective assessment (Klenowski et al., 2010). Besides the classroom context, teachers' assessment practices are also influenced by the school culture and the education department's policy. Clark (2011), drawing from the work of Damon and Phelps (1989) on equality and mutuality as components of collaborative learning, argues that a socio-cultural classroom is supported by mutuality, particularly from policymakers. This mutuality is evident in the support of the government for assessment reforms. The countries that have adopted and implemented assessment reforms acknowledge the importance of creating and implementing policies coherently with effective assessment principles. Davison (2013), leading large-scale assessment reforms in Hong Kong, Brunei and Singapore, attributed the success or failure of these initiatives to a shared understanding of assessment principles and practices across schools and all levels of bureaucracy. Such political support strengthens the implementation of assessment reforms and reshapes practices inconsistent with the principles of effective assessment practices. Similarly, the economic aspect of assessment reforms' implementation is equally important as it is costly and needs strong financial support from higher authorities. Another important layer that adds to the complexities of the context-dependency of assessment practices is addressing the expectations and beliefs of the community, parents and carers (Hutchinson & Young, 2011).

These seven key points demonstrate that assessment practices to support learning and teaching are strongly aligned with a socio-cultural learning theory. In this perspective, teachers use assessment as a tool to support students in their learning, give greater responsibility to students in terms of monitoring their learning and develop a learning environment in which students are actively engaged in making decisions related to their learning. In addition, teachers establish a CoP to support each other in their ongoing assessment literacy development. Lastly, teachers develop and use appropriate assessment

10 Assessment and Teacher Assessment Literacy

knowledge skills within the social, cultural and economic context of their particular educational system.

Teacher Assessment Literacy

Teacher assessment knowledge and skills are always evolving; hence, teacher assessment literacy can be characterised as a highly situated construct which must be operationally defined for a particular educational system. This section defines and characterises teacher assessment literacy. It begins by looking at the diverse views of researchers and practitioners on what knowledge and skills constitute teacher assessment literacy. Due to the shortcomings of current views, this chapter proposes a more holistic approach to conceptualising assessment literacy and then outlines its key characteristics and principles.

The Changing Conceptualisation of Teacher Assessment Literacy

The views of several authors form the theoretical background of the discussion of teacher assessment literacy. Since the early 1960s, there has been a continuous stream of publications on assessment, including both books and training materials. The ongoing publication of assessment resources both reflects and reinforces the widely perceived need to enhance teacher assessment literacy. Although the rationale for enhancing teachers' assessment literacy has been constant, the content and components of effective assessment practices have changed. Davies (2008) identifies two factors that shaped these changes: the growing professionalisation of assessment, and the demand for knowledge and skills in assessment. The focus of early assessment literacy was on measurement principles, amidst concerns about ensuring the reliability and validity of teacher-made tests and the interpretation of assessment information. Later, the focus shifted to the assessment knowledge and skills teachers needed in the classroom. This is evident in the views of Fullan (2002), who equates assessment literacy with teachers' and principals' capacity to use student achievement data to increase learning and to inform policy. Apart from this, Webb (2002) highlights the importance of using assessment data to improve teaching and the effectiveness of educational programs to help students learn. Over time, these professional and technical emphases have evolved to include a more holistic view of assessment literacy. Stiggins (2005) describes the characteristics of assessment literate teachers as teachers who "know the difference between sound and unsound assessment. They are not intimidated by the sometimes mysterious and always daunting technical world of assessment" (p. 240). Stiggins emphasises that assessment literate teachers are confident in their capacity to undertake the necessary preparation and planning. They determine the object of their assessment, its purpose, the best way to assess the construct of interest, the best way to generate exemplary performance of students, the misrepresentation of assessment and the negative effects of inaccurate assessment. This view of Stiggins is consistent with the view of Popham (2011) that teacher assessment literacy involves teachers' "understanding of the fundamental assessment concepts and procedures deemed likely to influence educational decisions" (p. 265). Popham's emphasis is on teachers' ability to use assessment to inform decisions related to student learning and effective teaching.

In recent years, the emphases of assessment literacy have broadened to include critical views of assessment and its social consequences (McNamara & Roever, 2006) and the social roles of assessment (Inbar-Lourie, 2008), including the roles of teachers in providing assessment information to stakeholders (Taylor, 2009). Also, assessment literacy is now seen as no longer confined just to teachers; there is now a growing emphasis on the assessment literacy of other stakeholders (Davison, 2013; Taylor, 2009). This trend has been shaped by pressures at the system level, where the effectiveness of teacher assessment practices is constrained by external pressures due to inconsistencies between effective assessment practices and the understanding and expectations of other stakeholders. This call for stakeholder assessment literacy was first evident in Popham's (2009) view that assessment literacy is directly linked to roles and responsibilities, which means that different stakeholders have different assessment literacy needs. Teacher assessment literacy is a critical factor for addressing the assessment needs of and building the assessment literacy of stakeholders (Taylor, 2009).

The Dimensions of Teacher Assessment Literacy

Apart from studies that explore individual teacher assessment skills, other studies use a range of dimensions to characterise teacher assessment literacy.

The seven competencies used by Stiggins (1999b) to describe teacher classroom practices cover the dimensions described in the Standards for Teacher Competence in the Educational Assessment of Students (American Federation of Teachers, 1990), which was used by Mertler and Campbell (2005) to develop their Assessment Literacy Inventory. They presented a comparison between the dimensions they used, and the ones described by Stiggins. They made this remark: "while there is some debate as about the extent to which *The Standards* adequately address those competencies which research shows that teaches need to possess, (shows) that there is a great deal of overlap in the original 1990 Standards and the competencies listed by Stiggins (1999b)" (p. 7). However, Stiggins critiqued the standards used for teacher competence in the Educational Assessment of Students as not being able to account for the critical roles of teachers in meeting the demands of their assessment responsibilities in the classroom. He maintains that the list of competencies he originally proposed is more substantial, and these competencies are supported by research evidence about their role in improving student learning. However, although the competencies described by Stiggins are comprehensive and can

12 Assessment and Teacher Assessment Literacy

be supported theoretically, no study has been conducted to gather empirical evidence to demonstrate whether these competencies reflect the actual dimensions of teacher assessment literacy, particularly in the context of AfL.

Another study that attempted to explore the underlying dimensions of teacher assessment literacy is the work of Newfields (2006). The methodology he used was somewhat problematic because, just like Stiggins and Mertler and Campbell, he only used a theoretical approach to establish the four dimensions. Although he employed a series of expert validations and pilot testing, no empirical evidence was provided to support the existence of four dimensions in the data. Another issue of his work is its strong focus on assessment knowledge and measurement principles, which makes the individual teacher assessment skills skewed towards summative assessment practices. Hence, even if these dimensions are supported by empirical evidence, they will be specific only for teacher summative assessment practices and not for the broader framework of teacher assessment literacy.

Definitions of assessment literacy that emerged from an empirical approach are exemplified in the work of DeLuca and Klinger (2010) and Fulcher (2012), which provided preliminary empirical evidence about the existence of key factors or dimensions. The 12 dimensions described by DeLuca and Klinger encompass aspects of teacher assessment literacy related to practice, theory and philosophy. However, some of these dimensions can be collapsed to form more unified dimensions. For example, the dimensions related to summative assessment (i.e. test design and marking, provincially mandated assessment practices, technical knowledge of assessment practice and philosophies of large-scale assessment) can be clustered into one dimension. Another problem with these dimensions is the dichotomisation of assessment practices into formative and summative assessment that needs to be more consistent with current thinking around assessment.

The four dimensions established by Fulcher encompass the dimensions described by Newfields, but one dimension emerged that relates to classroom assessment practices. Although the inclusion of classroom assessment practices as one dimension highlights the possible integration of other teacher assessment practices that are more psychometric by nature, the explicit naming of this dimension as teacher classroom practices poses an issue about the implied separation of classroom assessment from other teacher assessment activities, particularly those that relate to summative assessment.

Although the studies described above that explored the dimensions of teacher assessment literacy have obvious limitations in terms of the assessment knowledge and skills included and their clustering to form factors, using these dimensions to describe and characterise teacher assessment practices is helpful in understanding teacher assessment knowledge and skills. Also, it suggests that teacher assessment literacy consists of dimensions where similar teacher assessment practices cluster together and form distinct factors. However, there is no agreement regarding the interpretations of the dimensions of teacher assessment literacy. This is because assessment is a context-dependent construct. The description of teacher assessment knowledge and skills is influenced by policy and contextual factors along with other factors. For example, in a teacher-based assessment culture such as Australia, quite different knowledge and skills are valued compared with the more testing-based culture of the USA.

However, given the focus of this book on using assessment to support learning, the teacher assessment literacy of Alonzo (2016) is adopted (Figure 1.1).

The six-factor model was theoretically and empirically aligned with the concept of teachers' teacher assessment practices that support learning and teaching. The six dimensions are defined as follows:

- *Teachers as assessors*, represents teacher assessment literacy to develop assessment tasks and strategies and use assessment tasks to measure student learning outcomes.
- *Teachers as pedagogy experts*, indicates teachers' AfL literacy to make use of assessment tasks and assessment data to inform teaching and learning activities.
- *Teachers as student partners*, relates to teachers' knowledge and skills in involving students in the assessment and learning process.
- *Teachers as motivators*, is about using assessment tasks and assessment data to support and motivate individual students in the classroom.
- *Teachers as teacher learners*, reflects teachers' ability to reflect on their own assessment practices and experiences and to use assessment data to evaluate their own needs in professional development.
- *Teachers as stakeholder partners*, pertains to teacher AfL literacy to recognise, understand and work with related stakeholders to maximise students' learning outcomes.

Of the six dimensions, four of which are directly related to activities involving students in the classroom. Placed inside the rectangle are the assessment skills of teachers that directly affect the students in the classroom. The two other dimensions outside the rectangle relate to teachers' ability to use their assessment experiences to identify their professional development needs (teachers as teacher learners) and to enhance the assessment literacy of their stakeholders (teachers as stakeholder partners).

Teacher Assessment Literacy in the Context of Supporting Student Learning

Defining teacher assessment literacy from the point of using assessment to support learning and teaching is important in ensuring a consistent interpretation, as the literature presents different views and conceptions of what knowledge and skills constitute teacher assessment literacy. Although the term

14 Assessment and Teacher Assessment Literacy

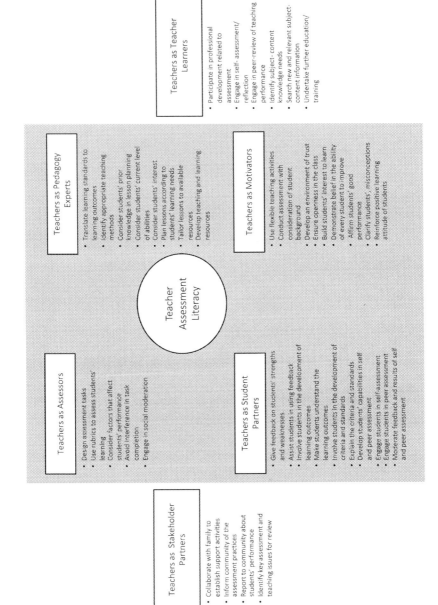

Figure 1.1 Teacher Assessment Literacy Framework

'assessment literacy' was originally used to describe the components of assessment practices that teachers need to know in order to carry out their functions in terms of assessing student learning (Inbar-Lourie, 2008; Stiggins, 1997; Stoynoff & Chapelle, 2005), some of the literature equates the term with teacher understanding of measurement principles. In this view, the emphasis in teacher assessment literacy is on preparing students for high-stake tests, with teachers needing to understand and apply fundamental measurement principles in their classroom practices, such as reliability, validity, item difficulty, item discrimination and interpretation of test results. Even a recent definition of assessment literacy by Fulcher (2012), which was expanded to account for diverse contexts, principles and practices, still leans towards describing teachers' competencies for large-scale standardised testing as that is still the dominant form of assessment in the USA. Consequently, the emphasis of teacher professional development is focused on test design and analysis, which should only be one element of the key components of teacher assessment literacy. The view of teacher assessment literacy as simply ensuring the reliability and validity of assessment is too narrow to account for a teacher's daily assessment practices as they try to make sense of how students learn through engaging in various decision-making activities and hence to adjust their teaching while ensuring that student self-regulation is being developed. Thus, for assessment literacy to be relevant to classroom activities, it must be viewed across different dimensions to develop a more holistic definition.

Putting together these different views on assessment literacy, this chapter presents a more comprehensive definition to describe teacher assessment literacy broadly. This definition expands the definition of assessment literacy by Webb (2002) which emphasises that assessment literacy should focus on utilising assessment information to monitor students' progress in achieving learning outcomes and to improve teaching and effectiveness of the educational programs to help students learn. According to Webb, a clear indicator of an assessment literate individual is his/her capacity to use assessment data to increase the motivation of all stakeholders to carry out their roles in education. What was not emphasised by Webb is the underlying purpose for enhancing teacher assessment literacy. From this point of view and incorporating the principles of effective assessment to support learning and teaching, in this book:

> Teacher assessment literacy accounts for knowledge and skills in making highly contextualised, fair, consistent and trustworthy assessment decisions to inform learning and teaching to support both students' and teachers' professional learning effectively. Part of the responsibility of teachers is to build students' and other stakeholders' capabilities and confidence to take an active role in assessment, learning and teaching activities to enable and provide the needed support for more effective learning.
>
> (Alonzo, 2016, p. 58)

16 Assessment and Teacher Assessment Literacy

This definition emphasises teachers' skills in using assessment as the central unifying process of all learning and teaching activities. The daily decisions made by teachers to improve learning are informed by various assessment data and student learning characteristics, progress and needs, as well as by information from other stakeholders such as parents and school leaders. To fully understand the definition of teacher assessment literacy above, its key characteristics are elaborated in the following section.

Key Characteristics of Teacher Assessment Literacy

Considering the empirical and theoretical evidence, the changing conception of assessment and the competing dimensions, the definition of teacher assessment literacy proposed in this chapter embodies several key characteristics.

First, assessment literate teachers translate effective assessment principles and knowledge into practice to ensure student learning. These principles and knowledge are manifested by teachers' skills in using assessment and analysing assessment information to make important decisions in their learning and teaching context. There are six general clusters of knowledge and skills that comprise assessment literacy. First, the ability of the teachers to develop and use a wide range of assessment strategies to gather robust assessment data (Stiggins, 2005). Second, the ability of the teacher to reflect on the assessment data – both student achievement and student characteristics – and use this information to develop learning and teaching activities. Webb (2002) offers a definition of assessment literacy that encompasses this ability of teachers. He defines assessment literacy "as the knowledge of means for assessing what students know and can do, how to interpret the results from these assessments and how to apply these results to improve student learning and program effectiveness" (p. 1). Third, the skills of the teachers to actively engage students in the assessment, learning and teaching activities. Fourth is the teacher's use of assessment to enhance and sustain student motivation. As argued by Leenknecht et al. (2021), teachers need to assess students' motivation to understand them better and to make contextualised assessment decisions. The teacher needs to know if the assessment task enhances students' engagement in learning and if the students are exerting effort to accomplish the task. Fifth is the ability of the teachers to reflect on their practices and assessment data to identify their professional needs both in assessment knowledge and in curriculum-content knowledge (Timperley, 2008, 2011). Sixth is the ability of the teachers to establish strong partnerships with stakeholders by providing them with their assessment information needs. A clear understanding of the principles of assessment will help implement assessment more effectively. For example, policymakers can review assessment policies to ensure that external factors are helping teachers make assessment information more relevant (McMillan, 2003).

Second, any teacher assessment literacy model must emphasise the responsibility of teachers in working with students, colleagues, parents and the community.

As mentioned above, assessment literate teachers provide assessment information to various stakeholder groups (Nieminen et al., 2021). Apart from the ability of teachers to communicate assessment results to students, they must also provide assessment information to different stakeholder groups tailored to each group's information needs (Davison, 2013). The dialogue between the teacher and stakeholders ensures that stakeholders gain a deeper understanding of assessment practices, which consequently draws positive support from them.

Third, the construct of teacher assessment literacy stresses the trustworthiness and social consequences of teachers' assessment practices. McNamara and Roever (2006) cite some misuse of language testing, which is also relevant to other disciplines, like sorting out and labelling students into various social classes instead of using assessment to improve student learning. Similarly, they cite the controlling effects of centralised standards and testing in teaching. In the definition proposed above, the need to enhance teacher competence is emphasised to ensure teacher assessment practices are fair and trustworthy from the point of view of all key stakeholders.

Fourth, a teacher assessment literacy program should not be confined to just formal training but consider the socio-cultural aspects of teacher learning where teachers and school leaders "form a knowledge community by discussing, critiquing and questioning fundamental issues relevant to their context" (Inbar-Lourie, 2008, p. 389). Formal training may build the foundation of teachers' assessment knowledge, but studies have consistently shown that teachers forming a community of learners can improve their assessment literacy. In the study by Dekker and Feijs (2005), they found that the most significant source of support for teachers in continuing their assessment practices after the initial training period was the development of learning groups within the school, where teachers were provided with the environment where they could discuss related assessment issues with peers through professional meetings or informal contacts.

Finally, the definition of teacher assessment literacy and its characteristics discussed above must address the inconsistencies both in understanding and the actual practices among teachers of what constitutes sound assessment practices (Davison & Leung, 2009). Ideally, teachers should have a common understanding of their assessment practices. However, in reality, teachers have different views and needs as influenced by various factors. Davison (2004) has emphasised that to resolve conflicts in teachers' needs in assessment literacy, school systems should prioritise enhancing teachers' assessment skills. This is consistent with the findings of Hayward and Hedge (2005) that in the primary sector in Scotland, staff development related to AfL is one of the most common areas of concern, with teachers arguing that intensive training is needed to implement AfL reform effectively.

These key characteristics of teacher assessment literacy capture the elements of the construct and how it should be operationalised. The work of Xu and Brown (2016) reconceptualises assessment teacher assessment literacy, bridging the gap between assessment and teacher education research. They proposed a conceptual framework highlighting teacher assessment literacy in practice. They argued that for teachers to use assessment effectively, their assessment knowledge must be applied considering the system and contextual factors, and teachers negotiate their identity when making compromises among competing tensions. Stakeholders influence teachers' assessment literacy.

Conclusion

The empirical and theoretical support for using assessment to support learning and teaching is undeniably strong, making such assessment one of the most effective interventions in increasing student outcomes. Researchers and teachers agree that putting such assessment as a central feature of learning and teaching, where teachers use it to engage students in their learning and use assessment data to adapt their teaching, is the key to optimising students' outcomes.

References

Adie, L., Addison, B., & Lingard, B. (2021). Assessment and learning: An in-depth analysis of change in one school's assessment culture. *Oxford Review of Education*, *47*(3), 404–422. https://doi.org/10.1080/03054985.2020.1850436

Ahmadi, R. (2022). Students' perceptions of student voice in assessment within the context of Iran: The dynamics of culture, power relations, and student knowledge. *Higher Education Research & Development*, *41*(2), 211–225. https://doi.org/10.1080/07294360.2021.1882401

Alonzo, D. (2016). *Development and application of a teacher assessment for learning (AfL) literacy tool*. University of New South Wales. http://unsworks.unsw.edu.au/fapi/datastream/unsworks:38345/SOURCE02?view=true

Alonzo, D. (2020). Teacher education and professional development in industry 4.0: The case for building a strong assessment literacy. In J. P. Ashadi, A. T. Basikin, & N. H. P. S. Putro (Eds.), *Teacher education and professional development in industry 4.0*. Taylor & Francis Group.

Alonzo, D., Leverett, J., & Obsioma, E. (2021). Leading an assessment reform: Ensuring a whole-school approach for decision-making. *Frontiers in Education*, *6*(62). https://doi.org/10.3389/feduc.2021.631857

Alonzo, D., & Loughland, T. (2022). Variability of students' responses to assessment activities: The influence of achievement levels. *International Journal of Instruction*, *15*(4), 1071–1090. https://doi.org/10.29333/iji.2022.15457a

Alshakhi, A. (2021). EFL teachers' assessment practices of students' interactions in online classes: An activity theory lens. *TESOL International Journal*, *16*(16), 148–176.

American Federation of Teachers, National Council on Measurement in Education, & National Education Association. (1990). The standards for competence in the educational assessment of students.

Arsyad Arrafii, M. (2023). Assessment reform in Indonesia: Contextual barriers and opportunities for implementation. *Asia Pacific Journal of Education*, *43*(1), 79–94. https://doi.org/10.1080/02188791.2021.1898931

Ash, D., & Levitt, K. (2003). Working within the zone of proximal development: Formative assessment as professional development. *Journal of Science Teacher Education*, *14*(1), 1–26.

Beck, J. S., Morgan, J. J., Brown, N., Whitesides, H., & Riddle, D. R. (2020). "Asking, learning, seeking out": An exploration of data literacy for teaching. *The Educational Forum*, *84*(2), 150–165. https://doi.org/10.1080/00131725.2020.1674438

Black, P., & Wiliam, D. (1998). Assessment and classroom learning. *Assessment in Education: Principles, Policy & Practice*, *5*(1), 7–74. http://dx.doi.org/10.1080/0969595980050102

Black, P., & Wiliam, D. (2006) Developing a theory of formative assessment. In J. Gardner (Ed.), *Assessment and learning* (pp. 81–100). London: Sage.

Boistrup, L. B. (2017). Assessment in mathematics education: A gatekeeping dispositive. In H. Strachler-Pohl, N. Bohlmann, & A. Pais (Eds.), *The disorder of mathematics education – Challenging the socio-political dimensions of research* (pp. 209–230). Springer.

Chen, P. P., & Bonner, S. M. (2020). A framework for classroom assessment, learning, and self-regulation. *Assessment in Education: Principles, Policy & Practice*, *27*(4), 373–393. https://doi.org/10.1080/0969594X.2019.1619515

Clark, I. (2011). Formative assessment and motivation: Theories and themes. *Prime Research on Education*, *1*(2), 26–36.

Clark, I. (2014). Equitable learning outcomes: Supporting economically and culturally disadvantaged students in 'formative learning environments. *Improving Schools*, *17*(1), 116–126. https://doi.org/10.1177/1365480213519182

Cohen, J. (1988). *Statistical power for the behavioral sciences* (2nd ed.). Larence Erlbau Associates Publishers.

Cowie, B. (2005). Pupil commentary on assessment for learning. *The Curriculum Journal*, *16*(2), 137–151. https://doi.org/10.1080/09585170500135921

Cowie, B., & Khoo, E. (2018). An ecological approach to understanding assessment for learning in support of student writing achievement. *Frontiers in Education*, *3*(11). https://doi.org/10.3389/feduc.2018.00011

Damon, W., & Phelps, E. (1989). Critical distinctions among three approaches to peer education. *International Journal of Educational Research*, *13*(1), 9–19.

Davies, A. (2008). *Assessing academic English: Testing English proficiency 1950–1989—The IELTS solution*. UCLES/Cambridge University Press.

Davison, C. (2004). The contradictory culture of teacher-based assessment: ESL teacher assessment practices in Australian and Hong Kong secondary schools. *Language Testing*, *21*(3), 305–334.

Davison, C. (2007). Views from the chalkface: English language school based assessment in Hong Kong. *Language Assessment Quarterly*, *4*(1), 37–68. https://doi.org/10.1080/15434300701348359

Davison, C. (2013). Innovation in assessment: Common misconceptions and problems. In K. Hyland, & L. Wong (Eds.), *Innovation and change in English language education* (pp. 263–275). Routledge.

Dekker, T., & Feijs, E. (2005). Scaling up strategies for change: Change in formative assessment practices. *Assessment in Education*, *12*(3), 237–254.

DeLuca, C., & Klinger, D. A. (2010). Assessment literacy development: Identifying gaps in teacher candidates' learning. *Assessment in Education: Principles, Policy & Practice*, *17*(4), 419–438. https://doi.org/10.1080/0969594X.2010.516643

20 Assessment and Teacher Assessment Literacy

Dunn, K., & Mulvenon, S. (2009). A critical review of research on formative assessment: The limited scientific evidence of the impact of formative. *Practical Assessment, Research & Evaluation, 14*(7), 1–11. https://doi.org/10.7275/jg4h-rb87

Evers, C. W., & Mason, M. (2011). Context based inferences in research methodology: The role of culture in justifying knowledge claims. *Comparative Education, 47*(3), 301–314. https://doi.org/10.1080/03050068.2011.586763

Ferguson, R. F., & Brown, J. (2000). Certification test scores, teacher quality, and student achievement. In D. Grissmer & J. M. Ross (Eds.), *Analytic issues in the assessment of student achievement*. National Center for Education Statistics.

Flagg, E., & Ayling, D. (2011). Teacher engagement in a Web 2.0 world: Developing your online teaching and learning Community of Practice. In G. Williams, P. Statham, N. Brown & B. Cleland (Eds.), *Changing Demands, Changing Directions*. Proceedings ascilite Hobart 2011. (pp. 386–391).

Friedman, H., & MacDonald, D. (2006). Humanistic testing and assessment. *Journal of Humanistic Psychology, 46*(4), 510–529.

Fulcher, G. (2012). Assessment literacy for the language classroom. *Language Assessment Quarterly, 9*(2), 113–132. https://doi.org/10.1080/15434303.2011.642041

Gipps, C. (1999). Socio-cultural aspects of assessment. *Review of Research in Education, 24*, 355–392.

Goddard, Y., Goddard, R. D., & Tschannen-Moran, M. (2007). A theoretical and empirical investigation of teacher collaboration for school improvement and student achievement in public elementary schools. *Teachers College Record, 109*(4), 877–896.

Guo, W., & Wei, J. (2019). Teacher feedback and students' self-regulated learning in Mathematics: A study of Chinese secondary students. *The Asia-Pacific Education Researcher*. https://doi.org/10.1007/s40299-019-00436-6

Fullan, M. (2002). Principals as leaders in a culture of change. *Educational Leadership, special issue, May 2002*. https://michaelfullan.ca/wp-content/uploads/2016/06/13396053050.pdf

Hannigan, C., Alonzo, D., & Oo, C. Z. (2022). Student assessment literacy: Indicators and domains from the literature. *Assessment in Education: Principles, Policy & Practice, 29*(4), 482–504. https://doi.org/10.1080/0969594X.2022.2121911

Harrison, C. (2005). Teachers developing assessment for learning: mapping teacher change. *Teacher Development, 9*(2), 255–263. https://doi.org/10.1080/1366453 0500200251

Hattie, J. (2008). *Visible learning: A synthesis of over 800 meta-analyses relating to achievement*. Routledge:London. https://doi.org/10.4324/9780203887332

Hattie, J., & Timperley, H. (2007). The power of feedback. *Review of Educational Research, 77*(1), 81–112.

Hayward, L., & Hedge, N. (2005). Travelling towards change in assessment: Policy, practice and research in education. *Assessment in Education, 12*(1), 55–75.

Hendry, G. D., Armstrong, S., & Bromberger, N. (2012). Implementing standards-based assessment effectively: Incorporating discussion of exemplars into classroom teaching. *Assessment & Evaluation in Higher Education, 37*(2), 149–161. https://doi.org/10.1080/02602938.2010.515014

Herzog-Punzenberger, B., Altrichter, H., Brown, M., Burns, D., Nortvedt, G. A., Skedsmo, G., Wiese, E., Nayir, F., Fellner, M., McNamara, G., & O'Hara, J. (2020). Teachers responding to cultural diversity: Case studies on assessment practices, challenges and experiences in secondary schools in Austria, Ireland, Norway and Turkey. *Educational Assessment, Evaluation and Accountability, 32*(3), 395–424. https://doi.org/10.1007/s11092-020-09330-y

Hong Kong Curriculum Development Council (2001). *Learning to learn: The way forward to curriculum development.* Hong Kong Curriculum Development Council.

Hutchinson, C., & Young, M. (2011). Assessment for learning in the accountability era: Empirical evidence from Scotland. *Studies in Educational Evaluation, 37*(1), 62–70. https://doi.org/10.1016/j.stueduc.2011.03.007

Inbar-Lourie, O. (2008). Constructing a language assessment knowledge base: A focus on language assessment courses. *Language Testing, 25*(3), 385–402.

James, M. (2006). Assessment, teaching and theories of learning. In J. Gardner (Ed.), *Assessment and learning.* London: Sage Publication Ltd.

Jones, L., Allen, B., Dunn, P., & Brooker, L. (2017). Demystifying the rubric: A five-step pedagogy to improve student understanding and utilisation of marking criteria. *Higher Education Research & Development, 36*(1), 129–142. https://doi.org/10.1080/07294360.2016.1177000

Keppel, M., & Carless, D. (2006). Learning-oriented assessment: A technology-based case study. *Assessment in Education, 13*(2), 179–191.

Klenowski, V. (2014). Towards fairer assessment. *The Australian Educational Researcher, 41*(4), 445–470. https://doi.org/10.1007/s13384-013-0132-x

Klenowski, V., Tobias, S., Funnell, B., Vance, F., & Kaeschagen, C. (2010) Culture-fair assessment: Challenging Indigenous students through effortful mathematics teaching. In *AARE International Education Research Conference,* 28 November–2 December 2010, Melbourne.

Koshy, S. (2013). Differentiated assessment activities: Customising to support learning. In P. Bartholomew, N. Courtney & C. Nygaard *(Eds.), Quality Enhancement of University Teaching and Learning,* Libri Publishing, Faringdon.

Lave, J., & Wenger, E. (1991). *Situated learning: Legitimate peripheral participation.* Cambridge: Cambridge University Press.

Learning and Teaching Scotland (2006). Assessment is for learning - Self-assessment toolkit. The Scottish Government: Education Scotland.

Leenknecht, M., Wijnia, L., Köhlen, M., Fryer, L., Rikers, R., & Loyens, S. (2021). Formative assessment as practice: The role of students' motivation. *Assessment & Evaluation in Higher Education, 46*(2), 236–255. https://doi.org/10.1080/02602938.2020.1765228

Marshall, B., & Drummond, M. J. (2006). How teachers engage with assessment for learning: Lessons from the classroom. *Research Papers in Education, 21*(2), 133–149.

Martin, A., & Dowson, M. (2009). Interpersonal relationships, motivation, engagement, and achievement: Yields for theory, current issues, and educational practice. *Review of Educational Research, 79*(1), 327–365.

McMillan, J. (2003). Understanding and improving teachers' classroom assessment decision making: Implications for theory and practice. *Educational Measurement: Issues and Practice, 22*(4), 34–43.

McNamara, T., & Roever, C. (2006). *Language testing: The social dimension.* Blackwell.

Mertler, C. A., & Campbell, C. (2005). *Measuring teachers' knowledge and application of classroom assessment concepts: Development of the assessment literacy inventory.* American Educational Research Association.

22 Assessment and Teacher Assessment Literacy

Ministry of Education of Brunei (2008). SPN 21 interem guidelines. Brunei: Curriculum Development.

Ministry of Education of Brunei (2011). School-based assessment for learning: Brunei SBAfL guidebooks for years 7 and 8 core subjects. Brunei: Curriculum Development.

Newfields, T. (2006). Teacher development and assessment literacy. In *5th annual JALT Pan-SIG conference*, Shizuoka, Japan, March 13–14, 2006.

Nieminen, J. H., Atjonen, P., & Remesal, A. (2021). Parents' beliefs about assessment: A conceptual framework and findings from Finnish basic education. *Studies in Educational Evaluation, 71*, 101097. https://doi.org/10.1016/j.stueduc.2021.101097

Nuthal, G. (1999). The way students learn: Acquiring knowledge from an integrated science and social studies unit. *Elementary School Journal, 99*(4), 303–342. https://www.jstor.org/stable/1002174

Patri, M. (2002). The influence of peer feedback on self- and peer-assessment of oral skills. *Language Testing, 19*(2), 109–131. https://doi.org/10.1191/0265532202lt224oa

Pedder, D. (2006). Organizational conditions that foster successful classroom promotion of learning how to learn. *Research Papers in Education, 21*(2), 171–200. https://doi.org/10.1080/02671520600615687

Pereira, D., Niklasson, L., & Flores, M. A. (2017). Students' perceptions of assessment: A comparative analysis between Portugal and Sweden. *Higher Education, 73*(1), 153–173. https://doi.org/10.1007/s10734-016-0005-0

Perrenoud, P. (1998). From formative evaluation to a controlled regulation of learning processes. Towards a wider conceptual field. *Assessment in Education: Principles, Policy & Practice, 5*(1), 85–102. https://doi.org/10.1080/0969595980050105

Popham, W. J. (2009). Assessment literacy for teachers: Faddish or fundamental? *Theory Into Practice, 48*(1), 4–11. https://doi.org/10.1080/00405840802577536

Popham, W.J. (2011). Assessment literacy overlooked: A teacher educator's confession, *The Teacher Educator, 46*(4), 265–273. https://doi.org/10.1080/08878730.2011.605048

Pryor, J., & Crossouard, B. (2005). A sociocultural theorization of formative assessment. In *Sociocultural theory in educational and practice conference*, University of Manchester, September 8–9, 2005.

Queensland Department of Education and the Arts (2005). Assessment and reporting. Queensland Government: Education.

Reeves, D. (2013). *From differentiated instruction to differentiated assessment* (Vol. 6). ASCD Express.

Rhodes, C., & Beneicke, S. (2002). Coaching, mentoring and peer-networking: challenges for the management of teacher professional development in schools. *Journal of In-service Education, 28*(2), 297–310. https://doi.org/10.1080/13674580200200184

Schlager, M. S., & Fusco, J. (2004). Teacher professional development, technology, and communities of practice: Are we putting the cart before the horse? In S. Barab, R. Klin & J. Gray (Eds.), *Designing for virtual communities in the service of learning.* Cambridge MA: Cambridge University Press.

Sadler, D. (2012). Assuring academic achievement standards: From moderation to calibration. *Assessment in Education: Principles, Policy and Practice, 20*, 5–19.

Sadler, D. R. (1989). Formative assessment and the design of instructional systems. *Instructional Science, 18*(2), 119–144. https://doi.org/10.1007/BF00117714

Singapore Ministry of Education (2008). Singapore Assessment and Examination Board.

Smith, E., & Gorard, S. (2005) The dissemination of formative assessment: A short response to Black, Harrison, Hodgen, Marshall and Wiliam. *Research Intelligence, 4*, 466–478.

Snook, I., Clark, J., Harker, R., O'Neill, A.-M., & O'Neill, J. G. (2009). Invisible learning? A commentary on John Hattie's book: Visible learning: A synthesis of over 800 meta-analyses relating to achievement. *New Zealand Journal of Educational Studies, 44*(1), 93–106.

Stiggins, R. J. (1991). Assessment literacy. *Phi Delta Kappan, 72*(7), 534–539.

Stiggins, R. J. (1997). *Student centered classroom assessment*. Prentice Hall.

Stiggins, R. J. (1999). Evaluating lassroom assessment training in teacher education programs. *Educational Measurement: Issues and Practice, 18*(1), 23–27. https://doi.org/10.1111/j.1745-3992.1999.tb00004.x

Stiggins, R. J. (2005). From formative assessment to assessment for learning: A path to success in standards-based schools. *Phi Delta Kappan, 87*(4), 324–328.

Stoynoff, S., & Chapelle, C. (2005). *ESOL test and testing: A resource for teachers and program administrators*. TESOL.

Taras, M. (2007). Terminal terminology: The language of assessment. In M. Reiss, R. Hayes, and A. Atkinson (Eds.), *Marginality and difference in education and beyond (pp. 52–67)*. Stoke-on-Trent: Trentham Books.

Taylor, L. (2009). Developing assessment literacy. *Annual Review of Applied Linguistics, 29*, 21–36.

Terhart, E. (2011). Has John Hattie really found the holy grail of research on teaching? An extended review of Visible Learning. *Journal of Curriculum Studies, 43*(3), 425–438. https://doi.org/10.1080/00220272.2011.576774

Thompson, M., & Wiliam, D. (2007). *Tight but loose: A conceptual framework for scaling up school reforms*. American Educational Research Association.

Villarroel, V., Bloxham, S., Bruna, D., Bruna, C., & Herrera-Seda, C. (2018). Authentic assessment: Creating a blueprint for course design. *Assessment & Evaluation in Higher Education, 43*, 840–854.

Vygotsky, L. (1978). *Mind and society: The development of higher mental processes*. Cambridge, MA: Harvard University Press.

Webb, N. (2002). Assessment literacy in a standard-based urban education setting. In *American Educational Research Association annual meeting*, April 1–5, 2002.

Willis, J. (2009) Assessment for learning: A sociocultural approach. In: Proceedings of Changing Climates: Education for Sustainable Futures, 30 November–4 December 2009, Australia, Queensland, Kelvin Grove.

Xu, Y., & Brown, G. T. L. (2016). Teacher assessment literacy in practice: A reconceptualization. *Teaching and Teacher Education, 58*(Supplement C), 149–162. https://doi.org/10.1016/j.tate.2016.05.010

Yan, Z., Chiu, M. M., & Ko, P. Y. (2020). Effects of self-assessment diaries on academic achievement, self-regulation, and motivation. *Assessment in Education: Principles, Policy & Practice, 27*(5), 562–583. https://doi.org/10.1080/0969594X.2020.1827221

Zhang, Z. (2021). Promoting student engagement with feedback: Insights from collaborative pedagogy and teacher feedback. *Assessment & Evaluation in Higher Education, 47*(4), 540–555. https://doi.org/10.1080/02602938.2021.1933900

Chapter 2

The Historical and Conceptual Development of Assessment

Introduction

The debates over the types and purposes of assessment divide many assessment practitioners, researchers and teachers. There are different perspectives on the key elements of assessment (Baroudi, 2007), its nature and process (Bennett, 2011), the distinction between summative assessment (SA) and formative assessment (FA) (Sadler, 1989), and the appropriateness of the use of assessment types (Wiliam, 2011). These different perspectives have created different understandings and thus different practices. Although it is not the aspiration of this book to create universally common practices because assessment is so context-driven, teachers' assessment practices do need to be underpinned by understanding that any assessment and assessment data should be used to support learning and teaching. Hence, it is critically important to establish a shared understanding of assessment to ensure that schools' assessment culture optimises student learning.

The following sections present the four waves of conceptualisations of assessment, starting from the period of adoption of assessment from the field of evaluation. This is followed by the period of dichotomisation where SA and FA divided practitioners and researchers in their view on which one is more effective in supporting student learning. The third wave is seen during the dominance of assessment *for* learning (AfL), with assessment seen as a continuum of practice rather than a dichotomy. However, FA and SA still dominated the educational discourse during this period, with AfL often used interchangeably with FA. Other assessment terminologies also emerged, including assessment *as* learning (AaL) and assessment *of* learning (AoL), to reconcile competing conceptualisations of assessment to support learning and teaching. However, these terminologies created more confusion than clarity around the purposes of assessment. The current wave, the fourth wave, conceptualises assessment within a broader model of pedagogy. The central role of assessment in learning and teaching is made more explicit. Also, there is an emerging consensus that competing terminologies related to assessment are irrelevant when assessment is used to support learning. The debates between

DOI: 10.4324/9781003396277-2

FA and SA are resolved, to some extent, as both types of assessments can be used to support learning.

Wave 1: Adoption, Dichotomisation and Formalisation

Although FA and SA have always been an implicit part of educational practice, it was in 1967 that Scriven made the distinction between formative and summative evaluation for program implementation. The former term was coined to describe the original concept of looking for data that could be used to modify the program during its entire implementation, while the latter term was used to describe the collection of data to judge the program's worth.

In 1971, the formative and summative concepts were adopted by Bloom, Hastings and Madaus and applied in the context of student learning by replacing the word 'evaluation' with 'assessment'. They describe the distinguishing features of SA versus FA, including their purpose and timing and the interpretability of data gathered (Bloom et al., 1981). Since then, both terms have been used operationally to distinguish the types and functions of assessment. In general, those assessments being conducted by teachers regularly or daily to gather data aimed at improving learning are collectively referred to as FA, while those assessments conducted to determine whether learning had occurred over a period of teaching are classified as SA. This distinction led to the dominant belief that SA is mutually exclusive from FA.

Despite the introduction of FA, the pressure of external examinations for accountability purposes continued to institutionalise SA as the dominant paradigm, especially in the United States of America (USA) as well as in the traditional examination-driven cultures of the non-English speaking world. The effort of schools to perform well in local, state, national and even international assessments has reinforced the prominence of SA practices in the classroom. This is evident in the countless number of books on SA focused on testing published during this period, with only a handful on FA. According to Sadler's (1989) inventory, from the time the word 'assessment' was used as a key concept, only the works of Rowntree (1977), Bloom et al. (1971), Black and Dockrell (1984), and Chater (1984) mentioned feedback and FA. The dominance of SA in the USA has continued to persist despite widespread calls for assessment reform (Stiggins, 2005).

During this period, the term AfL was not coined yet, and FA was given only superficial attention. Crooks (1988) published a review of the literature at the time, highlighting that students' assessment data from SA were rarely used to help them learn. He was one of the first assessment theorists who emphasised that feedback about students' performance must be communicated to induce further learning, a concept later strengthened and formalised by Sadler (1989).

The conception of and distinction between FA and SA in the USA spread to other countries, including Australia, which was not very reliant on high-stakes

26 Historical and Conceptual Development

tests during this period. Hence, judgements about student learning involved a relatively large degree of teacher-based assessment, even for formal secondary graduation requirements. In Queensland, Sadler (1989) formalised the distinction between FA and SA, attributing it to the work of Ramaprasad (1983), who puts feedback as the central feature of FA. Sadler argued that FA differs from SA regarding purpose and effect (like Bloom et al., 1981) but excluded timing as a distinguishing feature. He further posited that "many of the principles appropriate to summative assessments are not necessarily transferable to FA, the latter requires a distinctive conceptualisation and technology" (Sadler, 1889, p. 120). The work of Sadler further enhanced the dichotomy between FA and SA, which further divided teacher assessment practices into either FA or SA.

However, reviewing Sadler's conception of feedback as the central feature of FA, where the feedback is based on the collected and analysed evidence of learning, it can be argued that SA can also be used to provide feedback. In other words, conceptually, SA can be part of FA as the information gathered in SA about individual students' current level of learning can and should be used by both students and teachers to develop learning goals and approaches to meet the required standards. This point was later highlighted by Davison (2007) and Taras (2009) but was not acknowledged by Sadler. He maintained his view that SA and FA were mutually exclusive.

Wave 2: Complexification and Exploration

The second wave of complexification and exploration of the key concepts underpinning AfL was seen when the United Kingdom (UK) implemented an assessment reform in 1999 focused on using FA based on the work of Black and Wiliam (1998). Their meta-analysis of over 250 studies on the effects of FA in learning and teaching was commissioned by the Assessment Reform Group (ARG) to explore the utilisation of FA to improve student learning. Shortly after the publication of their seminal paper, which showed the powerful effect of FA in improving student learning and its benefits for underachieving performing students, various educational systems adopted FA as a centrepiece of their educational reforms. However, even before Black and Wiliam's work was commissioned, the value of FA in the UK had been acknowledged. In fact, from the 1970s until the release of Black and Wiliam's ground-breaking paper in 1998, although SA dominated educational systems, numerous studies documented the effects of assessment in supporting learning. In 1982, FA started to gain considerable attention with the recommendation of the Inquiry into the Teaching of Mathematics in Schools in the UK that "assessment should be diagnostic and supportive and teaching should be based on the scheme of work which is appraised and revised regularly" (Cockcroft, 1982, p. 243). In 1987, the UK government required the integration of national assessment and teachers' assessment to report individual achievement of students. This stirred

Historical and Conceptual Development 27

national debates because of the difficulty in integrating the results of FA with SA. It was emphasised by the National Curriculum Task Group on Assessment and Teaching (1998), the agency commissioned to develop a format for reporting the results of FA and SA as one, that the results of FA could be combined to be used for summative purposes, but the results of SA could not be used for formative purposes. This further confused teachers and did not encourage any interplay between FA and SA.

During this period, the definitions of FA and AfL started to be formalised. In the report of their study, Black and Wiliam (1998) defined FA as:

> We use the general term assessment to refer to all those activities undertaken by the teachers – and by their students in assessing themselves – that provide information to be used as feedback to modify teaching and learning activities. Such assessment becomes formative assessment when the evidence is actually used to adapt the teaching to meet the student needs.
>
> (p. 140)

This definition of FA is consistent with the work of Sadler where feedback is considered the main feature of FA. It is evident from this definition that the results of FA have to be used by teachers to modify their teaching to address the learning needs of students. However, attributing to FA, the worth of assessment activities to inform learning and teaching is quite simplistic as other factors contribute to the effectiveness of utilising assessment information to improve student learning.

The ARG encapsulated the fundamental problem with the term FA:

> The term 'formative' itself is open to a variety of interpretations and often means no more than that assessment is carried out frequently and is planned at the same time as teaching. Such assessment does not necessarily have all the characteristics just identified as helping learning. It may be formative in helping the teacher to identify areas where more explanation or practice is needed. But for pupils, the marks or remarks on their work may tell them about their success or failure but not about how to make progress towards further learning.
>
> (ARG, 1999, p. 7)

For ARG, the worth of assessment in improving student learning is guided by the key characteristics of AfL, of which FA is just a part. It is significant to note that the ARG was not the first to use the term AfL. It was first used by H. Black (1986) in a published book chapter. However, the paper presented by James (1992) on AfL at the American Educational Research Association (AERA) conference and the book published by Sutton (1995) with the title 'Assessment *for* Learning' provided the primary impetus for the use of the concept. The ARG defined AfL as "the process of seeking and interpreting

28 Historical and Conceptual Development

evidence for use by learners and their teachers to decide where the learners are in their learning, where they need to go and how best to get there" (ARG, 2002, p. 2). With this definition, the ARG (2002) formulated ten principles of AfL based on the research evidence of effective teacher assessment practices. According to ARG, assessment:

- Is part of effective planning
- Focuses on how students learn
- Is central to classroom practice
- Is a key professional skill
- Is sensitive and constructive
- Fosters motivation
- Promotes understanding of goals and criteria
- Helps learners how to improve
- Develops the capacity for self-assessment
- Recognises all educational achievement

The ARG's definition of AfL and its characteristics broadened Black and Wiliam's pedagogical definition of FA. It emphasised the responsibility of students for their learning and the need to ensure they are highly involved in assessment processes and in monitoring their learning, so they had substantial information (including feedback from teachers and the results of self- and peer assessments) to identify what they needed to do in order to attain the desired learning outcomes. The three processes described in the definition offered by ARG are consistent with the core premises identified by Ramaprasad (1983) and adopted by Sadler (1989) to allow feedback to function (see Table 2.1).

Table 2.1 Comparison of the Three Macro Processes in Feedback, FA and AfL

ARG (1999, p. 2)	Sadler (1989, p. 121)	Ramaprasad (1983, p. 6)
Learners and their teachers to decide	Learners have to	Conditions required for feedback to function include the availability of
Where the learners are in their learning	Compare the actual (or current) level of performance with the standard	Data on the actual data level of the same parameter
Where they need to go	Possess a concept of the standard (or goal, or reference) being aimed for	Data on the reference level of the focal system parameters
How best to get there	Engage in appropriate action which leads to some closure of the gap	Mechanism [for] comparing the two data to generate information about the gap between the two levels

The work of ARG in promoting the concept of A*f*L received significant attention in many educational systems, including England, Wales, Hong Kong, Singapore and most states of Australia, all of which took up A*f*L as a basis for their assessment reform. However, the attention received by A*f*L and the continuous promotion of Black and Wiliam and Black et al. of FA created some confusion among teachers, researchers and even among themselves. In 2003 Black et al. extended their definition of FA. However, they used it synonymously with A*f*L and still emphasised that the main feature of the extended definition is the utilisation of assessment results as feedback to improve student learning.

> Assessment *for* learning is any assessment for which the first priority in its design and practice is to serve the purpose of promoting pupils' learning. It thus differs from assessment designed primarily to serve the purposes of accountability, or of ranking, or of certifying competence. An assessment activity can help learning if it provides information to be used as feedback, by the teachers, and by their pupils in assessing themselves and each other, to modify the teaching and learning activities in which they are engaged. Such assessment becomes 'formative assessment' when the evidence is actually used to adapt the teaching work to meet learning needs.
>
> (Black et al., 2003, pp. 2–3)

It is interesting to note that Black and Wiliam acknowledge the participation of students in assessment processes, particularly self- and peer assessments, but still use the term FA to describe the practice of using assessment data to adjust teaching practices to meet student learning needs. This revised definition of FA by Black et al. (2003) was criticised by Taras (2009) [although Taras herself earlier had used the term interchangeably (see Taras, 2005)], as it contradicted Black and Wiliam's earlier definition as there was no mention of student responsibilities in assessment. She commented, "FA is part of teaching methodology and has more to do with teachers than learners, thus seeming to contradict the initial definitions" (p. 61). Even Stiggins (2002) was at one point tempted to use A*f*L as synonymous with FA but quickly clarified that these two terms were not the same. Stiggins emphasised that the processes in FA of frequent assessment to provide information to teachers to adjust learning are just part of A*f*L. According to him, in the process of learning, FA becomes A*f*L if students become actively involved in the assessment processes and become controllers of their learning.

Not only did Black and Wiliam and Black et al. change their definitions of FA and A*f*L several times, they also widened the dichotomy between FA and SA. Their exclusion of the effects of SA on students' learning in their research made teachers and other researchers think that SA must function very differently and separately from FA. Shortly after publishing their 1998 paper, Biggs (1998) critiqued the premise of the study, which focused only on FA without

30 Historical and Conceptual Development

accounting for the interplay of SA. Biggs' critique focused on the effects of SA on learning which he called 'backwash' (Biggs, 1996), arguing that it can negatively affect learning and its effect can be much stronger than the effects of feedback. Biggs wanted to see Black and Wiliam deal with the broader context in which learning occurs. Biggs (1996) argued that:

> A strong interaction between FA and SA could be incorporated in an overall synthesis, so both backwash (from SA) and feedback (from FA) are conceptualised within the same framework. Then indeed one might have a powerful enhancement of learning, using such a synthesis to engineer backwash from SA so that the effects were positive, the backwash from SA supporting the feedback from FA.
>
> (p. 106)

Biggs's argument highlights the interconnectedness of FA and SA; that is, it is impossible to entirely isolate one from the other, as they both support each other. Despite the wide range of evidence and criticisms of the weaknesses (both theoretically and practically) of their conception of FA, Black and Wiliam and Black et al. continued using the term FA instead of A*f*L to collectively describe all assessment practices that improve learning and teaching.[1]

In 2009, Black and Wiliam made a slight revision of their definition of FA, which they claimed to be consistent with the definition of A*f*L by the ARG:

> Practice in a classroom is formative to the extent that evidence about student achievement is elicited, interpreted, and used by teachers, learners, or their peers to make decisions about the next steps in instruction that are likely to be better, or better founded, than the decisions they would have taken in the absence of the evidence that was elicited.
>
> (p. 109)

Not only did Black and Wiliam revise their definition of FA, but they also added more elements or key characteristics to FA. They incorporated many of the elements of assessment practices that had been proven by research to improve teaching and learning. For example, the critique by Biggs (1998) of their article regarding the exclusion of the effect of SA in learning pressed them to incorporate SA as part of FA (Black & Wiliam, 2009), adjusting their earlier position that SA cannot be used for formative purposes. Black and Wiliam and their colleagues, Harrison, Lee and Marshall, revised the four areas suggested in their original paper, Inside the Black Box, to include the formative use of summative tests (Black et al., 2003). They argued that the result of SA shows evidence of students' achievement and, therefore, can be used to elicit and give feedback. Also, they emphasised the value of SA, "these can also communicate to students what is and is not valued in a particular discipline, thus communicating criteria for success" (Black & Wiliam, 2009, p. 8).

Another revision of Black and Wiliam's conception of FA is their adoption of Perrenoud's (1998) argument that feedback is not the main issue, but rather it is just one of the many elements that affect learning. In 2009, Black and Wiliam linked their analysis of feedback to other learning theories "so that the concept of formative interaction may be enriched and contextualised in the light of relevant theories" (p. 6), including the self-regulated learning model (Boekaerts & Corno, 2005; Boekaerts et al., 2005) which was linked to the role of feedback.

The complexification and exploration of the use of FA and AfL and the exclusion of SA from FA have driven researchers and teachers to find empirical and theoretical evidence to resolve the issue. This triggered much research and many arguments around using FA and SA to improve student learning. As more and more research findings were made available and more FA, SA and AfL theorisations developed, teachers, researchers, policymakers and other stakeholders started to understand what was fundamental to assessment practices that promote student learning. However, this realisation did not stop other researchers (i.e. Black & Wiliam, 2009) from widening the dichotomy between FA and SA, hence, seemingly creating more confusion and resistance (Bennett, 2009).

During this time, a large number of studies explored the effects of FA and SA on student learning. Most of the studies were focused on investigating the effects of SA on student learning to find strong evidence to support the superior role of SA over FA in learning and teaching. However, as researchers gathered evidence to show that SA raises standards, what was also highlighted was its negative effects in limiting learning (Harlen & Deakin Crick, 2003), narrowing the curriculum (Johnston & McClune, 2000; Reay & William, 1999) and compromising teaching (Gordon & Reese, 1997; Leonard & Davey, 2001; Pollard et al., 2002; Shepard, 2000).

Another area of exploration during this period was the interplay between FA and SA. Researchers concluded that SA could be used to enhance learning and teaching in various ways. One of the findings was that if the content, format and design of SA reflect the development of skills, then students' preparation could increase their motivation as they try to understand the links between different concepts (Shepard, 2006). Also, a synergy between SA and FA exists (Harlen, 2005) as evidence of student learning can be used for any purposes. This is exemplified by the use of portfolios for high-stake assessments in Queensland where the evidence of student learning collected is used to provide regular feedback to students. Then, at the end of the specific period of teaching, the documented evidence of student learning is summarised to describe the overall performance of the students. To support the interplay of FA and SA, Taras (2009) argues that feedback always relies on SA as all assessment processes start with a SA. According to her, the effectiveness of FA is being constrained by resistance to acknowledging the interplay between FA and SA.

32 Historical and Conceptual Development

Wave 3: Realisation and Reconciliation

The realisation that the SA results can also be used to improve teaching and learning provided the impetus for the third phase of AfL development. This is the period when SA and FA were seen as mutually supporting each other's purposes. The work on AfL is more influential in this period than Black and Wiliam's (1998) and Black et al.'s (2003) conceptions of FA. Education departments, ministries, educators and teachers in the USA, Hong Kong, Singapore, Australia, New Zealand and Brunei moved forward from the previous conceptions of FA, building on the definition of AfL given by ARG, but incorporating specific elements that have been proven by research to contribute significantly to improving learning. For example, the role and value of SA (Bennett, 2009; Biggs, 1998; Stiggins, 2005), the effect of self-assessment in self-efficacy and intrinsic motivation (Schunk, 1996), and the role of the teachers as activators rather than facilitators of learning (Hattie, 2008) were highlighted during this period.

The distinction made between FA and SA is now seen as invaluable because these types of assessments do not function in isolation, as Biggs (1998) had further explained, especially "when the summative assessment is defining the parameters for the formative assessment, it does not seem helpful to confine a review of the one with the attempted exclusion of the other" (p. 108). As illustrated by Bennett (2009), assessments that are conducted to document student learning can also function formatively, and those assessments conducted by teachers regularly to modify their teaching can also be used for summative purposes. For this reason, Bennett tried to resolve the definitional issue of FA, but he did not acknowledge the use of the term AfL. His key point was "calling formative assessment by another name may only exacerbate, rather than resolve, the definitional issue" (Bennett, 2009, p. 7). This is not, however, the main argument with the definitional issue because these two terms are now clearly being used in different ways. AfL is now perceived as the overarching umbrella of which FA is just a part.

The resultant re-thinking of assessment practices, due to weakness in the ability of high-stakes tests to improve learning, triggered a return of interest in FA in the USA (Stiggins, 2005). The result of standardised SA conducted once a year does not help teachers gain significant insights about the learning of the students as SA collectively measures the overall achievement in all standards. Consequently, the lack of evidence of students' mastery in each standard makes it impossible for teachers to identify specific interventions to help individual students perform better. Furthermore, the timing of SA does not provide sufficient opportunity for teachers to use the data to enhance student learning. These realisations of teachers and researchers have slowly changed the way SA is conducted in the USA. SA is now conducted more frequently, and the results are used to inform instruction. Although this approach helps adjust teaching to help students learn better, the nature of the multiple-choice

Historical and Conceptual Development 33

tests used in SA and the responsibility given to teachers "fall short of tapping the immense potential of formative thinking" (Stiggins, 2005, p. 327). This has led to adopting an AfL approach, which Stiggins defines in contrast to two major elements of traditional formative thinking. First, he said, AfL includes not just FA that informs teaching but also informs students about their learning. Students are empowered to take active roles in their learning by being trained to use assessment information to make changes in how they learn and how they approach the achievement of learning outcomes. Second, while AfL incorporates frequent testing of student achievement of learning outcomes, it changes the focus of frequent assessment. Regular formal or informal assessments explore the learning steps to achieve the learning outcomes, "it tells users if and when students are attaining the foundations of knowledge, the reasoning, the performance skills, and the product development capabilities that underpin the mastery of essential standards" (p. 328). In other words, AfL provides a whole picture of students' progression toward the achievement of learning outcomes.

In a high-stakes test environment, AfL has been seen to effectively improve learning without the negative effects of assessment while maintaining accountability (Popham, 2011). This is best exemplified by the practice of Queensland, Australia, with their state-wide Core Skills Test of student assessment administered in the final years of secondary school. The Queensland Studies Authority collects and analyses assessment data and disseminates the results to the schools, including information on how students responded to the test. Teachers use the information provided to adjust learning and teaching activities. This practice supports the idea that for a successful implementation of AfL, assessment data should be used at all levels of authority (i.e., monitoring and evaluation of teaching practices, professional development and policy) to influence classroom practices. What is highlighted in this practice is the critical role of state authorities in providing support to teachers in their assessment literacy (Klenowski, 2011). Another example of the participation of state authorities in assessment is the case of the Board of Studies Teaching and Educational Standards (BOSTES) of New South Wales in Australia, where they created the Assessment Resource Centre website aimed at supporting and enhancing professional practice in assessment and reporting student achievement.

The current thinking about AfL has helped to reconcile the different functions of SA and FA, and to see them as a continuum (Davison, 2007) rather than a dichotomy. Other core concepts have also shifted during this current period, including the role of the teacher. The role of the teachers in student learning, in the 1980s and 1990s widely conceptualised as a facilitator, has shifted to being seen as an activator of learning. Stiggins (2005) argues that when AfL is used effectively, it "always triggers an optimistic response to assessment results from within the learners" (p. 328). The processes identified by Stiggins that help teachers trigger learning were highlighted due to Hattie's (2008) meta-analysis.

34 Historical and Conceptual Development

There are several key points that underpin the current re-thinking of AfL. The philosophy underlying assessment processes in AfL is empowerment. Collectively, AfL activities should be an enabling mechanism to develop the ability of students to take responsibility for their learning. This makes AfL a truly student-centred approach. In this approach to assessment, students are guided to identify their strengths and weaknesses, understand success criteria and standards, assess their own and their peers' work, become responsive to the feedback they receive and set goals to achieve the desired learning outcomes. In other words, teachers are more concerned about the processes of assessment and learning, not just the procedure, and work to ensure that students actively participate in learning and teaching activities.

As part of this review of AfL, the role and nature of teacher professional development related explicitly to assessment has also been highlighted. As activators of learning and instructional designers, teachers have multiple, complex and interrelated tasks that need regular moderation. To ensure that AfL is effectively implemented, teachers have a two-fold task: (1) to develop their AfL skills and (2) to ensure that students will respond positively to the activation to develop their skills required in learning. If teachers are focused only on enhancing their skills, then AfL is a failure. Prior knowledge and subsequent training for teachers are important aspects of AfL. While students are learning, it is also expected that teachers should do the same. AfL then requires teachers to continue engaging in professional development (formal or informal) to address their professional needs.

Around this time, AfL also started to gain prominence in Asian countries, which have a long history of SA-dominant practices. After Hong Kong, countries like Singapore and Brunei quickly adopted the concept. In Hong Kong, school-based assessment (SBA) for English language education is rooted in the principles of AfL (Davison, 2007, 2013). Apart from public examinations, teachers design assessment tasks and conduct formal and informal classroom assessments while engaging students in self- and peer assessments. AfL, in this context, is used to gather a holistic view of student achievement because traditional testing cannot provide information about the more important aspects of learning. The most significant contribution of this initiative has been the adoption of a more inclusive model of AfL where all assessments, either formative or summative, are conceptualised under the umbrella of AfL and are conducted to help students in their learning (Kennedy et al., 2006).

In Singapore, the principles of AfL were incorporated into their traditional practice. Much of the effort of the government goes into professional development, where the focus is on enhancing teacher assessment literacy in using AfL in the classroom. With Singapore's recent assessment reform, Tan (2011) argues that the effect of assessment on student learning should also be considered. In other words, useful and meaningful assessment practices enable and support the development of students' lifelong learning skills, with AfL having a proven benefit in acquiring such skills (Hanrahan & Isaacs, 2001).

Historical and Conceptual Development   35

In Brunei, the principles and practices of AfL have been incorporated into their SBA reform, which they now call school-based assessment for learning (SBAfL). The SBAfL is uniquely contextualised to meet the objectives of the Brunei assessment reform. It was initially designed for students in Year 7 and 8 to prepare them to transition to upper secondary school. SBAfL is a dominant practice from Term 1 of Year 7 to Term 3 of Year 8. The use of AfL incorporates the typology of assessment practices developed by Davison (2007). In Terms 1 and 2 of Year 7, students are provided with assessment activities that are designed to scaffold their acquisition of skills in taking responsibility for their learning. The process starts with informal assessment activities that help students prepare for their engagement in assessment starting in Term 3 of Year 7. It eventually progresses into more formal assessment activities, which are criteria-based and address the students' needs while adhering to external standards. As students enter Term 3 in Year 7, they will engage with a prescribed set of assessment tasks over 18 months called the Brunei Common Assessment Tasks (BCATs), which comprise a variety of authentic assessment tasks. These assessments have both formative and summative functions. While the combined result of SBAfL comprises 30% of their final grade, the BCATs are used by teachers to engage students in self- and peer assessments and to provide meaningful feedback to assist them in their learning. In 2012, SBAfL was extended to all Brunei primary schools.

Another equally important development in the reconceptualisation of AfL has been the realisation that the responsibility for student learning does not just lie only with teachers and students alone. A concerted effort and common understanding by all stakeholders are needed to ensure that government policies, curriculum design and parents' expectations do not constrain the effective implementation of AfL (Bennett, 2011; Davison, 2013). AfL operates in a wider educational context, hence as argued by Davison (2013), policymakers also play an important role in AfL. The policies and guidelines they create may make or break AfL implementation. Teachers, students and all other stakeholders involved in the educational process, particularly policymakers, need to have common aims, beliefs and understandings to enable the successful implementation of AfL (Buhagiar, 2007; Hayward & Hedge, 2005; Hayward et al., 2004). Thus, the definition of AfL should not only focus on the roles of teachers but also consider system issues referred to by Bennett (2011). For example, in a high accountability educational culture, the implementation of AfL is only possible if teachers are experts in all domains of AfL. To successfully implement assessment reform, all components of the education system should function coherently.

Wave 4: Conceptualisation within a Pedagogical Model

This wave started as early as 2009 when Black and Wiliam linked their analysis of feedback to other learning theories "so that the concept of formative interaction may be enriched and contextualised in the light of relevant theories"

36 Historical and Conceptual Development

(p. 6), including the self-regulated learning model (Boekaerts & Corno, 2005; Boekaerts et al., 2005), which was linked to the role of feedback. One of the significant theorisations is the relationship between curriculum and assessment (Daugherty et al., 2011). Black explores the relationship of FA and SA by framing both within an overarching model of pedagogy. From this period onwards, Black et al. (2011) and his colleagues have made significant theorisation on the use of SA for formative purposes. They extensively explored how teachers can enhance their competence in SA, particularly on how to use it to improve learning and teaching. Black (2014) argues that test performance needs to be the basis for feedback to students for SA to work formatively. Students should have the opportunity to do further work based on feedback on test performance. He emphasised that this process will also shape students' understanding of the value of SA. He also emphasised that the distinction between formative and summative lies in the purpose for which the assessment findings are used.

This wave was formalised more recently when Black (2017) re-emphasised the role of SA in helping students to learn effectively. He identified three critical elements – feedback, roles of teachers and students, and modification of learning and teaching activities based on assessment information gathered. In 2018, Black and Wiliam revisited the recommendation of Perrenoud (1998) to theorise FA in a broader theoretical field, particularly in the theory of pedagogy. A limitation that has also been cited by Baird et al. (2017) where they argue that assessment and learning are fields apart in their current forms. Black and Wiliam clearly articulated how assessment is linked to broader pedagogical approaches of teachers and emphasised that the distinction between FA and SA "is not useful because all assessment would be about producing valid inferences about students" (p. 570).

At this stage, the theorisation of assessment within a broader pedagogical model continues to develop. Baird et al. (2017) highlight that assessment and learning are fields apart because of the apparent lack of connection between learning and assessment theories. They argue that at this stage, where assessment is highly prominent and used for any purposes in any educational system, there should have been sophisticated integrated theorisation of learning and assessment. Their main message is "that if assessments are to serve the goals of education, then theories of learning and assessment should be developing more closely with each other … this discussion on the relationship between assessment and learning should be developed further and be at the forefront of high-stakes, large-scale educational assessments" (p. 317).

In fact, at this stage, Brown (2019) questions if AfL is truly an assessment, and he concludes that AfL is not a form of assessment, but rather it is more accurately described as a pedagogical curriculum approach. This means that AfL practices are best used to guide teaching interactions within the classroom and cannot be relied upon for decision-making beyond this context due to issues with accuracy in teacher and student judgement. He argues that if decisions are made based on teacher and student judgement, it might lead to invalid conclusions about student learning. He said that "without social or statistical moderation, stakeholders cannot be assured that valid conclusions are reached.... Because teaching requires robust evidence to support decisions made about students and teachers, the practices commonly associated with AfL cannot provide sufficient evidence on which to base anything more than teaching interactions" (n.p.). However, the issues raised by Brown on the accuracy of teacher and student judgement have been clearly argued in the literature. There are proxy measures used to ensure the accuracy of teacher judgement. Brookhart (2003), Moss (2003) and Smith (2003) developed the 'classroometric' principles of assessment to ensure the accuracy and consistency of classroom assessments that do not allow for statistical analysis (see Chapter 7 for extensive discussion).

In the current conceptualisation of assessment, the dichotomy between SA and FA and the competing use of FA and AfL is becoming more irrelevant. What appears to be a robust conceptualisation of assessment includes the following:

1 Students and teachers are working as partners to elicit evidence of learning.
2 Any assessment and assessment data are used by students, teachers and the whole school community to identify individual students' strengths and weaknesses to improve their learning.
3 Learning and teaching activities are driven by assessment. Students and teachers use assessment information to modify learning and teaching activities.
4 Any decision made concerning student learning must be supported by assessment data to be trustworthy.
5 Assessment is context-driven; hence, students and teachers must acknowledge contextual factors that enable or hinder its effectiveness.

Conclusion

In summary, the theorisation of assessment has gone through a long process of debate, complexification, exploration, confusion and convergence. The dichotomy of FA and SA once divided teachers, researchers and even policy makers. As each camp sought to establish dominance over the other, significant insights from various research studies on FA and SA, conducted separately or in combination, have emerged. After resisting the dichotomisation of SA and FA, reconciliation has started. However, much attention has focused on using competing terminologies like AfL, AaL and AoL rather than looking at FA and SA separately. The use of AfL as an overarching framework for using assessment to support learning and teaching still causes some confusion due to its strong association with FA. Recently, assessment is purposely conceptualised within a broader pedagogical model. Competing assessment terminologies slowly become irrelevant as it is acknowledged that all types and forms of assessment can be and should be used to support learning and

38 Historical and Conceptual Development

teaching beyond the accountability requirements of educational systems. This theorisation places assessment as the central feature of learning and teaching – an assessment conceptualised within a broader pedagogical model.

In this book, as earlier cited in Chapter 1, I use the term assessment to refer to all types of assessment, from in-class contingent FA, planned FA, mock SA, to the most formal SA, including high stake testing and international examinations whose results are used to support learning and teaching (Davison, 2007). When specific terminologies are used, that is formative, summative, feedback, I am referring to a specific type of assessment, but still, the results are used to support learning. The use of these terminologies is more prominent in the succeeding chapters to adhere to the original terminologies reported in the literature.

Note

1 In 2007, Stiggins, who referenced and cited Black and Wiliam's (1999) work on FA, commented that he had stopped using the term FA because, through the years of its development, the term has lost its meaning.

References

ARG. (1999). *Assessment for learning: Beyond the black box.* http://hdl.handle.net/2428/4621

ARG. (2002). *Assessment for learning: 10 principles.* https://www.storre.stir.ac.uk/bitstream/1893/32458/1/Assessment%20for%20learning%2010%20principles%202002.pdf

Baird, J.-A., Andrich, D., Hopfenbeck, T. N., & Stobart, G. (2017). Assessment and learning: Fields apart? *Assessment in Education: Principles, Policy & Practice, 24*(3), 317–350. https://doi.org/10.1080/0969594X.2017.1319337

Baroudi, Z. M. (2007). Formative assessment: Definition, elements and role in instructional practice. *Post-Script. Postgraduate Journal of Education Research, 8*(1), 37–48.

Bennett, R. E. (2009). *Formative assessment: Can the claims for effectiveness be substantiated?* Retrieved March 12, 2010. http://www.iaea.info/documents/paper_4d5260ae.pdf

Bennett, R. E. (2011). Formative assessment: A critical review. *Assessment in Education: Principles Policy and Practice, 18*(1), 5–25. https://doi.org/10.1080/0969594X.2010.513678

Biggs, J. (1996). Assessing learning quality: Reconciling institutional, staff and educational demands. *Assessment and Evaluation in Higher Education, 21*(1), 5–15.

Biggs, J. (1998). Assessment and classroom learning: A role for summative assessment? *Assessment and Evaluation, 5*(1), 103–110.

Black, P. (2014). Assessment and the aims of the curriculum: An explorer's journey. *Prospects, 44*(4), 487–501. https://doi.org/10.1007/s11125-014-9329-7

Black, H. (1986). Assessment for learning. In D. L. Nuttall (Ed.), *Assessing educational achievement* (pp. 7–18). London: Falmer Press.

Black, P. (2017). Assessment in science education. In K. S. Taber & B. Akpan (Eds.), *Science education: An international course companion* (pp. 295–309). SensePublishers. https://doi.org/10.1007/978-94-6300-749-8_22

Black, H., & Dockrell, W. B. (1984). *Criterion-referenced assessment in the classroom.* Scottish Council for Research in Education.

Black, P., Harrison, C., Hodgen, J., Marshall, B., & Serret, N. (2011). Can teachers' summative assessments produce dependable results and also enhance classroom learning? *Assessment in Education: Principles, Policy & Practice*, *18*(4), 451–469. https://doi.org/10.1080/0969594X.2011.557020

Black, P., Harrison, C., Lee, C., Marshall, B., & Wiliam, D. (2003). *Assessement for learning: Putting it into practice.* Oxford University Press.

Black, P., & Wiliam, D. (1998). Assessment and classroom learning. *Assessment in Education: Principles, Policy & Practice*, *5*(1), 7–74. https://doi.org/10.1080/0969595980050102

Black, P., & Wiliam, D. (1999). Assessment for learning: Beyond the black box. Cambridge: University of Cambridge School of Education.

Black, P., & Wiliam, D. (2009). Developing the theory of formative assessment. *Educational Assessment, Evaluation and Accountability*, *21*, 5–31.

Bloom, B. S., Hastings, J. T., & Madaus, G. (1971). *Handbook on formative and summative evaluation of student learning.* McGraw-Hill.

Bloom, B. S., Madaus, G., & Hastings, J. T. (1981). *Evaluation to improve learning.* McGraw-Hill.

Boekaerts, M., & Corno, L. (2005). Self-regulation in the classroom: A perspective on assessment and intervention. *Applied Psychology*, *54*(2), 199–231.

Boekaerts, M., Maes, S., & Karoly, P. (2005). Self-regulation across domains of applied psychology: Is there an emerging consensus? *Applied Psychology*, *53*(2), 149–154.

Brookhart, S. M. (2003). Developing measurement theory for classroom assessment purposes and uses. *Educational Measurement: Issues and Practice*, *22*(4), 5–12. https://doi.org/10.1111/j.1745-3992.2003.tb00139.x

Brown, G. T. L. (2019). Is assessment for learning really assessment? [Perspective]. *Frontiers in Education*, *4*(64). https://doi.org/10.3389/feduc.2019.00064

Buhagiar, M. (2007). Classroom assessment within the alternative assessment paradigm: Revisiting the territory. *The Curriculum Journal*, *18*(1), 39–56.

Chater, P. (1984). *Marking and assessment in English.* Methuen.

Cockcroft, W. H. (1982). Mathematics counts. Report of the Committee of Inquiry into the Teaching of Mathematics in Primary and Secondary School sin England and Wales. HSMO: London.

Crooks, T. J. (1988). The impact of classroom evaluation practices on students. *Review of Educational Research*, *58*(4), 438–481.

Daugherty, R., Black, P., Ecclestone, K., James, M., & Newton, P. (2011). Assessment of significant learning outcomes. In R. Berry & B. Adamson (Eds.), *Assessment reform in education: Policy and practice* (pp. 165–183). Springer Netherlands. https://doi.org/10.1007/978-94-007-0729-0_12

Davison, C. (2007). Views from the chalkface: English language school based assessment in Hong Kong. *Language Assessment Quarterly*, *4*(1), 37–68. https://doi.org/10.1080/15434300701348359

40 Historical and Conceptual Development

Davison, C. (2013). Innovation in assessment: Common misconceptions and problems. In K. Hyland, & L. Wong (Eds.), *Innovation and change in English language education* (pp. 263–275). Routledge.

Gordon, S., & Reese, M. (1997). High stakes testing: Worth the price? *Journal of School Leadership, 7,* 345–368.

Hanrahan, S. J., & Isaacs, G. (2001). Assessing self- and peer-assessment: The students' views. *Higher Education Research and Development, 20*(1), 53–70.

Harlen, W. (2005). Teachers' summative practices and assessment for learning-tensions and synergies. *British Curriclum Foundation, 16*(2), 207–223. https://doi.org/10.1080/09585170500136093

Harlen, W., & Deakin Crick, R. (2003). Teaching and motivation for learning. *Assessment in Education, 10*(2), 169–208.

Hattie, J. (2008). *Visible learning: A synthesis of over 800 meta-analyses relating to achievement.* Routledge.

Hayward, L., & Hedge, N. (2005). Travelling towards change in assessment: Policy, practice and research in education. *Assessment in Education, 12*(1), 55–75.

Hayward, L., Priestley, M., & Young, M. (2004). Ruffling the clam of the ocean floor: Merging practice, policy and research in assessment in Scotland. *Oxford Review of Education, 30*(3), 397–415.

James, M. (1992). Assessment for learning. Paper presented at the Annual Conference of the Association for Supervision and Curriculum Development. New Orleans, LA.

Johnston, J., & McClune, W. (2000). *Selection project sel 5.1. Pupil motivation and attitudes – Self-esteem, locus of control, learning disposition and the impact of selection teaching and learning.* Queen's University.

Kennedy, K. J., Sang, J. C. K., Wai-ming, F. Y., & Fok, P. K. (2006). Assessment for productive learning: forms of assessment and their potential for enhancing learning. In *32nd annual conference of the International Association for Educational Assessment.* Singapore.

Klenowski, V. (2011). Assessment for learning in the accountability era: Queensland, Australia. *Studies in Educational Evaluation, 37*(1), 78–83. http://www.sciencedirect.com/science/article/pii/S0191491X11000162

Leonard, M., & Davey, C. (2001). *Thoughts on the 11 plus.* Save the Children Fund.

Moss, P. A. (2003). Reconceptualizing validity for classroom assessment. *Educational Measurement: Issues and Practice, 22*(4), 13–25. https://doi.org/10.1111/j.1745-3992.2003.tb00140.x

National Curriculum Task Group on Assessment and Teaching (1998). Department of Education and Science and the Welsh Office.

Perrenoud, P. (1998). From formative evaluation to a controlled regulation of learning processes: Towards a wider conceptual field. *Assessment in Education: Principles, Policy & Practice, 5*(1), 85–102. https://doi.org/10.1080/0969595980050105

Pollard, A., Triggs, P., Broadfoot, P., Mcness, E., & Osborn, M. (2002). *What pupils say: Changing policy and practice in primary education.* Continuum.

Popham, W.J. (2011). Assessment literacy overlooked: A teacher educator's confession, *The Teacher Educator, 46*(4), 265–273. https://doi.org/10.1080/08878730.2011.605048

Ramaprasad, A. (1983). On the definition of feedback. *Behavioral Science, 28,* 4–13.

Reay, D., & William, D. (1999). 'I'll be nothing': Structure, agency and the construction of identity through assessment. *British Educational Research Journal, 25,* 343–354.

Rowntree, D. (1977). *Assessing students: How shall we know them?* Harper and Row.

Sadler, D. R. (1989). Formative assessment and the design of instructional systems. *Instructional Science, 18*(2), 119–144. https://doi.org/10.1007/BF00117714

Schunk, D. H. (1996). Goal and self-evaluative influences during children's cognitive skill learning. *Educational Research Journal, 33*(2), 359–382.

Shepard, L. (2000). The role of assessment in a learning culture. *Educational Researcher, 29*(7), 4–14.

Shepard, L. (2006). Classroom assessment. In R. L. Brennan (Ed.), *Educational measurement* (4th ed., pp. 623–646). American Cuncil on Education/Praeger.

Smith, J. K. (2003). Reconsidering reliability in classroom assessment and grading. *Educational Measurement: Issues and Practice, 22*(4), 26–33. https://doi.org/10.1111/j.1745-3992.2003.tb00141.x

Stiggins, R. J. (2002). Assessment crisis: The absence of assessment for learning. *Kappan Professional Journal, 83*(10), 758–765.

Stiggins, R. J. (2005). From formative assessment to assessment for learning: A path to success in standards-based schools. *Phi Delta Kappan, 87*(4), 324–328.

Sutton, R. (1995) *Assessment for learning.* Salford, RS Publications.

Tan, K. (2011). Assessment for learning in Singapore: Unpacking its meanings and identifying areas for improvement. *Educational Research Policy Practice, 10,* 91–103. https://doi.org/10.1007/s10671-010-9096-z

Taras, M. (2005). Assessment-summative and formative- some theoretical reflections. *British Journal of Educational Studies, 53*(4), 466–478. https://doi.org/10.1111/j.1467-8527.2005.00307.x

Taras, M. (2009). Summative assessment: The missing link for formative assessment. *Journal of Further and Higher Education, 33*(1), 57–69.

Wiliam, D. (2011). *Formative assessment: Definitions and relationships.* Institute of Education, University of London. http://eprints.ioe.ac.uk/6806/1/Wiliam2011 What2.pdf

Chapter 3

Isn't Assessment to Support Learning Just Good Teaching?

Introduction

In the work of Alonzo (2016) in establishing the dimensions of teacher assessment literacy, described in Chapter 1, one of the dimensions, Teachers as Pedagogy Experts, relates to how teachers use assessment and assessment data to inform learning and teaching. This dimension emphasises teachers' roles in using assessment information to inform their teaching, highlighting the pedagogical use of assessment data. Student assessment data are important inputs for teachers' instructional design and planning (Datnow et al., 2021; Poortman & Schildkamp, 2016). These data are not only limited to student achievement (from qualitative teacher records to high-stake tests) but include socio-demographic and contextual information about schools, teachers and students and non-cognitive characteristics of students, teachers and school leaders (Beswick et al., 2022). McMillan (2000) confirms that integrating assessment data into instructional planning develops teachers' capacity to decide the focus and teaching level appropriate for a specific group of students. Other researchers have also highlighted how planning learning and teaching activities requires a high level of teacher understanding of student learning characteristics, including their interests, motivation, learning needs and prior knowledge (Hornstra et al., 2015; Jimerson et al., 2019; Leenknecht et al., 2021). Teachers' use of assessment data to adapt learning and teaching activities enables them to develop and implement differentiated instruction to support individual students (Alonzo & Loughland, 2022; Tomlinson & McTighe, 2006).

In addition, this pedagogical dimension highlights the ability of teachers to embed assessment into teaching effectively. This ability is aligned with the principles of effective teacher assessment practices that argue for the "central role of assessment to classroom practice" (ARG, 2002). In this principle, assessment has a pivotal role in ensuring effective learning and teaching, but this happens only when assessment is viewed as an integral part of learning and teaching activities. Assessment should not be an afterthought in planning. Many studies provide strong empirical evidence for the effectiveness of

DOI: 10.4324/9781003396277-3

Using Assessment to Support Learning   43

using assessment as a learning activity to raise student outcomes (Keppel & Carless, 2006; Marshall & Drummond, 2006; To & Liu, 2018; Yan & Carless, 2022). Students benefit from their engagement with various assessment tasks as learning tasks. These tasks require them to utilise various cognitive processes beyond recalling and recognising information, consequently increasing their knowledge-building and skills development (Mayer, 2002).

When trying to develop a framework for researching classroom-based assessment, Hill and McNamara (2012) highlighted the fact that assessment strategies also often serve as teaching strategies. For example, effective questioning can be an effective assessment strategy to find out what students already know and need to learn but it can also be used as an effective engagement strategy and for classroom management, refocusing student attention on the topic at hand – all of which is good teaching. Another example is teachers' use of feedback as a strategy to increase students' intrinsic and autonomous motivation (Chamberlin et al., 2023). The actionable feedback is a good teaching strategy that promotes trust between teachers and students, and it also promotes cooperation among students. Hill and McNamara conclude that because assessment can function for 'teaching', 'learning', 'reporting', 'management' and 'socialisation' purposes, analytically it is not always possible to separate one purpose from another (p. 405). This chapter explores the nature of this problem from both a micro- and macro-level.

The Problem

In principle, assessment should be conceptualised within a broader pedagogical model (Black, 2017). This conceptualisation highlights the central role of assessment in learning and teaching. However, the intersections between assessment and learning and teaching, both conceptually and in practice, are still unclear. Despite the central role of assessment in providing data for teachers to adapt their learning and teaching activities and the pedagogical functions of assessment (engaging students in learning and teaching), the task of embedding assessment in learning and teaching activities remains challenging.

This chapter responds to the criticism that assessment and pedagogy are two different fields. Ideally, assessment and pedagogy are intertwined, as argued above, but the reality is they often operate primarily in isolation. Baird et al. (2017) make explicit the disconnect between assessment and learning. They have highlighted the lack of connection between theories of learning and educational assessments and argued that:

> … if assessment is to serve the learning goals of education, then this discussion on the relationship between assessment and learning should be developed further and be at the forefront of high-stakes, large-scale educational assessments.
>
> (p. 317)

44 Using Assessment to Support Learning

The first case study presented below demonstrates that the impact of assessment on learning and teaching can be optimised when teachers use assessment as an integral activity of their learning and teaching activities, and they use the results of assessment to adapt their teaching and to provide support for individual students. The second case study presents the challenge in embedding assessment activities in learning and teaching activities while the third case study offers an insight how to reconceptualise and enact assessment pedagogy.

Case 1: Learning from assessment

Description of the Study

This case study, drawn from the work Reinholz (2016) in developing a model of learning through peer assessment, demonstrates the clear intersections between assessment and teaching strategies. Reinholz drew from theories of self-assessment to develop an assessment cycle model to elaborate on how learning takes place through peer assessment. He applied the model in a calibrated peer review (CPR) process. This is an online tool that improves students' reading and writing skills in science by involving them in the process of writing, assessing calibration essays and grading peer essays. Teaching students in the experimental group involved using research materials and CPR to teach topics, while the control group had lectures and group work on textbook problems. Results showed that the use of peer assessment improved student performance on examination problems compared to traditional teaching methods.

What is evident in Reinholz's study is the effective use of peer assessment support learning opportunities. The assessment cycle consists of six components (i.e. task engagement, peer analysis, feedback provision, feedback reception, peer conferencing and revision) that describe different aspects of peer assessment and their potential for learning. Following this model, peer assessment can support goal awareness, performance awareness and gap closure which can lead to improved learning outcomes.

Problem Being Addressed

There are many studies that highlight the use of assessment to support learning and teaching. However, the issue of the difference between good teaching strategies and good assessment strategies is often debated. Much research evidence demonstrates the high impact of using assessment to increase student outcomes. However, there are also reports that the implementation of assessment does not always result in increased student learning gains. The negligible impact of assessment on student outcomes is often framed as a failure to conceptualise how assessment intersects with learning and teaching.

Factors Influencing the Problem

There are factors that influence the use of assessment strategies as teaching strategies:

1 *Opportunities for students to engage in assessment.*
   In the study by Reinholz above, one of the limitations identified in using feedback as a learning activity is the insufficient opportunities for students to participate in the activities to develop their expertise. With limited opportunities to engage, students view the learning and assessment strategies as the delivery of content rather than providing opportunities for students to apply their learning through assessment activities. The use of peer assessment is problematic, limiting the ability of the students to identify their strengths and weaknesses, receive feedback and improve their performance.

2 *Unclear expectation and process.*
   Any unclear expectations and processes will shift the teaching strategy functions of assessment to its evaluation of learning function. Although the actual rubrics used in the study were not given to students, it was assumed by students that they were used to assign grades. The use of rubrics for grading may have shifted the focus of the students from providing supportive feedback to simply earning a good grade; hence, this shift in focus may have limited the impact of the peer assessments on the students' learning.

3 *Culture of trust.*
   The interactive nature of many assessment strategies presents a social issue between teachers and students and among students. Students who have negative experiences during peer assessment activity may not benefit from it. In the study above, some students spoke poorly of their peers and criticised their feedback, which may have been demotivating and hindered their learning. Reinholz suggests that this negative experience could have been mitigated if students had the opportunity to conference with their peers and develop personal connection. Conferencing would allow students to discuss their feedback and clarify any misunderstandings, which could lead to more constructive criticism and a better learning experience.

4 *The nature of the curriculum.*

The underpinning philosophy of effective assessment practices requires opportunities for students and teachers to engage with assessment tasks through multiple processes. This engagement results to improved learning and teaching outcomes. However, this can only be achieved if a clear intersection between assessment, curriculum and teaching exists. Unless assessment is conceptualised within a broader model of curriculum and pedagogy, and unless the curriculum provides a space for assessment principles to be operationalised, then assessment strategies would remain as separate from teaching strategies, and their impact on improving student outcomes is not optimised.

Implications of the Problem

The conflicting evidence of the effectiveness of using assessment to support learning and teaching creates a barrier to changing teachers' assessment practices. In addition, the continuous publication of research findings demonstrating the ineffectiveness of assessment reform in raising student outcomes challenges the theoretical and empirical support for the large-effect size of using assessment to support learning and teaching. These issues could be resolved if assessment strategies are used effectively as teaching strategies.

Using assessment strategies as teaching strategies requires careful planning and implementation of effective processes. In the case of using peer assessment as a teaching strategy, its design and implementation were guided by an assessment model (Reinholz, 2016), consisting of six components. First, task engagement involves students working on a task similar to the one they will assess, allowing them to support their peer analyses with insights from their own work. The initial self-assessment activity is supported by explicit prompts for explanation, which help students reflect on the quality of their work. Their engagement in self-assessment allows them to develop a greater understanding of the task and expected outcomes. Second, teachers engage them in peer analysis, leveraging their experience in and insights drawn from self-assessment. The peer analysis helps students develop objectivity and a sense of quality by providing feedback and constructive criticism on their peers' work. Exposure to a variety of examples in peer analysis helps students see various levels of quality and develop deeper conceptual understanding. Third, they are given the time for feedback provision, involving students describing their analyses to their peers. This process promotes engagement and develops their accountability to provide actionable feedback. Fourth, feedback reception allows students to see their work from another's perspective and form a more objective lens for self-assessment. In this process, students see that not all feedback is equally useful. They filter feedback that helps them independently analyse, critique and improve their work. Fifth, teachers engage students in peer conferencing to discuss their feedback and analyses, enhancing goal awareness, performance awareness and gap closure. The last process concludes with revision, allowing students to close the feedback cycle and learn from the process of revising their work.

The assessment model described above presents an illustrative case of how to use an assessment strategy as a teaching strategy. Any assessment activities should intersect with learning and teaching. When assessment is seen as a separate activity, teacher practices will continue to oscillate between summative assessment (for meeting accountability) and formative assessment (for supporting learning). We need to create a space for teachers to understand and implement the principles of effective assessment practices within the curriculum structure that allows them to navigate according to the demands of the assessment activities to effectively use them as teaching strategies. If the curriculum structure is too rigid, and there is a strong pressure from the system to comply with and complete the curriculum content within the specified timeframe, teachers' autonomy is compromised, forcing them to cover everything with less regard to using assessment activities to support effective learning.

Case 2:   The challenge of embedding assessment in learning and teaching

Description of the Study

One of the principles of effective assessment practices is recognising and implementing assessment as the central feature of effective learning and teaching (ARG, 2002). However, effectively embedding assessment in learning and teaching activities is challenging. This case study drawn from Eriksson et al. (2022) illustrates how an assessment activity can be better implemented. Eriksson et al. conducted a research study of a small Swedish primary school in a socio-economically mixed but ethnically homogenous rural environment to understand how primary-school students interpret and make sense of the feedback they receive from their teachers.

First, classroom observations and fieldwork at the school were conducted, observing the students in their classrooms and in other school areas during lunchtimes and breaks. The observation allowed for deeper understanding of the students' social worlds and encouraged them to accept the researcher as one of their own. This process allowed the researcher to take on the role of a 'least-adult' that is less authoritative than that of a teacher, to gain the trust of the students and to better understand their perspectives. Twenty-three students (11 boys and 12 girls; 7–9 years old) participated in the study in Grades 2 and 3. All the children and their parents gave informed consent. Focus group interviews were then conducted with seven groups of students (three to four students per group). The data were then analysed using constructivist grounded theory methods to understand how these young learners conceptualised teacher feedback.

The results of this study indicate that primary school students conceptualise teacher feedback as communicating a lot of 'musts', which are centred on learning. These 'musts' involve what the students perceive to be things they must learn and do to learn, both academically and behaviourally. The findings also suggest that there are tensions between different types of these 'musts' for the student. In other words, when teachers give feedback to their students, those messages can sometimes conflict with each other or create confusion about how best to proceed with learning tasks. It was also found that primary school students preferred praise for effort rather than ability. This indicates that students are more focused on the effort they must put in to learn rather than the topics they must learn.

Problem Being Addressed

Feedback is one of the most effective assessment practices that support student learning (Brooks et al., 2019; Hattie & Timperley, 2007). However, there is surprisingly little research on how students perceive, interpret and make use of teacher feedback, and almost none that gives a voice to younger students. Research on feedback focuses more on teacher feedback literacy, including their views, beliefs and practices, with little regard for how students perceive feedback effectiveness, particularly in supporting their learning. This area of inquiry is critically important because students' control over their learning varies, and primary school students may have different conceptions of school. In addition, they may have different aims for being in school than older students. This could mean that they may understand teacher feedback differently.

Factors Influencing the Problem

Factors that influence primary school students' conception of feedback include the following:

1 *Feedback content.*

When teachers are focused on articulating what needs to be done rather than guiding students to discover areas for improvement, they will perceive feedback as a list of 'musts'. The content of feedback should direct students' attention to further explicate the suggested areas for improvement, leading to identifying aspects of their work that needs to be improved. In addition, students must be guided to explore ways they can act on feedback rather than a prescriptive approach where students are directed to do something.

2 *Feedback processes.*

Communicating feedback influences students' understanding of it. The ambiguity the students experience when receiving feedback from their teachers limits the effectiveness of feedback. As demonstrated in the study by Eriksson et al. (2022) described above, students were expected to do much work and do it with quality, creating a dilemma or conflict between two different rationales. This inconsistency in communication from the teachers caused confusion and criticism among students. Despite this, the students still understood their teachers' actions and choices, referring to good intentions.

3 *Classroom rules.*

Students indicated that sitting still, being quiet, raising one's hand and not disturbing others are things they must do to help create good conditions for learning. From an outside perspective, these same things could be described as the unwritten things they have to learn as part of becoming students and, thus, as part of the hidden curriculum that results in social control. This is in line with Boistrup (2017), who argues that assessment discourses in classrooms, along with regulatory decisions and administrative measures, form an apparatus in the school system to perpetuate social orders. However, the students in the study did not see sitting still or being quiet as things they had to learn, but as things they were told they must do and as things that helped them to learn and to create better learning conditions in the classroom. The study's findings support previous research showing that children tend to value rules aimed at structuring and maintaining schoolwork in the classroom as important because they tend to see these rules as functional and helpful rather than arbitrary and pointless.

Implications of the Problem

The results of this study have practical implications for both practice and teacher professional development. Teachers should consider the content of their feedback. Any content that students perceive to be irrelevant or overwhelming in terms of how it is framed and the number of 'musts' will negatively influence students' use of feedback. Teachers should consider the potential tensions between different types of 'musts' when giving feedback and ensure they provide clear messages about what needs to be done for learning tasks to succeed.

In addition, teachers should be aware of how students interpret their feedback. They need to ensure that students understand the principles and processes of eliciting and giving feedback and how they can act on them effectively. The ultimate aim of teachers in giving feedback is to ensure that students use it to revise their work further and improve their learning. The accuracy and effectiveness of students' interpretation of teacher feedback (and engagement in assessment more broadly) relies heavily on their own assessment literacy. Students should have assessment knowledge, skills and positive dispositions to effectively engage in assessment (see Chapter 6 for detailed explanations of student assessment literacy).

Furthermore, teachers should provide more opportunities for dialogue with students to quickly address and clarify any misunderstandings or confusion. Dialogic feedback is proven to be more effective than one-way feedback (Van Booven, 2015). This approach to feedback allows students to interrogate the content of the feedback. When feedback is framed around criteria and standards, students will develop a better understanding of the expectations and can use that understanding to further revise their work more effectively. In addition, through dialogic feedback, teachers can further explore students' learning which might not have been fully reflected in their work. They can ask students to further explicate their learning.

Case 3: Reconceptualising and enacting assessment pedagogy

Description of the Study

This case study drawn from Fleer (2015) illustrates one approach for teachers to reconceptualise assessment within their pedagogical practice. The study conducted in Australia examined how teachers used cultural-historical concepts, including the social situation of development, motives, the zone of proximal development and the relations between the real and ideal forms of development to change their assessment practices. Eleven primary school teachers from one school [mixed school population of middle- and working-class families from European heritage (Greek, Italian, French), Africa (Sudanese, Ethiopian, Somalian) and Asia (Korean, Chinese, Vietnamese)] participated in the study. Data were collected through interviews with participants and classroom observation.

Results show the tensions and struggles that teachers encounter when they attempt to move away from traditional institutionalised assessment practices where age dominates. Teachers also struggle as they work with key concepts to theorise new ways of conceptualising and enacting assessment to build a new pedagogy for their school. These results highlight the importance of intersections between educational constructs and assessment concepts to conceptualise assessment within a broader pedagogical model.

Problem Being Addressed

Changing teachers' assessment practices is a complex process influenced by many personal, social, cultural, leadership, policy and contextual factors (Alonzo et al., 2021). Often, these factors are competing, and the conflicts between factors compromise the development of new assessment practices aligned to supporting student learning. In an era of educational accountability, where teachers gather many assessment data to show evidence of their effectiveness, the common practice for schools is to meet the attainment of educational outcomes articulated in the curriculum. Mostly, these outcomes are age-specific, and teachers align their assessment practices to find evidence of achievement.

To change teachers' assessment practices and to ensure that assessment is conceptualised and implemented to support learning and teaching, teachers need to develop a new understanding of how assessment intersects with educational constructs. However, in doing so, they face a significant challenge if working in a traditional accountability-driven school assessment culture.

Factors Influencing the Problem

This process of shifting teachers' assessment practices from traditional institutionalised assessment to conceptualising it to a broader pedagogical model is influenced by several following factors:

1 *Policy, particularly accountability measures.*

As schools come further under the microscope of accountability, teachers increasingly accumulate large quantities of observations and records. They use these assessment data to provide evidence for attaining educational outcomes specified in the curriculum. However, many policy requirements drive teachers' assessment practices to focus on measuring individual students' attainment of outcomes. Consequently, teachers continue to use traditional approaches to assessment, and in a system based on age-related outcomes, the responsibility for 'lack of success' is often shifted to learners. Teachers often ignore the interplay of other factors that influence students' learning, including family, artefacts and peers.

2 *The school assessment culture.*

Even when teachers understand and implement effective assessment practices, they are forced to adhere to school assessment practices, particularly in marking and reporting. Thus, it is critically important that a shift in school assessment culture be implemented in tandem with changing teachers' assessment beliefs and practices. The alignment between what teachers do and what the school culture allows to happen ensures a holistic approach to implementing assessment to support learning and teaching.

3 *Individualistic approaches.*

A lack of consistency in incorporating cultural considerations in thinking and acting in the learning and teaching environment undermines the connection between pedagogy and assessment. Any individual effort to conceptualise assessment within a broader pedagogical model and implement it to support students learning will most likely be ineffective. A whole-school approach is needed where every component, including processes, people, procedures and resources, of the school system supports the implementation of effective assessment practices.

4 *Teachers' understanding of educational theories.*

The conceptual complexities of educational theories present a challenge for their operationalisation in the classroom. When these educational theories are used to conceptualise effective assessment practices, they become more complicated. Thus, a critical part of shifting teachers' practices is supporting them to understand the intersection of assessment and educational theories. When assessment is conceptualised outside educational theories, it will always be viewed as a discrete episode rather than an integral part of learning and teaching activities.

5 *Conflicts among assessment concepts.*

Apart from the debate between FA and SA, teachers' understanding of the dynamic nature of assessment and age-specific outcomes is critical for shifting their assessment practices. There is also tension between individual and collective assessment. These conflicts, when not resolved, will continue to present challenges to teachers' assessment practices. Thus, a conceptual clarity is needed to develop a shared understanding across the system.

Implications of the Problem

Fleer (2015) outlines some solutions to support teachers in reconceptualising assessment against the backdrop of educational theories. First is to conceptualise an assessment interaction as part of an assessment pedagogy. This means that teachers should consider the assessment process as part of the overall learning and teaching process and not as a separate activity. Changing teachers' assessment practices is more than just developing assessment knowledge and skills or acquiring practical skills in assessment. Rather, teachers must understand and establish the intersections of assessment and educational constructs. This is a critical process for teachers to see the broader function of assessment in pedagogy. As Fleer (2015) argues:

> But what if assessment practices actually examined the conditions that were made available to groups of children and analysed to see if it is possible for children to develop a meaningful motive, where the situations make sense to the child? This takes the focus away from blaming the child if they cannot achieve age-related outcomes. Rather, it can be asked: How is the environment constituted for providing the possibilities (meaningful motives) and ideal forms (stimulating motives) of the concept (culturally valued motive) in action?
>
> (p. 242)

Second is to look for the ideal forms of development available in the environment as part of the assessment approach. Teachers should look for the best ways to assess students based on the environment they are in and the resources available to them. Expanding the conception of assessment data to include the social and material environment and the students' interactions within it would give teachers a better understanding of how to support them effectively. In this sense, students are seen not as 'robots' programmed to learn but as social beings constantly interacting with other people and their environments. These interactions influence their learning and, thus, need to be accounted for in the assessment process.

Third is to teach students to build the ability to communicate what they know and what help they need. Teachers should help students to be able to express their knowledge and understanding in a way that is visible to others. Building a classroom environment that offers opportunities for students to demonstrate and communicate their knowledge and skills is key to ensuring effective learning.

Fourth is to include students in the assessment, supporting them to engage in an assessment interaction. This means that teachers should involve students in the assessment process and provide them with the necessary support to participate. Student active involvement in assessment is evident from the original definition of assessment *for* learning where the evidence of learning are used by students themselves to monitor their learning and to develop strategies to achieve the expected outcomes (ARG, 2002). Effective students' engagement in assessment requires building their assessment literacy (see Chapter 6).

Fifth is to look for various ways of breaking down the barriers between home and school so that assessment practices include families. This means that teachers should look for ways to involve families in the assessment process and to bridge the gap between home and school. Parental involvement in assessment has been shown to support learning and teaching (see Chapter 8 for detailed discussion).

Proposed Solutions

Assessment will only increase learning gains if it is considered the central feature of learning and teaching. Assessment should support effective teaching, and effective teaching will only occur if teachers are embedding assessment in their pedagogical practices (Alonzo, 2020). Although there is no doubt that using assessment to support learning and teaching exemplifies effective teaching (Black & Wiliam, 2018; Hattie, 2008), its implementation remains problematic.

One way for teachers to enhance the nexus between assessment and teaching is to clearly articulate their teaching philosophy and identify educational and pedagogical theories that support it (Baird et al., 2017). Their conceptual and practical understanding of these theories will help them conceptualise assessment within their broader pedagogical practice to ensure that any assessment implemented supports learning and teaching activities. The intersection of assessment and educational and pedagogical theories ensures that assessment will become an integral part of teaching, from planning, implementing, monitoring and evaluating learning and teaching activities. Unless teachers are able to establish this nexus, their use and implementation of assessment remain isolated from learning and teaching activities.

Teachers should not be left on their own to use assessment to support learning and teaching. Fleer (2015) shows that school culture constrains teachers' theorisation of assessment and pedagogy. School leaders should lead in establishing an assessment culture that supports learning and teaching (Alonzo et al., 2021). The whole-school approach to implementing assessment to support learning provides a common language for teachers, students, parents and other stakeholders, thus ensuring that everyone understands the assessment purpose, principles and practices. The common understanding amongst stakeholders will increase the likelihood that they will take accountability for their role in supporting students to learn more effectively.

In addition, effective teaching requires the active involvement of students in every learning and teaching activities (Hughes, 2014; Zdravković et al., 2018). Increasing students' responsibilisation in learning is equally important as increasing teachers' responsibilisation in teaching. However, beyond students' involvement in learning, they need to have certain assessment knowledge and skills to effectively engage in assessment, including understanding the learning outcomes and success criteria, engaging in self and peer assessment to give feedback to their selves and their peers, acting on teacher feedback, monitoring their learning and development, and reflecting on their overall assessment experience (Hannigan et al., 2022; Tsivitanidou et al., 2011).

Also, the accountability-driven nature of assessment should be redefined to attain the balance between accountability and learning functions of assessment. There is a large body of evidence demonstrating that external high-stake examinations put pressure to teachers and schools to revert to an examination-driven culture to meet the accountability agenda imposed by policymakers (Conway & Murphy, 2013; Datnow et al., 2019; Sahlberg, 2010). Adherence to accountability functions of assessment continues to widen the gap between assessment and learning (Baird et al., 2017). This is further intensified by the implementation of assessment frameworks and policies that undermine teachers' assessment practices. Much evidence suggests that teachers' practices are shaped predominantly by educational policies and narratives (Ball et al., 2012). It has been documented that even when a policy contradicts teachers' beliefs, they tend to follow to it for accountability reasons and adherence to prescribed practices (Datnow et al., 2019; Sahlberg, 2010). Hence, the alignment of assessment frameworks and policies to effective assessment principles has significant implications for shaping teachers' assessment practices. This raises the question: how do teachers translate into practice the student-centred philosophy of assessment under the competing demands driven by an assessment framework?

Further, in many educational bureaucracies, the assessment frameworks and policies advocate both accountability and assessment to support learning and teaching. Generally, there is a strong emphasis on teacher-led assessment practices, particularly using assessment and assessment information to inform learning and teaching. However, reporting favours the accountability mechanism, which strongly conveys that assessment for accountability is more valued than any other purpose of assessment for improving student learning. For example, the National Assessment of Educational Progress in the USA reports national progress and state comparisons (NAEP, 2019). Although the assessment program aims to provide records of individual students' outcomes, the data are also aggregated and used to report school quality. Popham (2000) has argued that this testing regime being used does not address the information needed for accountability, but rather it degrades education in the USA. The same scenario is seen in England, where key-stage assessments of national curricula aim to provide individual reports for students, but the data are used to measure and report teaching quality in schools. The focus on reporting for accountability is very prominent in most assessment policy frameworks where teaching quality is measured by single assessment data, so it is not surprising that teachers and principals perceive this to devalue their work and threaten their integrity (McNeil et al., 2008).

In the neo-liberal education system, the strong emphasis on using a national assessment for reporting school quality and teacher performance presents a strong representation of what matters in the bureaucracy. The reporting system gives primacy to the accountability function of assessment as it signals important values to stakeholders, particularly the public. The dominance of standardised tests as a data source for various reporting projects seems to be what really matter for policymakers, and this inevitably shapes the broader community's perspective on assessment. The primacy of national exams in assessment frameworks can be viewed through the lens of symbolism theory, in which a meaning or a phenomenon is represented by its primary element, and one of these is through the use of words whose meanings are connected to form a larger meaning (Langer, 1954). As argued by Reichling (1993), the meanings of these symbols, in this case related words, can be "understood through the whole, that is, through their relationships within a total structure and not as isolated ... the symbol allows one to conceptualise what it conveys; it does not stand in a mere proxy for an object" (p. 4). The assessment framework of any educational bureaucracy symbolises the system and its values. This symbolism plays a major role in how systems, and indeed, individual schools are perceived. The prominence of accountability contributes to the growth of external large-scale and high-stake testing systems, which are intended to prove that education expenditure is, in essence, responsible and rigorous. In other words, if we want to support the use of assessment to support learning and teaching, policymakers need to rethink how assessment is represented in the policy and how it must be enacted in schools to develop a strong assessment culture that allows effective assessment practices to be operationalised. In addition, teachers as professionals should participate in a process that gives them a say in how well students do in school and how to improve their performance. Teachers are best positioned to keep student assessments safe from unintended consequences and policy changes that are not based on evidence or success elsewhere.

Furthermore, we need to reconceptualise accountability in the context of supporting individual students (Popham, 2009) by not relying solely on external examinations but integrating classroom-based assessment and teacher judgement (Looney et al., 2017; Sahlberg, 2010). This means that data

Using Assessment to Support Learning 57

collection and tracking should be done from a classroom perspective, considering that teachers know their students well. Teachers' judgement, in-class quizzes, observation, interviews and any form of classroom assessments must be valued and used for reporting and accountability.

Conclusion

This chapter highlights the intersections between assessment and teaching. When assessment is seen as an isolated activity, assessment becomes high stakes, and the information gathered is unlikely to be used to inform learning and teaching. The potential of assessment and assessment data to improve learning and teaching is lost.

Insights from the three case studies above help to answer the question posed at the beginning of this chapter – Isn't assessment just good teaching? Indeed, using assessment and assessment data to inform learning and teaching is a key component of teaching effectiveness. Assessment, when conceptualised within a broader model of pedagogy, drives learning and teaching. This is evident in one of the principles of effective assessment practices developed by the Assessment Reform Group (ARG, 2002): assessment is part of effective planning. To make assessment as a central feature of learning and teaching, teachers must have good conceptual and practical clarity of educational and pedagogical theories and understand how assessment can operate within these theories to support students' learning.

References

Alonzo, D. (2016). *Development and application of a teacher assessment for learning (AfL) literacy tool.* University of New South Wales]. Sydney. http://unsworks.unsw.edu.au/fapi/datastream/unsworks:38345/SOURCE02?view=true

Alonzo, D. (2020). Teacher education and professional development in industry 4.0. The case for building a strong assessment literacy. In J. P. Ashadi, A. T. Basikin, & N. Putor (Eds.), *4th international conference on teacher education and professional development (InCoTEPD 2019)* (pp. 3–10). Taylor & Francis Group.

Alonzo, D., & Loughland, T. (2022). Variability of students' responses to assessment activities: The influence of achievement levels. *International Journal of Instruction, 15*(4), 1071–1090. https://doi.org/10.29333/iji.2022.15457a

Alonzo, D., Leverett, J., & Obsioma, E. (2021). Leading an assessment reform: Ensuring a whole-school approach for decision-making. *Frontiers in Education, 6*(62). https://doi.org/10.3389/feduc.2021.631857

Assessment Reform Group (ARG). (2002). *Assessment for learning: 10 principles.* https://www.storre.stir.ac.uk/bitstream/1893/32458/1/Assessment%20for%20learning%2010%20principles%202002.pdf

Baird, J.-A., Andrich, D., Hopfenbeck, T. N., & Stobart, G. (2017). Assessment and learning: Fields apart? *Assessment in Education: Principles, Policy & Practice, 24*(3), 317–350. https://doi.org/10.1080/0969594X.2017.1319337

58 Using Assessment to Support Learning

Ball, S., Maguire, M., & Braun, A. (2012). *How schools do policy: Policy enactments in secondary schools.* Routledge.

Beswick, K., Alonzo, D., & Lee, J. (2022). *Data literacy for student outcomes: Supporting principals and teachers to use data for evidence-informed decision-making.* School of Education, University of New South Wales.

Black, P. (2017). Assessment in science education. In K. S. Taber & B. Akpan (Eds.), *Science education: An international course companion* (pp. 295–309). Sense Publishers. https://doi.org/10.1007/978-94-6300-749-8_22

Black, P., & Wiliam, D. (2018). Classroom assessment and pedagogy. *Assessment in Education: Principles, Policy & Practice, 25*(6), 551–575. https://doi.org/10.1080/0969594X.2018.1441807

Boistrup, L. B. (2017). Assessment in mathematics education: A gatekeeping dispositive. In H. Straehler-Pohl, N. Bohlmann, & A. Pais (Eds.), *The disorder of mathematics education – Challenging the socio-political dimensions of research* (pp. 209–230). Springer.

Brooks, C., Carroll, A., Gillies, R. M., & Hattie, J. (2019). A matrix of feedback for learning. *Australian Journal of Teacher Education, 44*(4), 14–32.

Chamberlin, K., Yasué, M., & Chiang, I.-C. A. (2023). The impact of grades on student motivation. *Active Learning in Higher Education, 24*(2), 109–124. https://doi.org/10.1177/1469787418819728

Conway, P. F., & Murphy, R. (2013). A rising tide meets a perfect storm: New accountabilities in teaching and teacher education in Ireland. *Irish Educational Studies, 32*(1), 11–36. https://doi.org/10.1080/03323315.2013.773227

Datnow, A., Lockton, M., & Weddle, H. (2019). Redefining or reinforcing accountability? An examination of meeting routines in schools. *Journal of Educational Change.* https://doi.org/10.1007/s10833-019-09349-z

Datnow, A., Lockton, M., & Weddle, H. (2021). Capacity building to bridge data use and instructional improvement through evidence on student thinking. *Studies in Educational Evaluation, 69*, 100869. https://doi.org/10.1016/j.stueduc.2020.100869

Eriksson, E., Boistrup, L. B., & Thornberg, R. (2022). "You must learn something during a lesson": How primary students construct meaning from teacher feedback. *Educational Studies, 48*(3), 323–340. https://doi.org/10.1080/03055698.2020.1753177

Fleer, M. (2015). Developing an assessment pedagogy: The tensions and struggles in re-theorising assessment from a cultural–historical perspective. *Assessment in Education: Principles, Policy & Practice, 22*(2), 224–246. https://doi.org/10.1080/0969594X.2015.1015403

Hannigan, C., Alonzo, D., & Oo, C. Z. (2022). Student assessment literacy: Indicators and domains from the literature. *Assessment in Education: Principles, Policy & Practice, 29*(4), 482–504. https://doi.org/10.1080/0969594X.2022.2121911

Hattie, J. (2008). *Visible learning: A synthesis of over 800 meta-analyses relating to achievement.* Routledge.

Hattie, J., & Timperley, H. (2007). The power of feedback. *Review of Educational Research, 77*(1), 81–112.

Hill, K., & McNamara, T. (2012). Developing a comprehensive, empirically based research framework for classroom-based assessment. *Language Testing, 29*(3), 395–420. https://doi.org/10.1177/0265532211428317

Hornstra, L., Mansfield, C., van der Veen, I., Peetsma, T., & Volman, M. (2015). Motivational teacher strategies: The role of beliefs and contextual factors. *Learning Environments Research*, *18*(3), 363–392. https://doi.org/10.1007/s10984-015-9189-y

Hughes, C. (2014). Improving student engagement and development through assessment: Theory and practice in higher education. *Higher Education Research & Development*, *33*(1), 176–177. https://doi.org/10.1080/07294360.2013.783954

Jimerson, J. B., Cho, V., Scroggins, K. A., Balial, R., & Robinson, R. R. (2019). How and why teachers engage students with data. *Educational Studies*, *45*(6), 667–691. https://doi.org/10.1080/03055698.2018.1509781

Keppel, M., & Carless, D. (2006). Learning-oriented assessment: A technology-based case study. *Assessment in Education*, *13*(2), 179–191.

Langer, S. K. (1954). *Philosophy in a new key: A study in the symbolism of reason, rite, and art*. The New American Library.

Leenknecht, M., Wijnia, L., Köhlen, M., Fryer, L., Rikers, R., & Loyens, S. (2021). Formative assessment as practice: The role of students' motivation. *Assessment & Evaluation in Higher Education*, *46*(2), 236–255. https://doi.org/10.1080/02602938.2020.1765228

Looney, A., Cumming, J., van Der Kleij, F., & Harris, K. (2017). Reconceptualising the role of teachers as assessors: Teacher assessment identity. *Assessment in Education: Principles, Policy & Practice*, 1–26. https://doi.org/10.1080/0969594X.2016.1268090

Marshall, B., & Drummond, M. J. (2006). How teachers engage with assessment for learning: Lessons from the classroom. *Research Papers in Education*, *21*(2), 133–149.

Mayer, R. E. (2002). Rote versus meaningful learning. *Theory Into Practice*, *41*(4), 226–232. https://doi.org/10.1207/s15430421tip4104_4

McMillan, J. H. (2000). Fundamental assessment pricniples for teachers and schools adminsitrators. *Practical Assessment, Research & Evaluation*, *7*(8). https://doi.org/10.7275/5kc4-jy05

McNeil, L. M., Coppola, E., Radigan, J., & Vasquez Heilig, J. (2008). Avoidable losses: High-stakes accountability and the dropout crisis. *Education Policy Analysis Archives*, 16. https://doi.org/10.14507/epaa.v16n3.2008

NAEP. (2019). *About national assessment of educational progress: A common measure of student achievement*. NAEP. https://nces.ed.gov/nationsreportcard/about/

Poortman, C. L., & Schildkamp, K. (2016). Solving student achievement problems with a data use intervention for teachers. *Teaching and Teacher Education*, *60*, 425–433. https://doi.org/10.1016/j.tate.2016.06.010

Popham, W. J. (2000). Big change questions. Should large-scale assessment be used for accountability?—Answer: Depends on the assessment, silly!. *Journal of Educational Change*, *1*(3), 283–289. https://doi.org/10.1023/a:1010054525759

Popham, W. J. (2009). Assessment literacy for teachers: Faddish or fundamental? *Theory into Practice*, *48*(1), 4–11. https://doi.org/10.1080/00405840802577536

Reichling, M. J. (1993). Susanne Langer's theory of symbolism: An analysis and extension. *Philosophy of Music Education Review*, *1*(1), 3–17.

Reinholz, D. (2016). The assessment cycle: A model for learning through peer assessment. *Assessment & Evaluation in Higher Education*, *41*(2), 301–315. https://doi.org/10.1080/02602938.2015.1008982

Sahlberg, P. (2010). Rethinking accountability in a knowledge society. *Journal of Educational Change, 11*(1), 45–61. https://doi.org/10.1007/s10833-008-9098-2

To, J., & Liu, Y. (2018). Using peer and teacher-student exemplar dialogues to unpack assessment standards: Challenges and possibilities. *Assessment & Evaluation in Higher Education, 43*(3), 449–460. https://doi.org/10.1080/02602938.2017.1356907

Tomlinson, C. A., & McTighe, J. (2006). *Integrating differentiated instruction + understanding by design*. Association for Supervision and Curriculum Development: USA

Tsivitanidou, O. E., Zacharia, Z. C., & Hovardas, T. (2011). Investigating secondary school students' unmediated peer assessment skills. *Learning and Instruction, 21*(4), 506–519. https://doi.org/10.1016/j.learninstruc.2010.08.002

Van Booven, C. D. (2015). Revisiting the authoritative–dialogic tension in inquiry-based elementary Science teacher questioning. *International Journal of Science Education, 37*(8), 1182–1201. https://doi.org/10.1080/09500693.2015.1023868

Yan, Z., & Carless, D. (2022). Self-assessment is about more than self: The enabling role of feedback literacy. *Assessment & Evaluation in Higher Education, 47*(7), 1116–1128. https://doi.org/10.1080/02602938.2021.2001431

Zdravković, M., Serdinšek, T., Sobočan, M., Bevc, S., Hojs, R., & Krajnc, I. (2018). Students as partners: Our experience of setting up and working in a student engagement friendly framework. *Medical Teacher, 40*(6), 589–594. https://doi.org/10.1080/0142159X.2018.1444743

Chapter 4

Are Formative and Summative Assessments Different?

Introduction

The five competing terminologies [formative assessment (FA), summative assessment (SA), assessment *for* learning (AfL), assessment *as* learning (AaL), assessment *of* learning (AoL)] have been widely critiqued for creating confusion, compromising the effectiveness of assessment and widening the dichotomy between FA and SA (Bennett, 2011). In 1996, Biggs argued that FA could be used for summative purposes and SA for formative purposes (Biggs, 1996). Their interconnectedness means that it is impossible to entirely isolate one from the other, as both types of assessment support each other. Biggs further contends that focusing just on the use of SA causes a backwash effect on learning and teaching, including limiting learning (Harlen, 2007; Wei, 2015), narrowing the curriculum (Bijsterbosch et al., 2017; Johnston & McClune, 2000) and compromising teaching (Cranley et al., 2022; Pollard et al., 2002).

In response to Biggs' critique, Black and Wiliam (2009) emphasise the relevance of SA as part of FA, an adjustment to their earlier position that summative tasks could not be used for formative purposes. They revised their original stance (Black & Wiliam, 1999) to include the formative use of SA, arguing that the result of an SA is evidence of student achievement and, therefore, can be used to elicit and give feedback (Black et al., 2003). By reframing the relationship of FA and SA within a model for pedagogical practice, Black and Wiliam emphasise that the distinction between FA and SA "is not useful because all assessment would be about producing valid inferences about students" (2018, p. 570). The understanding that SA and FA are not mutually exclusive supports the earlier theorisation of Davison (2007) that assessment is a continuum of practice from in-class contingent FA to the most formal SA, including national and international examinations, in which the results are used to adapt learning and teaching activities.

The Problem

Despite the current conceptualisation of assessment that the distinction between SA and FA becomes irrelevant when conceptualised within a broader

DOI: 10.4324/9781003396277-4

62 Reconciling the Formative and Summative Debate

pedagogical model, the dichotomy continues to impact our understanding of assessment. The SA and FA divide is prevalent in schools and universities and dominates the discourse on what assessment is more effective in supporting learning and teaching. Also, assessment policies intensify this debate with SA and FA as key recommended approaches to assessing student learning. However, research evidence points out that this dichotomisation is unnecessary and often confuses teachers, practitioners and policymakers, consequently undermining the effectiveness of assessment (Black, 2017; Black et al., 2011; Curry et al., 2016). To clarify this debate, the following three case studies highlight the intersections between FA and SA and demonstrate that all types of assessment can be used either formatively or summatively.

Case 1: The mutually inclusive formative and summative functions of assessment

Description of the Study

This study by Black and Wiliam (2018) illustrates the complementary role of FA and SA in meeting their accountability and learning functions. Black and Wiliam (2018) developed an assessment model underpinned by "theories of pedagogy, instruction and learning, and by the subject discipline, within the wider context of education" (p. 551). This model is a response to Perrenoud's (1998) critique of the extant models, which were not conceptualised within a broader pedagogical model. Perrenoud argues that assessment becomes effective only when embedded in learning and teaching such that it supports teacher decision-making. Taking this critique, Black and Wiliam illustrate how teachers can adjust their classroom assessments to function both formatively and summatively, and how these classroom assessments inform the external SA. Also, the model attempts to develop theories that position assessment as an integral part of learning and teaching.

The proposed model explains a way for teachers to develop productive relationships between the formative (short-term) and summative (long-term) functions of classroom assessment, to inform the formal external assessment of students. The relationships between FA and SA allow teachers to use their assessments to improve student learning and provide a valid and accurate way of measuring that learning.

Problem Being Addressed

The formative and summative functions of classroom assessments continue to dominate the discourse in many educational bureaucracies, widening the dichotomisation between FA and SA. This dichotomy emphasises that FA informs teacher instruction (day-to-day activity) while SA informs pedagogy (broader curriculum implementation approach) and policy. This understanding, however, does not support the more integrated conceptualisation of FA and SA. Black and Wiliam noted that with their experience working with schools, teachers often critique and resist the use of FA as they are under pressure to raise students' test scores and, thus, prefer to use SA and to 'teach the test'. Despite a large amount of empirical evidence that FA enhances student learning outcomes, teachers view FA as a lesser component for effective learning and teaching, thus prioritising SA to help improve students' outcomes. This view leads to a poor understanding of the intersections of assessment and pedagogy. Consequently, assessment has little influence on classroom practice but has more significant consequences within the accountability discourse.

Factors Influencing the Problem

Many factors influence the poor conceptualisation of assessment within a broader pedagogical framework:

1 *Missing theoretical links.*
   Theories of pedagogy put little emphasis on assessment. Pedagogy is focused on discussing the social, cultural and political contexts that influence it without explicitly highlighting the role of assessment to inform teachers' practices; let alone the intersections of assessment with those social, cultural and political contexts.
2 *Views on assessment.*
   The dominant view is that assessment is something that exists on its own with little connection to pedagogy. This view reinforces the belief that assessment is separate from learning and teaching. However, research evidence shows that effective learning and teaching hinge on the use of assessment and assessment data to identify the learning needs of individual students.
3 *Accountability-driven assessment practices.*
   The constant pressure on schools to use valid and reliable assessments to report students' learning improvement continues to undermine teachers' use of other assessment strategies for their perceived lack of accuracy and consistency. The consistency and accuracy requirements for school reports reinforce the view that teachers' assessment practices are insufficient to measure students' learning. This view is a result of inaccurate application of psychometric principles in the context of classroom assessment (see Chapter 7).

64 Reconciling the Formative and Summative Debate

4 *Teacher assessment literacy.*
   Teachers' understanding of assessment principles and practices is critical to understanding the intersection between assessment and pedagogy. Developing teachers' assessment knowledge, skills and positive disposition towards assessment requires ongoing training and support from the school and the system, including articulating and implementing policies that support such.
5 *Lack of explicit guidance for FA application in specific key learning areas.*
   Assessment is a context-driven construct and is dependent on the content knowledge and skills. The intersections between assessment and pedagogical content knowledge are undertheorised, with most guidelines for FA implementation being generic.
6 *Students' involvement in assessment.*
   When students understand that the outcomes of FA would form part of their SA report, they would be most likely to engage in FA, demonstrating their learning. However, just like teachers' effective use of assessment relies on their assessment literacy, students need to develop assessment knowledge, skills and a positive disposition towards assessment (see Chapter 6).

Implications of the Problem

The absence of theorisation of assessment within the broader pedagogical model, integrating theories of pedagogy, instruction and learning, and by the subject discipline, together with the wider context of education, continues to compromise and limit the impacts of assessment in improving student learning outcomes. Teachers who do not understand the integrated nature of FA, SA and pedagogy will continue to view FA as informing their day-to-day activities while SA as informing their overall pedagogy high-stake decisions. This understanding will continue to shape the dichotomisation of assessment instead of seeing the integrated nature of FA and SA, where all assessment results are used to inform any decisions related to students' learning. In addition, the lack of a critical view on how FA informs pedagogy within the constraint of social, cultural and political contexts will continue to shape teachers' practices that assessment is an isolated activity, and the types of assessments dictate their functions.

The six-component framework of Black and Wiliam (2018) illustrates the interplay between assessment and pedagogy. The first three components (pedagogy and instruction, theories of learning and learning, and context–subject discipline, social, political and cultural) are critical for establishing the aims of teaching. Learning theories must be used to design educational activities and assessments to promote progression in learning.

It is also important for teachers to focus on learning the content of particular subjects and to develop the 'disciplinary habits of mind' peculiar to different subject disciplines. Moreover, the content topics chosen should be central to the subjects involved and teachers should aim to develop students' abilities to apply what they have learned in one context to another.

The fourth component, planning and design, requires the importance of planning activities in the classroom. The aims of the lesson, in terms of learning and content, should guide the planning of specific activities. Furthermore, a structure should be implemented to ensure that each successive topic is related to the previous one and can expand the learning goals. Additionally, particular attention should be given to students' learning ability, and each activity should be designed to engage, motivate and present them with a challenge that they can respond to successfully, thus reinforcing the intrinsic reward. Finally, activities should also be designed to engage and develop their interest in the particular lesson and build up their commitment to learning.

The fifth component, implementation by teachers – FA and SA, explains the importance of implementing teachers' intentions and plans in the classroom. Both FA and SA are integrated into this component as the distinction between the two creates tension in the conceptualisation of assessment. Black and Wiliam illustrate how an SA that aims to produce a mark or grade for students can function formatively for teachers for future planning and for students and parents for future decisions. There are three mechanisms for overcoming the tension between FA and SA. First, teachers and schools should be accountable only for the determinants of their work that they have control over. This might involve implementing a value-added system, which measures students' progress over time and adjusts for external factors like student background. Second, assessment instruments used for summative purposes should be designed to support learning. Third, teachers should take responsibility for serving the summative purposes or at least be involved in meeting this responsibility.

The sixth component accounts for external summative testing and how teachers' assessment practices contribute to increasing test scores. It emphasises the importance of teachers contributing to formal tests and examinations. There is a need to be concerned with the context of public, local or national assessments to ensure that the public perceives procedures and instruments to be accurate and consistent. There is also a need to consider the impact of high-stake assessments on teachers' work. High-stake assessments are tests with significant consequences for teachers and students. These assessments can put pressure on teachers, as they may prioritise teaching practices that will help their students perform well on the test rather than good learning practices.

Case 2: Students' view on reconciling formative and summative debate

Description of the Study

Studies highlighting the debate between FA and SA are always drawn from the perspectives of teachers and school leaders. This case study explores what students think of this debate. The study by Guo and Yan (2019) aimed to investigate the relationship between students' attitudes towards FA and SA. To achieve this aim, they developed an instrument and surveyed 3,019 Hong Kong primary school students in ten schools, exploring their instrumental and affective attitudes. Instrumental attitudes refer to opinions or feelings that FA or SA is useful and necessary. In contrast, affective attitudes refer to opinions or feelings that FA and SA are enjoyable or unpleasant. Results show that students generally have positive instrumental yet negative affective attitudes towards FA and SA. Girls tend to have less negative affective attitudes towards FA but more positive instrumental attitudes towards FA and SA than boys. In both attitudes, Grade 4 students consistently scored higher than Grade 5 and Grade 6 students. Furthermore, students' affective and instrumental attitudes to FA positively predicted their affective and instrumental attitudes to SA.

Problem Being Addressed

The dichotomy between FA and SA is also a common misunderstanding among students. Students' attitude towards assessment affects their engagement and, consequently, their overall performance. Understanding students' attitudes towards SA and FA will provide teachers with information on how best to support students to maximise the impacts of assessment on improving their learning. If students have a negative attitude towards any type of assessment, it disengages them and will consequently compromise the positive impacts of assessment. Research evidence illustrates that SA is perceived by students negatively because it causes test anxiety.

Unless students see that both types of assessments, and all assessments in general, are integral parts of the learning and teaching processes and are helping them to improve their learning, they will continue to have negative perceptions of SA. They will continue to believe that FA is a type of assessment used to help them learn by providing feedback on their performance and helping them identify areas of improvement while SA is a type of assessment used to evaluate performance and is typically used to assign a final grade at the end of a course.

To ensure the interactive nature of FA and SA, and both assessments serve a meaningful purpose in improving student learning outcomes, students' views about these two types of assessment must be explored. Investigating the relationships between students' attitudes towards FA and SA will provide an understanding of how to combine these two types of assessment to enhance learning processes. Aspirations to reconcile FA and SA and help students overcome the negative effects of high-stake testing make it necessary to understand the relationship between students' attitudes towards the two types of assessment.

Factors Influencing the Problem

Many factors influence students' attitudes towards FA and SA.

1 *The FA and SA debate.*
   The ongoing tensions between FA and SA and the continued use of such terminologies in the classroom continue to shape the views, beliefs, discourse and practices in assessment. Teachers who explicitly use the terms and categorise their assessments as either FA or SA send a strong message to students that both types of assessments are mutually exclusive, and their nomenclature is significant for the functions of assessments.
2 *Personal factors influence students' attitudes towards FA and SA.*
   Girls have a more favourable attitude towards both FA and SA than boys because girls are more compliant with schooling-related issues (Whitelaw et al., 2000) and, thus, more likely to agree with assessment styles and requirements from teachers or schools. There are other student backgrounds that influence their attitude towards assessment, including ability level, cultural background, motivation and among others.
3 *The stage of schooling influences students' attitudes towards assessment.*
   Students' preferences for FA and SA decrease as their year levels increase. The assessment culture influences this; in that in an exam-oriented education system (like the one in Hong Kong), students in higher grades experience more academic pressure and competition for the next stage of education than students in lower grades. Thus, students must develop a positive attitude in their early years and carry that forward in a high-stake environment where assessments are used for accreditation and certification.

4 *Students' attitudes towards FA can predict their attitudes towards SA.*
A student with a positive affective and instrumental attitude towards FA will likely accept SA and find it useful for their learning. This clearly shows that from students' viewpoint, these two types of assessments are interrelated. Their perception in terms of use, necessity and emotional impact of assessment is not isolated in one type of assessment. Rather, whatever beliefs they hold, it is across different types of assessment.

Implications of the Problem

If the discourse and use of assessment in schools continue to be seen as a dichotomy between FA and SA, students will also perceive that these two assessments are mutually exclusive. Their perceptions will, in turn, influence their attitudes towards assessment, consequently impacting their performance. They will continue to develop a negative view of SA and see it as less beneficial for their learning.

Two perspectives are offered by Guo and Yan (2019). The first perspective is that FA and SA should be reconciled rather than separated in classroom practices. A clear articulation that assessment is a continuum of practice rather than a dichotomy is critically important for developing students' understanding of the roles and functions of any assessment in their learning. This understanding may change students' attitudes towards assessment, both instrumental and affective, as there is no key distinction. They will develop a positive perception that any assessment implemented by teachers will help them and their teachers to make decisions on how to support them in their learning further to achieve the prescribed outcomes.

The second perspective is that it is more feasible to manipulate students' attitudes towards FA to shape their attitudes towards SA. This implies that by understanding the correlation between students' attitudes towards FA and SA, teachers can design pedagogical interventions to change students' attitudes towards both FA and SA. Teachers can use SA to demonstrate that the results of such can be used to identify their learning needs and develop interventions to enhance their learning further. Similarly, teachers can use the results of FA to make decisions related to the outcomes of students' learning. This process will develop students' understanding that both assessments can function either formatively or summatively.

Case 3: Using classroom assessment results for high-stake decision-making

Description of the Study

Classroom assessments are often perceived to be less useful for informing high-stake decisions due to their perceived low reliability and validity. This case study addresses this perception and demonstrates that any assessments can be used for high-stale decisions. Curry et al. (2016) used a case study design to understand how a district-wide, teacher-centred approach to data use can meet high-stake accountability mandates requiring data use to improve schools. Data were collected in a mid-size suburban public school district in Midwest USA. The district employed 529 teachers in 2013–2014 and had a student enrolment of just over 10,000 in nine school sites (three elementary, two intermediate, one middle, one freshman academy and one high school). This district was purposefully sampled as it was identified as emphasising a formative, teacher-centred approach to data generation and utilisation at the classroom level to enhance instructional practices and student performance outcomes. Data were derived from interviews, field notes, observations and document analysis. Analysing formative data (second, third and fourth grades) and achievement results on state-mandated tests for students (third and fourth grades) allowed the researchers to observe student progress over three years. It also allowed researchers to understand better how reading specialists and classroom teachers work together to use data to enhance student outcomes.

Their findings suggest that teachers begin to practice reflective teaching when data is used to inform instruction rather than evaluate instruction. Additionally, a common language emerged across grade levels that facilitates a collaborative approach to data use. 'Inform' and 'evaluate' are terms used to describe how data can be used in the classroom. When data is used to 'inform' instruction, it provides insight into student performance and informs decisions about instructional strategies. When data is used to 'evaluate' instruction, it assesses the effectiveness of instructional strategies.

Based on the results, the authors propose a data-informed instructional theoretical model, based on self-determination theory, that stakeholders in K-12 education systems can use to enhance instruction and learning in the classroom. This model focuses on providing teachers autonomy, competence and relatedness to build collective capacity.

Problem Being Addressed

Teachers are expected to meet high-stake accountability mandates, requiring the use of data to improve learning and teaching. The use of high-stake tests to provide data for teachers to make instructional decisions is often critiqued because single-measure, multiple-choice tests do not effectively assess student progress (Darling-Hammond, 2010). The pressure between high-stake test results and classroom assessment data leads to confusion about which assessment would provide better information for teachers to improve students' learning outcomes. In addition, teachers often lack the skills and knowledge to use available summative data to improve learning and teaching at the classroom level effectively. This leaves them exasperated and can lead to decreased motivation for using data.

Factors Influencing the Problem

Many factors influence teachers' low capacity to use classroom data for decision-making:

1 *Teachers' perception of externally administered SA.*

The current high-stake accountability mandates data use for school improvement, but the focus is on using externally administered SA. Teachers are conflicted with this policy as they perceive that this type of assessment does not capture a holistic picture of students' learning. Often, high-stake tests and the results are too removed from the context of the schools and the students.

2 *Motivation to use data.*

Their autonomy to select what relevant data to use influences their actual data use. In addition, teachers' negative perception of high-stake tests does not motivate them to use high-stake data to inform learning and teaching. Some teachers' perceive that high-stake tests are irrelevant because they are not aligned to the content taught and the timing of its administration and availability of results are not in sync with teachers' lesson plan.

3 *Data literacy skills.*

Teachers and school leaders often do not have the knowledge and skills to use available summative data effectively to improve learning and teaching. Analysing summative data may require technical skills, and therefore, they need training to improve their data literacy skills. This is particularly needful when data are externally stored from the school, requiring remote access. In addition, when the data format does not align to what school leaders and teachers need to analyse, there is a higher likelihood that they will not use the data.

4 *Policy influence.*

The pressure to use data to drive school reform supported by federal and state policies and frameworks forces schools and districts to focus more on 'standards and accountability' through high-stake testing and summative data. Without a considerable shift in policy at the state and federal levels, requirements for SA are likely to be further entrenched.

5 *Structural conditions.*

These include the physical and organisational structures that are in place to support the use of data. District-level support and a consistent approach to data use are necessary for successful data use. This support included common planning times and blocks of time allowed monthly for collaborative efforts. Additionally, a common assessment framework across schools is needed to give teachers, students and parents a common language and shared understanding of student progress. The availability of teacher aides, when needed, will provide support and guidance to the teachers and students. Additionally, the district provided resources to support mentoring relationships among teachers to build teacher capacity for generating, analysing and utilising data.

6 *Normative conditions.*

These refer to the expectations and standards of behaviour that teachers and principals accept. The district-level, collaborative approach to formative data use to generate, analyse and utilise data encourages transparency among teachers and the use of data to inform instruction rather than evaluate performance. This helps to create a foundation for teaching practices and promotes a school culture that enhances the effectiveness of data use.

As shown above, teachers' use of formative data to make high-stake decisions is influenced by many factors. The interplay of these factors supports teachers in enhancing their practices and promotes a school culture that enhances the effectiveness of data use. More importantly, the structural and normative conditions meet teachers' psychological needs, including their autonomy (control over their work and to be ability to make decisions independently), competence (the need for teachers to feel competent in their work and to be able to demonstrate their skills) and relatedness (need for teachers to feel connected to their colleagues and to be able to work together in a collaborative environment).

Implications of the Problem

Meeting accountability requirements for formative data use in schools to improve student outcomes requires teachers' positive dispositions, knowledge and skills, motivation, autonomy and support. Besides teachers' data knowledge and skills, their motivation is critical for their data use to inform instruction. Teachers' perceptions and beliefs about teaching, their motivation to enhance capacity, and their assessment practices, pedagogical views and understanding of the relevancy, usefulness and accessibility of data influence how effective the use of data is in advancing instructional practice in the classroom.

To promote data use in schools, a bottom-up teacher-centred approach is recommended by Curry et al. (2016). This approach emphasises daily data generation, collection and utilisation by teachers. This approach accurately gathers assessment data that reflect students' behaviour, skills and knowledge and encourages self-reflection. This approach to data use meets the psychological needs of teachers, such as autonomy, competence and relatedness, which can lead to meaningful and sustainable school reform. The fact that this approach to data use has been linked to an increase in student performance on state-mandated high-stake assessments suggests that it is beneficial.

A shift on school data culture is needed, focusing more on using data to inform instruction rather than evaluate instruction. The study above shows that teachers begin to practice reflective teaching when schools have stronger focus on using data to support learning and teaching. Building a strong assessment culture, underpinned by a right balance between learning and accountability functions of assessment, would shape teachers' data use. Using assessment data for the sole purpose of evaluating teachers' performance puts another layer of accountability, which demotivates teachers to gather and analyse data. Using data in a non-threatening and transparent way encourages teachers to evaluate their instructional practices and adjust them to fit the needs of their students better. This process of self-reflection and adjustment enables teachers to more effectively use data to adjust their teaching to match their students' needs. Teachers feel this process empowers them because they are treated like a professional.

In any assessment reforms, teachers must be part of the processes, especially in making decisions relating to their work. In this study, teachers appreciated their inclusion in decision-making and having a voice in decisions that would affect their classroom practices. They were involved in developing a common framework for formative data use across the elementary schools in the district. Allowing teachers to have a voice in decisions around programs and methods of formative data collection can promote buy-in and motivation for sustained practices.

In addition, giving teachers the autonomy to make decisions for their classrooms is seen as an important factor. They need to be actively involved in goal setting and in setting the direction of the school assessment culture. Teachers are key decision-makers in data use, and thus, their expertise should be valued by giving them autonomy as to what to do with student learning. In this study, teachers expressed deep appreciation for the fact that they are 'treated as professionals' because they are trusted to make competent decisions for instruction. This means that teachers want freedom and responsibility to decide how to best use data to improve instruction and learning in their classrooms and should be respected as professionals capable of making these critical decisions.

A collaborative approach to data use facilitates teachers' need for relatedness. The regular meetings between administrators and teachers help discuss formative student data and collaboratively set short-term learning goals. This is done through teacher-initiated conversations and open and honest discussions of student progress. This approach is important, as it helps to build collective capacity by meeting the psychological needs of teachers, such as autonomy, competence and relatedness. Discussion around data use develops a shared understanding, instructional goals and a common language that guide discussions about student progress. This helps build a sense of community and a strong foundation for meeting the teachers' psychological need for relatedness, in contrast to the pressure teachers have felt from top-down high-stake assessment policies. A collaborative approach will enable teachers to build relationships with other teachers and parents.

A teacher-centred approach to data use has the potential to motivate teachers to persist in their efforts to reach achievement goals and enhance student outcomes. This approach should empower teachers to generate, analyse and use data at the classroom level to guide instruction. The authors argue that current approaches often overlook the influence of top-down policies on teachers, leading to widespread frustration and demoralisation. High-stake accountability mandates can demotivate teachers by removing them from the data-driven decision-making process and separating student outcomes from immediate instructional practices. The approach for using formative data for high-stake decisions should meet the psychological needs of teachers for autonomy, competence and relatedness. This approach would make data use meaningful and practical for teachers.

> Teachers need to work closely with students to set consistent goals to motivate them to take ownership of their learning goals and become actively involved in setting increasingly challenging goals. Students who can articulate their learning goals are better positioned to identify strategies to achieve them. This collaborative goal-setting process develops a common assessment language between teachers and students that enhances a common understanding of assessment principles, processes and tasks.

Proposed Solutions

Going back to the title of this chapter, the question of whether FA and SA are different, we need conceptual, behavioural, structural, organisational and policy changes to support teachers to see the intersections between SA and FA. Black and Wiliam (2018) clearly argue that assessment is essential to effective learning and teaching. When the use SA or FA is connected to learning improvement, the complementary nature of these assessments to support learning and teaching is optimised (Lau, 2016). The relationship between the instruction students receive and what they learn as a result of that instruction is complex. Simply documenting the educational experiences of each student would not accurately describe their capabilities. Therefore, we need to develop processes of eliciting and interpreting evidence to draw conclusions about what students have actually learned. It also explains that from this view, there should be no conflict between FA and SA, as all assessments should be about producing valid inferences about students' learning. We must go beyond our previous understanding that FA refers to assessments that inform instruction and SA refers to assessments to evaluate student learning. Any assessment, FA, SA, AoL, AfL, AaL, or whatever type of assessment, should be used to draw valid inferences about students' learning and use these inferences to further support individual students. This conceptual change provides the foundation for a common language among principals, teachers, students, parents, policymakers and the public. This shared understanding will develop a school assessment culture that prioritises using assessment to support learning and teaching.

In addition, teachers should be supported to conceptualise assessment within a broader pedagogical model. This process requires teachers to develop strong pedagogical content knowledge and theorise how their assessment literacy relates to this knowledge. The relationships between content, pedagogy and assessment will only become coherent when assessment is seen as a central feature of effective learning and teaching. Teachers' view of assessment as the central feature of learning and teaching will develop their positive dispositions towards using assessment to support individual students (Herppich et al., 2018; Mandinach & Gummer, 2016). Consequently, when teachers are adequately supported, and the school environment is favourable for their assessment practices, these positive dispositions are translated into actual classroom practices, eliciting behavioural change in their assessment practices.

Moreover, teachers need to understand assessment within the wider context in which it takes place. This context includes the cultural traditions, political and public expectations of education, and the norms of the various institutions in which teachers and schools operate. This understanding is consistent with the context-driven nature of assessment (Alonzo et al., 2021). The political aspects and public expectations of assessment are critical understanding for teachers to design and implement any assessment strategies. As policymakers expect to gather standardised assessment data, and hence, summative and external examinations are more favourable for them, teachers can design and implement SA and use the results for FA purposes or implement FA and use the results for summative purposes (Dolin et al., 2018). This approach is cited by Houston and Thompson (2017) to resolve the dichotomy between SA and FA, in that all assessments are used to communicate information about learning. In addition, Broadbent et al. (2018) demonstrated that designing SA aligned with formative processes enhances its formative use, addressing the tension of this dichotomy. They recommend using exemplars, discussing the marking criteria, eliciting and giving feedback, and supporting students to act on feedback.

Furthermore, organisational and structural changes need to support the conceptualisation of assessment to enhance learning and teaching. This requires recalibration of desired outcomes, provision of tools, support and resources, and review of rules, expectations and divisions of labour. The education bureaucracies can provide structural conditions, including workload allocation for common planning and time for teacher collaboration. Also, they can provide normative conditions, including a system-wide approach to assessment reform and development and the use of an agreed common assessment framework across schools that gives teachers, students and parents a shared language and understanding of student progress (Alonzo, 2016).

Conclusion

The three case studies included in this chapter highlight the interplay between FA and SA. As demonstrated, they are not mutually exclusive, and each supports the function of the other. They might be different in terms of format and implementation process. However, they can be used independently or collectively to meet both the accountability requirements and the classroom-level decisions for learning and teaching improvement. However, the debate around FA and SA needs to be resolved to effectively use FA and SA to meet these requirements and decisions. There is a need to refocus the conceptual

76 Reconciling the Formative and Summative Debate

understanding of the dichotomy between FA and SA and conceptualise them within a broader pedagogical model (Black & Wiliam, 2018). In doing this, all assessments, regardless of nomenclature, are used to support learning and teaching, and even FA (i.e., teacher observation and anecdotal records) is used to meet the accountability requirements set by the system (Curry et al., 2016). The conceptual, behavioural, structural, organisational and policy changes will support teachers in developing a deeper understanding that FA is not that different from SA, or vice versa, in terms of its functions to support learning and teaching. These changes will support teachers in resolving the dichotomy between FA and SA and see the central role of assessment in ensuring effective learning and teaching.

References

Alonzo, D. (2016). *Development and application of a teacher assessment for learning (AfL) literacy tool.* University of New South Wales. http://unsworks.unsw.edu.au/fapi/datastream/unsworks:38345/SOURCE02?view=true

Alonzo, D., Labad, V., Bejano, J., & Guerra, F. (2021). The policy-driven dimensions of teacher beliefs about assessment. *Australian Journal of Teacher Education, 46*(3). https://ro.ecu.edu.au/cgi/viewcontent.cgi?article=4761&context=ajte

Bennett, R. E. (2011). Formative assessment: A critical review. *Assessment in Education: Principles Policy and Practice, 18*(1), 5–25.

Biggs, J. (1996). Assessing learning quality: Reconciling institutional, staff and educational demands. *Assessment and Evaluation in Higher Education, 21*(1), 5–15.

Bijsterbosch, E., van der Schee, J., & Kuiper, W. (2017). Meaningful learning and summative assessment in geography education: An analysis in secondary education in the Netherlands. *International Research in Geographical and Environmental Education, 26*(1), 17–35. https://doi.org/10.1080/10382046.2016.1217076

Black, P. (2017). Assessment in science education. In K. S. Taber & B. Akpan (Eds.), *Science education: An international course companion* (pp. 295–309). Sense Publishers. https://doi.org/10.1007/978-94-6300-749-8_22

Black, P., & Wiliam, D. (1999). *Assessment for learning: Beyond the black box.* A. R. Group.

Black, P., & Wiliam, D. (2009). Developing the theory of formative assessment. *Educational Assessment, Evaluation and Accountability, 21*(1), 5–31.

Black, P., & Wiliam, D. (2018). Classroom assessment and pedagogy. *Assessment in Education: Principles, Policy & Practice, 25*(6), 551–575. https://doi.org/10.1080/0969594X.2018.1441807

Black, P., Harrison, C., Lee, C., Marshall, B., & Wiliam, D. (2003). *Assessment for learning: Putting it into practice.* Oxford University Press.

Black, P., Harrison, C., Hodgen, J., Marshall, B., & Serret, N. (2011). Can teachers' summative assessments produce dependable results and also enhance classroom learning? *Assessment in Education: Principles, Policy & Practice, 18*(4), 451–469. https://doi.org/10.1080/0969594X.2011.557020

Broadbent, J., Panadero, E., & Boud, D. (2018). Implementing summative assessment with a formative flavour: A case study in a large class. *Assessment & Evaluation in Higher Education, 43*(2), 307–322. https://doi.org/10.1080/02602938.2017. 1343455

Cranley, L., Robinson, C., Hine, G., & O'Connor, D. (2022). The desks have changed; it must be NAPLAN time: How NAPLAN affects teaching and learning of mathematics. *Issues in Educational Research, 32*(4), 1306–1320. https://search.informit. org/doi/10.3316/informit.806019402657872

Curry, K. A., Mwavita, M., Holter, A., & Harris, E. (2016). Getting assessment right at the classroom level: Using formative assessment for decision making. *Educational Assessment, Evaluation and Accountability, 28*(1), 89–104. https://doi.org/ 10.1007/s11092-015-9226-5

Darling-Hammond, L. (2010). The flat world and education: How America's commitment to equality will determine our future. Teachers College Press.

Davison, C. (2007). Views from the chalkface: English language school based assessment in Hong Kong. *Language Assessment Quarterly, 4*(1), 37–68. https://doi. org/10.1080/15434300701348359

Dolin, J., Black, P., Harlen, W., & Tiberghien, A. (2018). Exploring relations between formative and summative assessment. In J. Dolin & R. Evans (Eds.), *Transforming assessment: Through an interplay between practice, research and policy* (pp. 53–80). SpringerInternationalPublishing.https://doi.org/10.1007/978-3-319-63248-3_3

Education Council. (2019). *The Alice Springs (Mparntwe) education declaration.* Australian Government—Department of Education Skills and employment.

Guo, W. Y., & Yan, Z. (2019). Formative and summative assessment in Hong Kong primary schools: students' attitudes matter. *Assessment in Education: Principles, Policy & Practice, 26*(6), 675–699. https://doi.org/10.1080/0969594X.2019.1571993

Harlen, W. (2007). The impact of summative assessment on children, teaching, and the curriculum. In K. Möller, P. Hanke, C. Beinbrech, A. K. Hein, T. Kleickmann, & R. Schages (Eds.), *QualitÄt von Grundschulunterricht: entwickeln, erfassen und bewerten* (pp. 51–65). VS Verlag für Sozialwissenschaften. https://doi. org/10.1007/978-3-531-90755-0_4

Herppich, S., Praetorius, A.-K., Förster, N., Glogger-Frey, I., Karst, K., Leutner, D., Behrmann, L., Böhmer, M., Ufer, S., Klug, J., Hetmanek, A., Ohle, A., Böhmer, I., Karing, C., Kaiser, J., & Südkamp, A. (2018). Teachers' assessment competence: Integrating knowledge-, process-, and product-oriented approaches into a competence-oriented conceptual model. *Teaching and Teacher Education, 76*, 181–193. https://doi.org/10.1016/j.tate.2017.12.001

Houston, D., & Thompson, J. N. (2017). Blending formative and summative assessment in a capstone subject: 'It's not your tools, it's how you use them'. *Journal of University Teaching & Learning Practice, 14*(3). https://doi.org/10.53761/1. 14.3.2

Johnston, J., & McClune, W. (2000). *Selection project sel 5.1. Pupil motivation and attitudes: Self-esteem, locus of control, learning disposition and the impact of selection teaching and learning.* Queen's University.

Lau, A. M. S. (2016). 'Formative good, summative bad?' – A review of the dichotomy in assessment literature. *Journal of Further and Higher Education, 40*(4), 509–525. https://doi.org/10.1080/0309877X.2014.984600

Mandinach, E. B., & Gummer, E. S. (2016). What does it mean for teachers to be data literate: Laying out the skills, knowledge, and dispositions. *Teaching and Teacher Education, 60*, 366–376. https://doi.org/10.1016/j.tate.2016.07.011

Perrenoud, P. (1998). From formative evaluation to a controlled regulation of learning processes. Towards a wider conceptual field. *Assessment in Education: Principles, Policy & Practice, 5*(1), 85–102. https://doi.org/10.1080/0969595980050105

Pollard, A., Triggs, P., Broadfoot, P., Mcness, E., & Osborn, M. (2002). *What pupils say: Changing policy and practice in primary education.* Continuum.

Wei, W. (2015). Using summative and formative assessments to evaluate EFL teachers' teaching performance. *Assessment & Evaluation in Higher Education, 40*(4), 611–623. https://doi.org/10.1080/02602938.2014.939609

Whitelaw, S., Milosevic, L., & Daniels, S. (2000). Gender, behaviour and achievement: A preliminary study of pupil perceptions and attitudes. *Gender and Education, 12*(1), 87–113. https://doi.org/10.1080/09540250020427

Chapter 5

Beyond One Size Fits All?

Introduction

Early research documenting the significant effects of using assessment to support learning and teaching have influenced its adoption by other educational systems in English-speaking and non-English-speaking countries. Education departments, ministries, educators and teachers in the USA, Hong Kong, Singapore, Australia, New Zealand, Brunei and many other countries have focused on integrating assessment into their educational reforms. While many studies support its effectiveness, the extent to which such reforms raise student outcomes varies, especially in non-English-speaking countries (Alonzo & Loughland, 2022). This is because there are contextual factors that influence its adoption and effectiveness. Research reports highlight the failures of raising student outcomes using empirically supported effective assessment strategies (McMorran et al., 2017). Many factors undermine the effectiveness of assessment. These include cultural values (Watty et al., 2010), established authority of and power relations between teacher and students (Ahmadi, 2022), language proficiency requirement (Yan, 2014), educational policies (Davison, 2013), curriculum structure (Nortvedt et al., 2016), marking processes, teacher experiences (Barkaoui, 2011) and classroom context such as class size, physical layout and among others (Oo et al., 2021). If these factors are not accounted for when designing and implementing assessments, their effectiveness will be limited, and they may even negatively impact student learning.

For the successful implementation of assessment strategies, teacher adaptability is required (Loughland & Alonzo, 2019). The adaptive expertise of teachers optimises the impact of formative assessment (FA) on student learning. As the concept of FA was developed for a particular context, it needs some adaptation in other situations, particularly with English as an additional language or dialect (EAL/D) learners and in countries where teachers are EAL/D users. Capitalising on these modifications highlights the context-dependent

DOI: 10.4324/9781003396277-5

80 Adapting Assessment to Support Learning

nature of assessment that contributes to its effectiveness. This argument was highlighted by Wiliam (2013):

> Different teachers will find different aspects of classroom formative assessment more effective for their personal styles, their students, and the contexts in which they work – so each teacher must decide how to adapt ... for use in their practice.
>
> (pp. 19–20)

Due to various factors influencing the implementation of FA, there are needed modifications on how it should be implemented to ensure its effectiveness.

The Problem

Assessment is context-driven, and many factors influence its effectiveness, including personal, social, emotional, contextual and policy. The conceptual understanding of the intersections between assessment, learning and teaching must be viewed against the backdrop of these factors. Teachers implementing a one-size-fits-all assessment approach do not provide opportunities for students from diverse backgrounds to demonstrate their learning. Even within a particular school, the design and implementation of assessment are influenced by the contexts of key learning areas. Consequently, the impact of assessment to support learning and teaching is limited if no adaptation is made. Also, given the dynamic and evolving nature and practice of assessment, teachers should engage in ongoing experimentation and adaptation to develop new approaches and practices.

Case 1: Using assessment to inform differentiated instruction

Description of the Study

This case study by Alonzo and Loughland (2022) explores students' perceptions of the effectiveness of highly valued assessment practices that enhance learning and teaching. Given the range of research evidence supporting the effectiveness of sharing learning outcomes, use of rubrics, self and peer assessment, and feedback, one would think that using them automatically improves students' learning. Alonzo and Loughland (2022) investigated how secondary English students from different achievement levels respond to different assessment activities and how their responses influence their further engagement in learning. An interpretivist approach was used to analyse the transcripts of semi-structured interviews conducted with five high-performing, three average and three underperforming students and their teachers. Results show that individual students' responses to assessment activities are influenced by their learning goals, achievement levels and perceived benefits of the assessment strategies. High-performing students tend to selectively engage in assessment activities that best improve their learning, whilst underperforming students may disengage when the activity overwhelms them. Average-performing students may engage only to a certain extent to meet the average expectation or performance required. These findings suggest that effective teacher assessment practices would benefit from the concept of stimulus-response compatibility. This means that teachers should be aware of how their assessment strategies may trigger initial response from students and how their responses will influence their future engagement in learning. This study demonstrates that the use of differentiation of assessment strategies, including sharing learning outcomes, use of rubrics, self and peer assessment, and feedback, is necessary to tailor to individual students' needs and abilities to support them in achieving higher outcomes.

Problem Being Addressed

The implementation of assessment activities does not always lead to an improvement in student learning. There are students who do not benefit even with empirically proven assessment strategies to raise student achievement. This could be because many studies only report the overall improvement of the cohort and do not consider the effects of discrete assessment practices on individual students. Studying the effects of assessment on individual students is more in line with the learner-centred approach to assessment, where the focus is on helping individual students achieve better. Investigating individual students' benefit from assessment would shed light on how teachers can design differentiated assessment tailored to the needs of individual students from different ability levels.

Factors Influencing the Problem

As shown in this study, the effectiveness of assessment is influenced by students' personal factors. These include the following:

1 *Student achievement levels.*
  Students from different achievement levels respond differently to assessment activities. The relationship between the design and

implementation of any assessment is perceived differently by students from different achievement levels. Their initial response to assessment subsequently influences their learning.

2   *Student perception of assessment.*

Students' perception of the effectiveness of teacher's assessment practices affects their future learning motivation. The match between the stimulus (assessment) they receive and their capability (achievement level) to respond to the stimulus can either promote or compromise their future engagement in learning. Hence, teacher adaptive disposition, which has been linked to enhanced student learning, is critical in providing appropriate stimulus and constructive responses to students to further enhance their learning engagement.

3   *Student preference.*

There is no homogenous preference across all students; thus, even the most credible assessment activity may not have the same outcome for all students. For example, self-assessment is favourable for high-performing students as they are well motivated to identify and address the criteria they have not fully met, while underachieving students find it overwhelming to assess their work, particularly if they have not understood the marking criteria. Another example is the implementation of peer assessment. Underachieving students who are paired with high-performing students benefit more as the high-achieving student can clearly identify areas for further improvement. However, when high-achieving students are paired with underachieving students, they doubt the feedback provided and question the credibility of their peers.

4   *Teacher monitoring of student responses.*

The students' initial responses to assessment activity were shown to be critical for their subsequent actions. The variance of students' responses mediated the actual effects of assessment activities on student learning. Hence, teachers need to monitor student responses and use this information in their learning, teaching and assessment activities to optimise students' learning better. The modification of learning and teaching activities should be informed by the information gathered by teachers.

5   *Alignment of teacher intent and student response.*

The disconnect between teacher intent in using assessment strategies and students' actual responses compromises the effectiveness of assessment. It was observed that the teacher's intention in using an assessment strategy is not always realised. Individual students respond differently to any assessment strategies. For example, using a range of exemplars is highly recommended in the literature, and even if teachers believe that they are helpful, their effectiveness depends on how students perceive them. Similarly, feedback is considered the centrepiece of effective learning. However, the findings of this study suggest that the teacher's intent in giving feedback is not always accurately perceived by the students, thus making it ineffective in improving student learning.

Implications of the Problem

To ensure that individual students benefit from any assessment, it is important to differentiate the assessment design and implementation based on student factors, in this case, their ability levels, which influence their learning goals. The influence of many factors could explain why, even though assessment activities have been proven to have positive effects on student outcomes, empirical evidence of their effectiveness are not always translated into actual student achievement. Teachers should pay attention to these factors and use them to inform assessment design and implementation.

The effectiveness of assessment practices depends on how teachers design and implement them to elicit positive responses from individual students. Thus, assessment activities must be tailored to student factors, including but not limited to their needs and achievement levels. Teachers should not adhere to the generic design of effective assessment practices, such as sharing learning outcomes, providing exemplars, eliciting and giving feedback, and engaging in self and peer assessment. They should modify them to optimise their impact. Teachers must be aware of how students from different achievement levels respond to these activities. When an assessment activity matches the ability level of students, it can draw positive response and they can demonstrate their learning without being hindered by the task difficulty. Students can meaningfully engage by using their critical thinking, problem solving and decision-making skills at an appropriate level. Consequently, teachers would be able to collect data that can be used to adapt subsequent learning and teaching activities.

The teachers' approach to translate their intent to actual student outcomes is a necessary step for designing differentiated assessment. This ensures that the assessment activities are tailored to individual students and, thus, have a higher likelihood of leading to a more positive responses and improved student outcomes. The impact of differentiated assessment is more than just meeting the teacher's intent for using it. When assessment activity is tailored to the needs of the students, it creates a positive learning environment because individual students will feel that they are supported to succeed. The experience of success will reinforce students' growth mindset, leading to more positive outlook about their learning.

84 Adapting Assessment to Support Learning

Case 2: Assessment culture as a policy and context-dependent construct

Description of the Study

This case study highlights the influence of policy and context on teachers' assessment practices. The introduction and use of assessment *for* learning (AfL) in Norway and Portugal primary schools using mathematics teaching are used as illustrative examples. Nortvedt et al. (2016) used a case study design to describe the similarities and differences between the two countries. Data were obtained from policy documents and research reports, including educational acts and curriculum, policy-making and policy such as teacher education programs, evaluation of policy as well as monitoring educational systems and research. Content analysis was done using the following categories: teacher education programmes, primary education curriculum, assessment systems and assessment practices at the classroom level.

Results show that AfL practices are not common in primary mathematics classrooms in either Norway or Portugal, even though both countries have implemented it as a national policy. At the school level, there is a difference in terms of assessment culture. Portugal teachers claimed to have an assessment culture but is predominantly driven by summative assessment, whereas Norwegian teachers claimed to have no assessment culture, explaining why they have difficulty developing and using assessment criteria. At the national level, students in Portugal are graded compared to students in Norway who do not receive grades. While both countries implement AfL as a national policy, teachers do not use assessments within the AfL framework. It was also found that teachers' assessment practices change due to their engagement in professional development related to assessment. However, a difference in the sustainability of implementation between schools is influenced by head teachers' support for teachers and the school administration's support for head teachers. Thus, changing teachers' assessment practices "should build on national professional development projects that include support at both the national and local levels, enabling teachers to formulate clear criteria ... this necessitates forming national policies that are also rooted at the local level" (p. 381).

Another interesting finding of this chapter is the influence of teacher autonomy in implementing AfL policy. It was found that primary school teachers in Norway have a higher level of autonomy because there are no national test standards compared to teachers in Portugal who are preparing their students for a national examination. However, in both countries, the mathematics curriculum strongly focuses on attaining the learning outcomes, which drives teachers' assessment practices to over-value what can be observed and measured. Consequently, this curriculum structure limits teachers' practices, teaching only what they thought could help students achieve the learning outcomes at the risk of not implementing any other AfL strategies.

Problem Being Addressed

Teachers' implementation of assessment is influenced by many factors. In this study, the problem addressed is implementing a national assessment policy and the factors that influence it. Although the key principles of effective assessment are well articulated (see ARG, 2002), there are teacher assessment practices that are not aligned with these principles. Teachers continue to struggle to align their practices to AfL principles due to the influence of curriculum structure, national examinations and the school culture. The difficulty in translating the AfL principles into practical skills is not exclusive to any particular country, culture or subject. There is paucity in the literature about the underlying reasons for the generalised difficulty. A key to understanding the reasons is a more focused attention to local differences to understand the assessment traditions of each particular country to develop an effective assessment culture.

Factors Influencing the Problem

Several factors influence the difficulty of teachers in implementing AfL principles. These include the following:

1 *Assessment culture.*

This chapter demonstrated that the absence of an assessment culture or an inappropriate assessment culture (i.e., leaning towards summative assessment) influences teachers' implementation of AfL practices. The authors claim that these countries are at two ends of the spectrum: Norway with no agreed assessment culture and Portugal with assessment culture – two different factors lead to the same result, that is, a lack of AfL practices in the classroom. The absence of such and the ill-defined assessment culture then leads to ineffective teacher assessment practices.

2 *National professional development programs.*

Professional development with an assessment focus can change teachers' assessment practices towards AfL. Such professional development programs can be scaled up to the national level to support other teachers nationwide. However, a national policy must include support at the national and local levels. This support will enable teachers to create clear criteria for assessment and recognise the different levels of mathematical competence of their students.

3 *Curriculum structure.*

Too much emphasis on discrete learning outcomes shifts teachers' practices to focus on teaching those observable and measurable outcomes. This could lead to a few learning aspects being favoured and thus reducing the potential of AfL practices. This practice narrows down the curriculum, which consequently limits learning.

4 *Personal factor.*

Teacher autonomy is a factor in the rarity of AfL practices in primary school mathematics teaching. The presence of national examinations influences the level of teacher autonomy. Teachers in Portugal have a lower level of autonomy than teachers in Norway due to the pressure of national examinations. They prepare their students to perform better in these examinations. Thus, teachers' assessment practices are more summative by nature, resonating with these national examinations. Teachers who are under pressure to make their students perform better in the national examinations would always revert back to the summative-driven assessment practices to prepare their students.

5 *Key learning areas.*

The content focus to be assessed influences the type of assessment used by teachers. The knowledge and skills valued by the discipline shape teachers' assessment practices, developing a shared understanding of the most effective assessment types for assessing such knowledge and skills. Teachers should develop a repertoire of assessment skills that are aligned with the content and skills of each key learning area.

Implications of the Problem

The adoption and implementation of assessment by any educational bureaucracies, even at the school level, must account for policy, curriculum structure, contextual and personal factors. Teachers operate within the constraints of these factors, and the effectiveness of their assessment practices relies on the interplay of these factors. This means that assessment principles must be contextualised when adopted by an educational institution, whether at the national, state or school levels.

When changing teachers' assessment practices, policymakers need to support schools in developing an assessment culture that operationalises the principles and practices of effective assessment. One important consideration is the impact of national assessment culture, particularly the accountability-driven national assessment system, as it may present an obstacle to effectively implement effective teacher assessment practices. As demonstrated in this study, the implementation of a national examination lowers teachers' autonomy.

One way to support teachers in adopting effective assessment practices is implementing nationwide professional development relating to assessment. The difficulties teachers identify when seeking to change their assessment practices indicate that a significant investment in teacher training related to AfL is necessary. Professional development has a positive impact on teacher assessment practices. However, supporting and enabling mechanisms should be established to translate teachers' knowledge into practical skills. At the school level, the support from school leaders is vital for teachers to implement new assessment practices. Thus, a school-based mechanism for monitoring and supporting teachers who attended professional development programs must be established.

Moreover, the curriculum needs to be restructured to allow teachers to determine the dimensions of learning to be assessed. Giving teachers a choice in curriculum implementation develops their autonomy. A curriculum aligned to narrow concepts or particular learning outcomes produces restricted ideas of what to assess, thus limiting teachers' teaching and students' learning.

Case 3: The influences of multiple systems in an assessment reform

Description of the Study

This case study illustrates that adopting the principles of effective assessment practices requires adapting them. The usual adaptation is underpinned by policy and contextual factors. The work of Flórez Petour (2015) establishes a case for situating the study of assessment reforms in the context of three broader dimensions. The first dimension is the historical dimension, which considers the diachronic (long-term) aspect of assessment reforms. The second dimension is the systemic dimension, which looks at the processes of production, circulation and consumption of discourses related to assessment in a web of interactions between actors. The third dimension is the ideological dimension, which considers the extent to which the theories and research on assessment and their translation into policies are related to the perspectives on education and society supported by powerful groups. Both short-term and long-term assessment reforms were investigated using polysystems theory and critical discourse analysis to analyse documents from different periods of Chilean history of education and interviews with policy authorities and teachers to understand the systems, actors, activities and interactions involved in assessment reform processes. Additionally, the author analysed how discourses on assessment are produced and circulated and how knowledge on assessment is related to power issues.

Problem Being Addressed

The lack of a comprehensive and more complex approach to assessment reform processes in both policy-making and research influences the various issues that arise in AfL reform. The predominant view of assessment phenomena is limited, where only certain systems and their actors are considered or where only one particular discourse on assessment is studied in isolation. This limited perspective on research and policy-making overlooks the complexity of three different dimensions: historical, systemic and ideological. All of these three dimensions are important when it comes to understanding assessment reform processes.

Factors Influencing the Problem

Many factors influence the issues of AfL reform. In addition to schools, researchers and policymakers, this chapter highlights other factors as follows:

1 *Political parties.*
Political power and ideologies play a role in the assessment policy process. In all periods under scrutiny, actors with political power and ideologies have a fundamental role in assessment policy processes. The political discussions surrounding examinations focused on who should control them and opening and closing specific social mobility gates guarded by examination processes. The system of AfL policy in Chile is crucial and was developed by authorities in response to the lack of policies related to classroom assessment and the demand for such policies from teachers. However, two policy authorities also added an unofficial political motivation for reform due to low results from Trends in International Mathematics and Science Study and the national curriculum assessment system by the end of the 1990s and the beginning of the 2000s.

2 *Institutions of education governance.*

The Chilean historical governance tradition had an effect on the implementation of AfL, in which the structure of the Ministry of Education became increasingly complex, with previous units existing alongside new ones, and the top-down models were inherited from previous periods. This created a chaotic governance structure, with different units of the Ministry and local authorities generating their own assessment policies without much space for practitioners to make sense of them.

3 *Competing programs.*

The implementation of AfL was only one program among many assessment reforms developed by the Ministry, and interviews with policy authorities revealed internal and external conflicts between the different units and sudden policy shifts due to political contingency. There was a lot of different information available on assessment within the Ministry, leading to contradictions.

4 *School factors.*

The traditional top-down structure of the system of assessment policies in Chile contributes to the issue of AfL implementation. Assessment policies are circulated from the Ministry to local authorities, which in turn transfer them to Headteachers and Heads of Technical-Pedagogical Units (UTP Heads). UTP Heads act as the intermediaries of policies and transmit a filtered version of the policies to teachers through three different strategies: not informing teachers at all, providing general information and generating an in-depth discussion about the policy to reach collective understanding and decision-making. In addition, when assessment policies are not high stakes, like the case of AfL, a difference in the degree of freedom given to teachers in terms of enactment decisions is detected between private, private government-subsidised and public schools in Chile, with the former being the ones where teachers are granted greater autonomy and the latter where they feel more pressure to implement policies.

5 *Economic sector.*

The involvement of the economic and productive sectors in education policy in Chile has changed over time. In the past, representatives of the industrial, agricultural and business sectors were directly involved in decision-making processes. However, at present, employers are not directly involved in education reform processes. However, new partnerships between the private and public sectors have increased the business sector's influence. Additionally, their demands and the imperatives of the global economy are used to justify reforms and support a functional approach to education and society.

6 *Foreign models or education systems.*

The governments or policymakers look at the policies and practices of other countries and try to adapt them to their contexts. The assessment reform process in Chile involved hiring a foreign expert to develop a classroom assessment programme in the Unit for Curriculum and Assessment. The foreign expert was tasked with introducing AfL to policy authorities, universities and teachers who do not know the concept. The foreign expert thus undertakes a literature review, and the Assessment and Curriculum Unit begins a study to collect data on teachers' assessment practices to establish a more scientific basis to make the knowledge from practice more credible. The foreign expert's knowledge is accepted without question by authorities at the national level, suggesting a very top-down process of transnational policy learning, where the foreign expert's views on reform processes are accepted without any consideration of the actual level of knowledge the foreign expert has. This suggests that the present period is the most passive, as evidenced by accepting foreign ideas compared to previous periods. The foreign expert was asked why they chose the AfL approach, and they said they based their decision on a general review of the available literature and their own practical experience in assessment. The foreign expert also explained that they saw their role in the process as bringing light to a place where assessment knowledge was lacking. To explain their decision, they also mentioned the strategic use of the discourse of international organisations as a means to validate the new policies at the local level.

7 *Family factors.*

The family social classes have an impact on implementing AfL reform. In the case of Chile, since the 19th century, conservative groups have advocated for parents to be responsible for their children's education. However, this responsibility has not been extended to parents from lower social strata. These parents have a relationship with school that is described as one of tension, where they do not see education as important or blame teachers for their children's low performance. There was an attempt to involve parents in their children's schooling through parents' associations to foster collaboration in school activities. Teachers from state schools, which are schools for the more vulnerable groups in the currently segregated Chilean education system, have tried to get parents involved in the assessment process beyond merely receiving marks. In contrast, the high- and middle-class parents in Chile historically have been a participative group that has stated its demands loudly and clearly. They are mostly located in schools where the private sector is involved or in elite selective state secondary schools. Their main interest in the first three periods of Chilean history was to make certification (the process of obtaining an official certification or qualification) as straightforward as possible for their children to be guaranteed access to higher education, an important aspect of their self-concept as a social group. Teachers from higher social strata are held accountable by parents, leading teachers to feel more compelled to provide them with detailed feedback about their pupils' learning.

8 *Public opinion.*

Public opinion, historically, has been significantly influencing the assessment culture of educational systems, especially in the 19th century when it was restricted to a few elite members. In the 1920s, it shifted to a more multi-voiced space as workers and teacher organisations began to publish their materials. In the 1960s, public opinion was explicitly addressed by education governance institutions and used to measure a government's success. This was done through the use of standardised testing results and the establishment of a unit for national assessment in the Ministry. In the current period, policy authorities recognise the role of public opinion in a more abstract and 'omnipresent' form. This public opinion can take the form of people demonstrating on the streets, media messages around surveys on citizen perceptions or the education system itself is seen as conservative and resistant to change. In all cases, policy authorities see this system as exerting pressure and being able to change the course of education policy, even though there is no systematic account of the views of its actors. This underscores the importance of using public spaces intelligently and responsibly as a strategy for enacting assessment reforms in schools.

9 *Teacher education and the academy.*

The quality of teacher education influences AfL implementation of teachers. Despite universities incorporating assessment as a topic, both experienced and recently graduated teachers evaluated their initial education around assessment as deficient. They characterised this education as either too theoretical or too atheoretical, but in either case, as distant from the reality of the school. Due to their lack of knowledge acquisition from the university, teachers must learn about assessment through their school experience, communication with their colleagues and trial and error in practice. Finally, new discourses on assessment, like AfL, are often superficially absorbed by teachers and become part of a commercial strategy. It also notes that the responsibility of teacher education institutions for teachers' lack of knowledge on curriculum assessment is evident yet rarely taken into account in assessment reform processes.

Implications of the Problem

The complexities of implementing assessment reforms can only be understood when systems and actors influencing teacher assessment practices are viewed from a broader perspective. The key actors, including policy-makers, school leaders and teachers must know how historical events have shaped the current assessment system. In addition, they need to have a deeper understanding of the overall system, including the various components, actors and processes that make up the system. Equally important, they need to explore ideologies, including beliefs, values and assumptions, that shape how people think, act and interact.

The historical, systemic and ideological dimensions are important when it comes to understanding assessment reform processes. The limited understanding of these three dimensions will consequently compromise the implementation of any assessment reforms.

In a more detailed way, understanding of historical dimension of assessment reforms enables stakeholders to understand how the present reform is influenced by previous policies, practices, discourses and significant educational and political events. Some issues in the current reform maybe addressed by exploring the unintended consequences of previous reforms and the culture created by such. In addition, understanding the systemic dimension will situate assessment reform from competing priorities and all other processes and structure of the educational system. Assessment reforms need to align with the broader educational agenda and how such reform will bring significant change in systems' processes and outcomes. Moreover, the ideologies, values and beliefs of stakeholders about assessment shape the direction of the reform. A strong belief on the effectiveness of assessment to increase outcomes will shape the system-level and school-level reforms.

Proposed Solutions

How teachers should implement effective assessment is a long-standing question that has never been fully answered. As demonstrated in the three case studies, the adoption and development of assessment policy are influenced by the systems, ideologies, history, social-emotional factors, policy and context of the country. At the school level, the operationalisation of assessment policy should be carefully planned to inform the development of a school assessment culture that supports teachers' assessment practices.

At the classroom level, modifications are required apart from the use of differentiated assessment, where the design and implementation of assessments should consider the diversity of student backgrounds. Apart from those discussed in the three case studies, there are some key adaptations needed to ensure that FA is effectively implemented in other contexts.

Linguistic Adaptation

The original theorisation of teacher AfL practices was developed for a particular context. One of the most prominent features of this context is the use of English as the medium for instruction, with teachers and students mostly first-language users. This implies that some adaptation is needed for classrooms where there are EAL learners and more importantly in classrooms where teachers are EAL users. Many assessment strategies require a high level of language proficiency to engage effectively, like peer assessment, dialogic feedback and questioning. This has been mentioned by Black and Wiliam (2018), that is that they do not directly address Bernstein's concept of linguistic code that regulates cognitive orientation and moreover "regulates dispositions, identities, and practices, as these are formed in official and local pedagogizing agencies (school and family)" (1990, p. 3). They have identified the significant role of students' language background and proficiency in learning. This issue is more complex in the context of EAL classrooms. For students to communicate effectively with their peers and teachers, they require a higher level of English proficiency than the target level where they are currently. In this context, English is a subject of FA and at the same time an object as well. Hence, students need more scaffolding and support. Teachers can draw from their L1 to support students. In doing such, they build a strong relationship, gaining students' trust.

Cultural Adaptation

Culturally, many FA processes like dialogic feedback and peer assessment are not universally accepted as good teaching, especially in non-Western countries. This raises an important issue on how assessment can be situated in different cultural norms. For individualistic cultures, individual feedback will work really well, but for collectivist cultures as is the case in many Indigenous cultures and in many Asian countries, giving individual feedback may seem confronting. It may be unusual for students to talk about their learning and identify areas for improvement. Putting someone on the spot and individualising the feedback draws attention to the individual in ways that might be culturally alien to them. They simply have not been exposed from early primary to these kinds of strategies, and so teachers need to actually teach them not only how to do it but why it might be important, or even adapt their strategies to adopt a more collectivist approach. Effective assessment calls for a teacher and student partnership (Alonzo, 2016). This has been demonstrated as a negotiation between teachers and students and is critically important, especially in how feedback is communicated. Dialogic feedback is more effective than a one-way process where students receive feedback (Van Booven, 2015).

94 Adapting Assessment to Support Learning

However, implementing dialogic feedback requires teachers to reflect on their power relations with students. They need to see their students as learning partners, allowing them to interrogate their feedback to fully understand it, thereby acting on it. For teachers to change their practice, they need to be persuaded that there is no loss of their status or loss of authority in adopting this kind of dialogic questioning and interaction in the classroom.

Pedagogical/Practical Adaptation

Another necessary adaptation is pedagogical changes. It is widely recognised that assessment is the central feature of learning and teaching. However, the way it is being introduced in other educational institutions is invasive to the local pedagogies. It raises the issue of importing Western pedagogies and assuming that they are more effective than local pedagogies. There is a need to evaluate the strengths of the local pedagogies and how assessment can be effectively integrated. For example, working with individual students in a whole class situation may make them more comfortable. Students learn from observing and watching each other in a whole class situation, and there is a very strong focus on teacher-centred pedagogy, which is often seen as problematic in Western cultures.

The student-focused pedagogically linked approach to assessment requires examining students' characteristics and analysing how assessment could be tailored to fit to their needs to enhance their learning. This is quite challenging in a context where students come from different language and cultural backgrounds. In this context, assessment largely depends on who is asking, why and in which assessment context. A two-way process is needed for this context-driven assessment practice. First, teachers draw from their assessment knowledge and skills to develop and implement assessment strategies to respond to the needs of the students. In turn, teachers' experience in implementing assessment and analysing students' characteristics and responses to the assessment informs their succeeding approach to supporting students, eventually confirming their theoretical understanding of assessment. This foregrounds the interplay between theory and practice. This is evident in Taylor's (2013) recommended assessment literacy model that includes knowledge of theory, technical skills, principles and concepts, pedagogy, sociocultural values, local practices, personal beliefs/attitudes, scores and decision-making. She argues that the balance among these dimensions is dependent on the specific stakeholder groups. These eight dimensions can be differentiated based on stakeholders' needs, which has a profound implication for professional design and approach.

Teacher Assessment Literacy Adaptation

Another important consideration is the specificity of some teacher assessment knowledge and skills to a key learning area. The nature of the subject affects the nature of assessment. For example, in language subjects, teachers'

Adapting Assessment to Support Learning **95**

language awareness and language background influence their assessment and decision-making practices (Stanyer, 2023). In Maths, quantitative assessments and summative assessments are favoured due to the right or wrong nature of most assessment items. Burkhardt and Schoenfeld (2019) make an explicit comparison about adopting FA in maths and other subjects:

> In literature classes, sharing drafts with peers as well as the teacher is a common and natural practice; multiple revision cycles are understood to be necessary to make a complex argument. Thus, well-established conditions for looking at work in progress, along with well-established heuristics for supporting writing, provide a rich context within which formative assessment can more easily flourish. In mathematics, however, teachers need to overcome an answer-oriented tradition, show-and-practice pedagogies, and the need for a wide range of pedagogical content knowledge (different at each grade level) to be able to implement formative assessment with success.
>
> (p. 64)

There is also an issue in terms of the influence of year of schooling on the nature of teachers' assessment practices. For primary school teachers, they may enjoy a more integrated approach in assessment due to the nature of curriculum where most key learning areas are integrated, and teachers are expected to have a solid pedagogical content knowledge and assessment skills across various disciplines. In contrast, secondary school teachers are more varied in their assessment approach due to specificity of key learning areas (Rodriguez, 2019).

Conclusion

Going back to the title of this chapter, 'Beyond One Size Fits All?', it is evident that assessment is a context-dependent construct, and its effectiveness in raising student outcomes is influenced by many factors. The context should underpin the articulation and implementation of assessment policy. At the classroom level, assessment's dynamic and emerging nature requires constant exploration and reconfiguration of approaches and practices. This is compounded by many factors that significantly influence the effectiveness of assessment. Thus, there is no universal approach to assessing student learning that can be effective. Due to the context-driven nature of assessment, a need for ongoing experimentation and adaption in approach and practice should be at the forefront of teacher practices.

References

Ahmadi, R. (2022). Students' perceptions of student voice in assessment within the context of Iran: The dynamics of culture, power relations, and student knowledge.

Higher Education Research & Development, *41*(2), 211–225. https://doi.org/10. 1080/07294360.2021.1882401

Alonzo, D. (2016). *Development and application of a teacher assessment for learning (AfL) literacy tool*. University of New South Wales. http://unsworks.unsw.edu.au/fapi/datastream/unsworks:38345/SOURCE02?view=true

Alonzo, D., & Loughland, T. (2022). Variability of students' responses to assessment activities: The influence of achievement levels. *International Journal of Instruction*, *15*(4), 1071–1090. https://doi.org/10.29333/iji.2022.15457a

ARG. (2002). *Assessment for learning: 10 principles*. https://www.storre.stir.ac.uk/bitstream/1893/32458/1/Assessment%20for%20learning%2010%20principles%20 2002.pdf.

Barkaoui, K. (2011). Effects of marking method and rater experience on ESL essay scores and rater performance. *Assessment in Education: Principles, Policy & Practice*, *18*(3), 279–293. https://doi.org/10.1080/0969594X.2010.526585

Bernstein, B. (1990). *Class, codes and control volume IV: The structuring of pedagogic discourse*. Routledge. https://doi.org/10.4324/9780203011263

Black, P., & Wiliam, D. (2018). Classroom assessment and pedagogy. *Assessment in Education: Principles, Policy & Practice*, *25*(6), 551–575. https://doi.org/10.1080/ 0969594X.2018.1441807

Burkhardt, H., & Schoenfeld, A. (2019). Formative assessment in mathematics. In H. L. Andrade, R. E. Bennett, & G. J. Cizek (Eds.), *Handbook of formative assessment in the disciplines*. Routledge. https://doi.org/10.4324/9781315166933

Davison, C. (2013). Innovation in assessment: Common misconceptions and problems. In K. Hyland & L. Wong (Eds.), *Innovation and change in English language education* (pp. 263–275). Routledge.

Flórez Petour, M. T. (2015). Systems, ideologies and history: A three-dimensional absence in the study of assessment reform processes. *Assessment in Education: Principles, Policy & Practice*, *22*(1), 3–26. https://doi.org/10.1080/0969594X. 2014.943153

Loughland, T., & Alonzo, D. (2019). Teacher adaptive practices: A key factor in teachers' implementation of assessment for learning. *Australian Journal of Teacher Education*, *44*(7). https://doi.org/10.14221/ajte.2019v44n7.2

McMorran, C., Ragupathi, K., & Luo, S. (2017). Assessment and learning without grades? Motivations and concerns with implementing gradeless learning in higher education. *Assessment & Evaluation in Higher Education*, *42*(3), 361–377. https:// doi.org/10.1080/02602938.2015.1114584

Nortvedt, G. A., Santos, L., & Pinto, J. (2016). Assessment for learning in Norway and Portugal: The case of primary school mathematics teaching. *Assessment in Education: Principles, Policy & Practice*, *23*(3), 377–395. https://doi.org/10.1080/09 69594X.2015.1108900

Oo, C. Z., Alonzo, D., & Davison, C. (2021). Pre-service teachers' decision-making and classroom assessment practices. *Frontiers in Education*, *6*(102). https://doi.org/ 10.3389/feduc.2021.628100

Rodriguez, J. (2019). *Teacher perceptions of the impact of a school-developed professional development program*. University of New South Wales.

Stanyer, S. (2023). *Teacher assessment literacy: The relationship between language awareness and writing assessment behaviour*. University of New South Wales.

Taylor, L. (2013). Communicating the theory, practice and principles of language testing to test stakeholders: Some reflections. *Language Testing, 30*(3), 403–412. https://doi.org/10.1177/0265532213480338

Van Booven, C. D. (2015). Revisiting the authoritative–dialogic tension in inquiry-based elementary Science teacher questioning. *International Journal of Science Education, 37*(8), 1182–1201. https://doi.org/10.1080/09500693.2015.1023868

Watty, K., Jackson, M., & Yu, X. (2010). Students' approaches to assessment in accounting education: The unique student perspective. *Accounting Education, 19*(3), 219–234. https://doi.org/10.1080/09639280902836939

Wiliam, D. (2013). *Assessment: The bridge between teaching and learning. Voices From The Middle: Urbana, 21*(2), 15–20.

Yan, X. (2014). An examination of rater performance on a local oral English proficiency test: A mixed-methods approach. *Language Testing, 31*(4), 501–527. https://doi.org/10.1177/0265532214536171

Chapter 6

When Do We Engage Students in Assessment?

Introduction

One of the characteristics of effective teachers is their ability to identify, develop and implement assessment strategies to collect data and analyse it to make highly contextualised and trustworthy decisions to effectively support student learning (Alonzo, 2020; Kahl et al., 2013). This ability of teachers is referred to as assessment literacy. This construct is strongly emphasised in the literature (Davison & Michell, 2014; Klenowski, 2011; Popham, 2011) due to a wide range of evidence that highlights its central role in ensuring effective learning and teaching (Black & Wiliam, 1999; Hattie, 2008). One of its dimensions is teachers as student partners (Alonzo, 2016), which requires teachers to actively engage students in all assessment activities to make them owners of their learning (Wiliam & Thompson, 2007). Actively engaging students in assessment is underpinned by the principles of effective assessment practices. The Assessment Reform Group (ARG, 2002) states that assessment should "promote [students'] commitment to learning goals and a shared understanding of the criteria by which they are assessed, helps [them] know how to improve, and develops [their] capacity for self-assessment" (p. 2). Enactment of these principles is warranted if students have a clear understanding of the purpose, principles and practices of assessment.

Although students' engagement in assessment is theoretically and empirically supported to increase learning outcomes (Hannigan et al., 2022; Nicol, 2009; Stiggins et al., 2007), the question of what assessment knowledge and skills students need to have to engage in assessment actively has been poorly understood (Smith et al., 2013). This construct of student assessment literacy is critical for enhancing students' engagement and motivation (Clark, 2011), consequently improving their overall performance (Smith et al., 2013). This concept is somewhat similar to teacher assessment literacy but there are particular assessment knowledge and skills for students that distinguish the two (Price et al., 2012). A more explicit definition of student assessment literacy benefits teachers and school leaders in supporting students in developing and acquiring such skills to engage in assessment actively.

DOI: 10.4324/9781003396277-6

Engaging Students in Assessment

With the limited understanding of student assessment literacy, it is not surprising that little literature also investigates how teachers support students and the best strategies to develop their assessment literacy. The role of teachers in developing and implementing assessment literacy programs for students is highly recommended due to its pivotal role in increasing student engagement and outcomes (Popham, 2011; Sadler, 2010). Most of the research conducted in this area (Nicol, 2009; Rust et al., 2003; Smith et al., 2013) is done in the context of higher education and is focused on a specific assessment skill development rather than on supporting students to develop a holistic assessment literacy. Just like teachers, students need to develop a holistic view of the interrelationships of the various assessment knowledge and skills to improve their learning significantly. However, this can only be achieved if teachers deliberately provide opportunities for students to develop their assessment literacy (Smith et al., 2013) because students are not born with assessment proficiencies (Baird et al., 2017).

To address the limited understanding of student assessment literacy and investigate how teachers develop students' assessment literacy, this chapter reports how student assessment literacy is explored in the literature and how this construct influences student engagement in assessment and learning.

The Concept of Student Assessment Literacy

The term student assessment literacy is sparsely used in the literature. There are only three journal articles that use this term explicitly. Smith et al. (2013) were the first to theorise this construct, and they outline its components, namely: "(1) students' understanding the purpose of assessment and how it connects to learning; (2) students being aware of the processes of assessment and how that affects submission, and (3) opportunities students have to practice judging their own work to identify strengths and areas for improvement" (pp. 45–46). Although this definition offers insight into student assessment literacy as a multi-dimensional construct, there is no clarity on what specific knowledge and skills comprise each component. For example, it is unclear what discrete knowledge and skills are required for students to engage in and understand the processes involved in assessment, what ways students can practise assessing their work, and how to identify strengths and weaknesses concerning their work.

Chan and Luo (2020) proposed another definition of student assessment literacy as follows:

> students' knowledge of the rules surrounding assessment in holistic competency development, their attitude to appreciate and engage in holistic competency development and assessment, their action towards assessment tasks and feedback to monitor or further their development, and their ability to critique the assessment and feedback provided to enhance holistic competencies.
>
> (p. 13)

100   Engaging Students in Assessment

This definition highlights students' disposition, knowledge and skills about assessment. While valuable to the emerging understanding of student assessment literacy, greater clarity is needed around the indicators within each of its four dimensions so that teachers can support students in building their assessment literacy. While the previous definitions offer insights into defining the construct and identifying processes within assessment, some areas need to be clearly articulated. For broader understanding and usability of the construct, various aspects of each definition can be improved, such as greater lucidity around what the specific knowledge and skills of assessment are, the various strategies needed to improve, understand and engage in assessment, ways to engage in assessment, ways that learning can be monitored and reported on by students, and the role of reflective practice in assessment and affective skills.

Building on the weaknesses of these definitions, Hannigan et al. (2022) scoped the literature and offered a more explicit definition of the construct. As such:

> Student assessment literacy refers to students' perception, attitude and contextualised knowledge and skills in developing strategies to actively engage in assessment, monitor their learning, engage in reflective practice, and develop affective skills, to improve their learning and performance outcomes.... Part of students' responsibility is to work closely with their classmates and as teacher partners to achieve learning outcomes.
>
> (pp. 12–13)

This definition suggests that assessment literate students demonstrate positive dispositions about assessment, the ability to understand the assessment tasks and engage in assessment strategies that position them as teacher partners, self and peer assessors, and life-long learners capable of meeting expectations by using their assessment knowledge and skills. This is demonstrated through possessing and developing knowledge about the practice, principles and processes of assessment, feedback and evaluation, and decision-making skills and strategies that can be implemented when engaging in assessment.

This definition highlights critical aspects of student responsibilities in assessment. For example, students participate in and co-construct formative and summative tasks and learning goals (Smith et al., 2013; Sridharan et al., 2019), demonstrating their ability to generate and use criteria to make judgements about their learning and the learning of their peers (Bourke & MacDonald, 2016; Deeley & Bovill, 2017; Doyle et al., 2019). Also, it positions students as agents of their learning by monitoring their achievement of the learning outcomes and modifying future learning (Deeley & Bovill, 2017; Fastré et al., 2010; Harrison et al., 2015), reflecting (Smith et al., 2013), self-regulating (Kalata & Abate, 2013; Lorber et al., 2019), and evaluating areas of strength and improvement (Fitzgerald et al., 2003; Harrison et al., 2015; Hill & West, 2020; Lew et al., 2010).

More importantly, this definition expanded the previous conceptualisations to include the development of affective skills such as emotional resilience, agency and proactivity, which enable students to build their capacity for self-efficacy and equip them with the skills and knowledge to be life-long learners. In addition, this definition makes a significant contribution to research on student assessment literacy by addressing the missing piece within Alonzo's (2016) assessment literacy framework, *Students as Partners*, in that students are assessors, partners and autonomous learners.

The Problem

This chapter highlights the critical role of student engagement in assessment and outlines students' specific knowledge, skills and dispositions that comprise their assessment literacy. The key argument is that students are not born with assessment proficiencies. Just like teachers, they need to have a certain level of assessment knowledge, skills and positive dispositions to effectively engage in any assessment activities. Specific areas include their general understanding of assessment, developing strategies to engage in assessment activities, monitoring learning progress and engaging in reflective practice. The three case studies will highlight the need for teachers to ensure students' readiness before engaging them in assessment. One critical component of teacher assessment literacy is the teachers' ability to establish a strong partnership with students (Alonzo, 2016) and develop their assessment literacy. Many studies highlight the significant impact of building student assessment literacy on learning and teaching (Alonzo & Loughland, 2022; Hovardas et al., 2014; Sardareh et al., 2014).

Case Studies

Three case studies are presented below to demonstrate the need to ensure students have the necessary assessment knowledge, skills and dispositions to effectively engage in the assessment process. The first case study (Hovardas et al., 2014) shows that peer assessment is only effective if students can provide quality feedback to their peers, particularly on areas needing improvement. The second case study (Van Booven, 2015) highlights the need to create a space for and build students' agency to engage in assessment. The third case study (Sardareh et al., 2014) illustrates the interplay between teacher assessment literacy and student assessment literacy.

Case 1: The low validity and reliability of peer assessment

Description of the Study

This case study demonstrates one of the issues of engaging students in assessment in terms of the consistency and accuracy of the results. Hovardas

102 Engaging Students in Assessment

et al. (2014) investigated peer assessment at the secondary school in Cyprus, focusing on the quality of the feedback produced by students and subsequent potential usefulness to quality learning and teaching within the specific context of reciprocal online peer assessment of web portfolios developed in a science course. Twenty-eight Year 7 (14-year-old) students participated in this study. Quantitative (grades) and qualitative (written comment) data on the web portfolios were analysed to assess the quality of peer feedback. Prespecified assessment criteria were used by expert and student reviewers to rate the web portfolios, and participants were asked for written comments to justify the ratings and suggestions for possible revisions. Additional investigation was conducted as to whether peer or expert feedback led the peer assessors to revise their work in any way.

Problem Being Addressed

This study highlights the low validity and reliability of peer assessment compared to experts' assessment. The marks awarded by students are inconsistent with the experts' marks, which indicates that students could not effectively assess and award marks that reflect the actual performance of their peers. The variability in marks awarded by students also shows the inconsistencies in interpreting the assessment criteria and using it to judge their peers' works. In addition, peer feedback lacks the critical analysis of peer assessees' skills with fewer suggestions for improvement. They give more positive feedback, but their critical judgement for areas needing improvement, although accurate, lacks evidence to support their negative feedback.

These findings highlight the issue relative to the need for students to have a certain level of assessment literacy, in this context, their knowledge and skills in peer assessment. The authors argued that "mere explanation of the assessment criteria or prior experience with peer assessment procedures is not enough; teachers, researchers and policy makers should focus on the type of training and scaffolding that peer assessors need in order to produce high quality feedback" (p. 133).

Factors Influencing the Problem

Some of the factors that influence the low reliability and validity of peer assessment results involving students' knowledge of feedback and content being assessed include the following:

1 *Students' understanding of assessment criteria.*
   Students' low understanding of assessment criteria and their decision-making in terms of awarding marks. As argued by the authors,

students should have adequate training to develop their peer assessment skills, particularly in interpreting and applying the criteria, giving feedback that is aligned to the criteria and providing evidence to support negative feedback.

2 *Low understanding of the content being assessed.*

This has contributed to the inconsistent application of the assessment criteria due to the lack of a common understanding of the content being assessed.

3 *Inadequate training for students or lack thereof.*

In this study, the students have prior knowledge and experience in using criteria in assessing their works, and they received explicit training on using assessment criteria. However, the authors argue that these are not sufficient to build their capacity to apply the assessment criteria consistently and provide feedback to their peers that can be used to further improve their work.

4 *Guidance and scaffolding from teachers.*

Teachers' assessment literacy is critical for supporting students in understanding and applying the assessment criteria and the content being assessed. This process is particularly important with new criteria, content and expectations, as students may not have prior knowledge of such.

5 *Understanding of quality feedback.*

Students need to focus on the content of their feedback on the skills assessed. They have to include in their feedback the criteria that their peers have failed to achieve and offer suggestions to improve. Their negative feedback must be substantiated by evidence, drawn from their peers' works.

6 *The assessee's agency to act on feedback.*

As peer assessment is a two-way process, the assessee can benefit from this activity not only from the feedback they have received, but also from the feedback they have given. They need to be supported to use the feedback they have received and the feedback they have given. Their criticality in terms of establishing the link between what they have received and what they have given will motivate them to implement what they think is important.

7 *Engagement in peer assessment.*

Peer assessment is cognitively demanding as students are exposed to new knowledge with the potential to reinforce and deepen the understanding of both students and teachers involved in the peer assessment process. At the same time, peer assessment encourages students to be critical, independent learners as they become more familiar with the application of assessment criteria and the concepts underpinning the material being reviewed.

Implications of the Problem

The low reliability and validity of peer feedback, particularly the low quality of qualitative feedback, compromise the effectiveness of peer assessment to support students in their learning. As shown, if the peer assessor does not provide evidence for their negative feedback, the assessee ignores the suggestion on how to further improve their work. The feedback might be extremely helpful if acted on, but because there is a lack of evidence (i.e., linking to the criteria, highlighting specific section of assessee's work and offering suggestions on how to address the weakness identified), the feedback becomes useless.

Also, the inaccuracies in using assessment criteria contribute to the lack of comprehensive assessment of all areas needing further improvement. Students' understanding of the assessment criteria must be ascertained before engaging them in peer assessment. The variability of understanding these criteria poses the risk of inaccurate assessment and inappropriate feedback. Thus, before engaging students in peer assessment, teachers should ensure a common understanding of the assessment criteria. This will not only improve the peer assessment skills of the students but they can use this understanding to engage in self-assessment, identifying areas needing improvement in their work.

Moreover, the low agency of peer assessee to act on feedback misses the opportunity to use feedback effectively. As shown in the study, changes students made to their web portfolios were significantly less in number compared to the total number of changes proposed by expert and peer assessors. The low agency of the students to act on feedback might be attributed to their lack of understanding of the feedback given, the inappropriateness of language used in feedback or their inability to develop strategies to act on feedback.

To address the issues above, teachers need to create conditions that enable students to learn through action in the role of peer assessor and the enactment of the role of peer assessee. Drawing on the work of Sluijsms (2002), the authors suggested the following to improve students' peer assessment skills. "Students should be made aware of what is necessary for enacting the peer assessor role (e.g., understanding of the assessment criteria, what is the process to be followed), what skills are necessary to carry out the role of the peer assessor (e.g., making judgements about ones work), and the reasoning behind the implementation of peer assessment (e.g., learning through the process, supporting peers)" (p. 148). All these skills relate to student assessment literacy.

The researchers conclude that explicit training of students must be guided by a certain framework that depicts how peer assessor training or scaffolding should look. In addition, a well-established process for peer assessment must be established and adhered to. A critical component of this process is the dialogue between the assessor and the assessee to discuss the feedback. This process allows for better communication of the feedback and gives opportunities for the assessee to clarify the feedback given.

Case 2: Creating a space for student engagement in assessment

Description of the Study

This case study shows the relationship between teachers' assessment literacy and students' engagement in assessment. The study by Van Booven (2015) investigated the impact of teacher questioning on the quality and complexity of student responses and is used as an illustrative case. This study was conducted in one southeastern state of the USA where a three-year intervention – Curriculum and Teacher PD – for fifth-grade inquiry-based Science and language development was implemented. Three states participated in the program, but to manage the data, the analysis was limited to one state. Forty-four classroom observations were conducted during the first academic year of the project. Again, to manage the amount of data for analysis, 10 transcripts (five control and five treatment) of student-teacher dialogue were randomly selected. The total number of observation hours analysed represented 23% of the total number of observations for the county. The data were analysed using Chin's (2006) questioning-based discourse analytical framework, focusing on "(a) the different functions of teacher questions and feedback and (b) the varying cognitive and structural characteristics of student responses" (p. 1187). Results show that teachers' questioning skills impact students learning. Students respond more positively to dialogically oriented questions, demonstrating "a greater breadth and depth of both canonical and self-generated knowledge" (p. 1182). In contrast, students' responses to authoritatively oriented questions are limited, restricting their ability to demonstrate their learning.

Problem Being Addressed

Teachers' approaches to implementing assessment can limit students' ability to demonstrate their learning through assessment activities.

106 Engaging Students in Assessment

Students do not only need assessment knowledge and skills but the space to actively engage and demonstrate their learning. The approach teachers use in the assessment will either provide or limit the space for teacher-student interactions. In this case, the authoritative-orientated questioning limits students' opportunities to demonstrate their higher understanding and knowledge. In contrast, "the use of dialogic orientated questioning provides a discursive space for students to demonstrate a greater breadth and depth of both canonical and self-generated knowledge" (p. 1182).

Thus, teachers' questioning technique design and implementation should not only focus on the rigour of the questions to elicit responses from students but also to ensure that students are provided with the opportunity to expand their understanding. Teachers can leverage students' initial responses by supporting them to discuss further.

There exists a tension between learning science through student-led inquiry and critical reflection to meet process-product-oriented objectives, as well as summative, large-scale exams or testing. Examining the extent to which questioning – authoritative (AO) or dialogic (DO) orientation – used by fifth-grade science teachers restrict or expand the quality and complexity of student responses could potentially provide questioning strategies designed to address different educational purposes.

Factors Influencing the Problem

Some factors that influence the creation of student engagement in assessment include the following:

1 *Teacher assessment literacy.*
   This concept outlines teachers' dispositions, beliefs, knowledge and practices in using assessment to engage students in assessment effectively and the learning process. The approach used by teachers determines the extent to which students can demonstrate their learning. Students' gain from assessment depends on how well teachers implement assessment as a learning strategy.
2 *Student assessment literacy.*
   Students play a critical role in the assessment. When they are provided with opportunities for dialogic space, they demonstrate "a range of cognitive processes, syntacto-semantic complexity, and knowledge type" (p. 1196).
3 *Student agency in assessment.*
   It was also demonstrated that when students are allowed to express their views, they take an active role in the assessment process.

4 *Time required.*

Addressing the demands of managing the learning environment creates increased demand for teacher time. Embedding opportunities in learning and teaching activities for engagement in assessment requires time and careful planning. A highly structured, time-bound lesson plan limits these opportunities. Some flexibilities are ideal for teachers to engage students in assessment.

Implications of the Problem

Student engagement in assessment largely depends on teacher assessment practices. If teachers do not provide an opportunity for students to engage in assessment effectively, the impact of assessment on student learning remains limited. It was demonstrated in this study that the fixed nature of authoritatively asked questions impacts student responses and restricts student understanding and deeper learning.

Teachers' deeper knowledge on how to effectively use assessment to provide opportunities for greater student engagement allows for the development of an adaptive approach to assessment that is fit for purpose, for example, to meet curriculum outcomes, encourage diverse student knowledge and recall facts for testing. Acknowledgement that there are a variety of purposes or functions for implementing assessment provides opportunities for teachers to reconcile to a more straightforward, possibly more effective teaching practice. Thus, teachers must enhance their assessment literacy to ensure students are appropriately supported. One recommendation is the observation of own's work and peers' work. They can develop reflective practice and discussion guides and strategies to craft a learning environment that meets curriculum and accountability requirements and engages students to actively think, speak and employ higher order cognitive processes.

Case 3: The influence of teacher assessment literacy on student assessment literacy

Description of the Study

This case study shows the influence of teachers' assessment literacy on students' assessment literacy. The work of Sardarch et al. (2014) in examining the use of questioning in the context of Assessment for

Learning (AfL) in a national school system highlights this case. The study was conducted in a purposely selected primary school near a large urban centre in Malaysia. Data were collected by interviewing three English as a Second Language teachers and observing over 20 periods in each teacher's classroom environment. Interviews and observations were tape-recorded and transcribed verbatim for further analysis. Findings provide evidence for the challenges to AfL practice and areas of focus for future action and decision-making.

Based on the findings of this study, it was highlighted that student engagement in assessment depends mainly on teacher assessment literacy. Hence, it is critical to explore how teachers' assessment literacy is translated into student assessment literacy. Student understanding of assessment and how it impacts their engagement in activities related to assessment and learning is critical for optimising the effect of assessment. Teachers have a crucial role in framing and demonstrating a case for the importance of assessment literacy for themselves and learners. Teachers can increase student engagement in assessment through their competence and confidence in AfL strategies. Empirical findings indicate that greater levels of assessment literacy among teachers are associated with greater academic achievement by learners.

Problem Being Addressed

Teacher assessment knowledge and skills, known as assessment literacy, are critical for the effective implementation of assessment to support learning and teaching. One particular important skill is effective questioning, by both learners and teachers. Previous research has raised significant concerns about teachers' efficacy and use of questioning strategies in Malaysian primary schools after government policy introduced AfL into the school system. Accurately examining and reflecting on the existing situation at system, school and classroom environment levels provide evidence for developing a quality strategy to support learning and teaching and address system-wide implications for school improvement through AfL.

Factors Influencing the Problem

Student engagement in assessment largely depends on their assessment literacy (Hannigan et al., 2022), which is also dependent on teacher assessment literacy. The explicit teaching of assessment principles, processes and practices to students is needed to understand why they need to engage effectively in assessment and how it influences their learning.

Based on this study, some of the factors that influence student engagement in the assessment include the following:

1 *Teacher philosophical orientation.*
  Teachers' philosophy remains informed by teacher-centred assessment and pedagogical practice. Teachers must reorient their philosophy to student-centred assessment and pedagogical practices to create an environment where students actively engage in assessment. Unless teachers provide the necessary support, space and expertise, the impact of assessment on student learning remains limited.
2 *Teachers' lack of response to change.*
  The alignment between the principles of AfL, learning and teaching, teaching philosophy and pedagogical practice is critical for ensuring quality teaching, student engagement in assessment and optimisation of assessment outcomes. With the introduction of a new assessment reform, it is imperative that teachers need to reorient their disposition, knowledge and practical skills to the philosophy of the reform. Although this reorientation largely depends on teacher agency, other factors may influence it, including the strategic implementation of the reform and support from the higher authorities, school leaders and other colleagues.
3 *Undeveloped assessment literacy.*
  Teachers use traditional frameworks for questioning that require low cognitive input from students. Questions asked require recall and memory approaches to answer them. In this case, traditional structuring and patterning of questioning impacted the co-construction of learning and self-monitoring of students. A questioning strategy is needed to build harmonious relationships between students and teacher, increasing classroom interaction and boosting students' independence and their social capacity (Sun, 2012).
4 *Low student assessment literacy.*
  Low assessment literacy equates to low student engagement in assessment. Students' understanding of the purpose, principles and practices of effective assessment will increase their confidence, agency and understanding of how to engage effectively. They will understand the benefits it has for increasing their outcomes, and they will have the skills to navigate any assessment activity.

Implications of the Problem

The dependency of student assessment literacy on teacher assessment literacy poses critical implications for ensuring student engagement and increasing student outcomes. It was demonstrated in this study that as a result of teachers' ineffective use of questioning, students are not encouraged to respond or ask questions or engage in self-reflection. A key outcome of AfL is enhanced autonomous learning. This study provided evidence that teachers maintaining a traditional approach to questioning, a factor that contributes to learner autonomy, is actively stifling for them and students. In addition, teacher use of inappropriately low levels of cognitive load in the context of questioning impedes the development of independent learning and thinking.

The inappropriate implementation of assessment strategies without regard if students has a certain level of agency, readiness and assessment knowledge and skills limits the power of assessment to elicit student responses. In an authentic AfL questioning session, it should be anticipated that a range of possible responses will be evident if assessment, questions and prompts are planned and designed to clarify various possible levels of conceptual understanding within any group. The resultant range of student responses provides evidence for the different levels of conceptual understanding across learners and the learning environment. This, in turn, allows students to self-reflect on achieving learning objectives. Observation of this constitutes evidence on which teachers can reflect and evaluate.

In most assessment practices, the responsibility is heavily laden to teachers, where planning and automaticity is required to monitor and interpret student responses 'in-the-moment prompts' and to reflect and act on the circumstances of the range of student responses (Westbroek et al., 2020). Thus, students should take full responsibility for their learning. They must monitor their learning and act on every opportunity to achieve the learning outcomes.

To ensure the effective engagement of students in assessment, they need to develop their assessment literacy. This study recommends that teachers and schools should create opportunities to make assessment literacy explicit for students to embed assessment literacy in learning and teaching activities. Also teachers should model assessment knowledge and skills, subsequently enhancing their own assessment practices in the process. In the context of this study, the development and use of a 'question' analysis framework based on the experiences of a range of teachers provide a launch point for the development of generic rich questioning, as well as template questions for more specific discussion starters for a unit of work.

Proposed Solutions

The three case studies demonstrate the vital need to develop students' assessment literacy. This will build students' confidence and increase their motivation and engagement in assessment, consequently optimising learning outcomes. Students are considered the most important players in their learning. Thus, teachers must actively involve each student in assessment, learning and teaching (ARG, 2002). It has been argued that to fully realise students' potential, teachers must shift from merely facilitating to activating learning (Hattie, 2008) and treating students as owners of their learning (Wiliam & Thomson, 2008). These practices can be developed by working closely with students and providing them opportunities to understand and assume some ownership of their learning outcomes (Black & Wiliam, 1998; Gray & Tall, 1994; Hounsell et al., 2008; Sadler, 1989) and success criteria (Fredericksen & Collins, 1989; Gray & Tall, 1994; Nicol & Macfarlane-Dick, 2006; O'Donovan et al., 2008), engaging them in self and peer assessment (Kaufmann & Schunn, 2011; Klenowski, 1995; Lew et al., 2010; McMahon, 2010), and providing them with timely and effective feedback related to their strengths and suggestions on how to further improve their learning (Bird & Yucel, 2015; Carless et al., 2011; Walker, 2015).

As argued in the introduction of this chapter, students are not born with assessment proficiencies. Thus, like teachers, they need explicit training to acquire assessment knowledge and skills and develop positive dispositions towards assessment. It is part of the teacher's responsibility to ensure that students have the necessary assessment literacy before engaging in assessment (Alonzo, 2016; Sardareh et al., 2014).

The framework developed by Hannigan et al. (2022) outlines 45 indicators clustered in six domains of student assessment literacy (see Figure 6.1). This framework can guide teachers in what specific assessment knowledge, skills and dispositions they need to develop for their students. They can use the indicators to assess students' readiness to engage in assessment. Also, students can use the indicators to reflect on their assessment literacy needs. The framework can be part of an ongoing process in schools designed to help students develop their understanding, application and use of assessment knowledge and skills to increase learning outcomes.

The six dimensions that describe student assessment literacy are detailed below.

Domain 1: General knowledge of assessment. This domain refers to students' knowledge about the principles, processes and practices of assessment, feedback and evaluation through familiarisation with the tools and language to monitor and report on measurable growth in learning and improve performance outcomes.

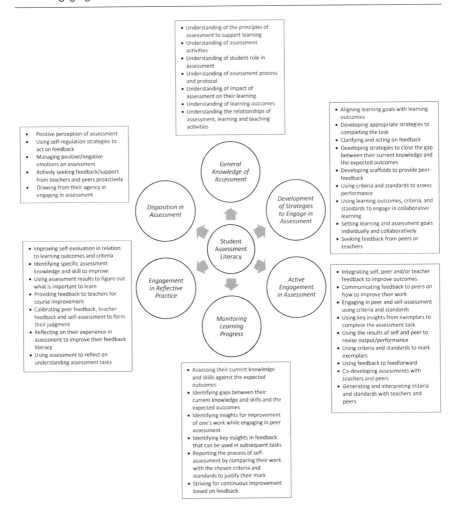

Figure 6.1 Student Assessment Literacy Framework (Hannigan et al., 2022).

Domain 2: Development of strategies to engage in assessment. This domain refers to developing valid and reliable strategies and decision-making skills that can be implemented to complete assessment tasks; engage in peer and self-assessment; generate, clarify and apply criteria and standards; and use the feedback cycle.

Domain 3: Active engagement in assessment. This domain refers to student involvement and participation in formative and summative assessments that provide opportunities to demonstrate their skill and knowledge application, synthesis, analysis and evaluation of peer and self-assessment using criteria and standards, feedback processes and exemplars. Engagement in an assessment provides effective and practical evidence of achievement to enhance outcomes, learning and engagement.

Domain 4: Monitoring learning progress. This refers to the identification, reporting, analysis and interpretation of feedback and assessment results against expected learning outcomes, criteria and goals, with the intention of using this data to measure, regulate and modify future learning, assessment and educational practices.

Domain 5: Engagement in a reflective practice. This domain refers to reflective practices, including engaging in feedback, self-regulation and evaluation to identify gaps in learning, make judgements about areas of improvement, develop increased self-awareness and improve assessment literacy.

Domain 6: Disposition in assessment. This domain refers to affective or non-cognitive skills, including a student's ability to develop and use emotional resilience and empathy, agency, intrinsic and extrinsic motivation, attitude, self-perception, self-regulation and interpersonal skills. Affective skills also refer to students actively seeking support, feedback or guidance from teachers and peers.

Another area teachers could look into when engaging students in assessment is the enactment of teacher intent in using assessment. Most often than not, students' responses in assessments do not reflect teacher intent, and students' responses vary according to their ability level. For example, the use of learning outcomes, success criteria, self and peer assessment, and feedback has been proven to improve student learning (Baird et al., 2017; Hattie, 2008; To & Liu, 2018), but when the impacts of these assessment strategies are investigated at the individual student level, some students accrued more benefits than the others. This implies that effective teacher assessment practices would benefit from recognising the concept of stimulus-response compatibility (Alonzo & Loughland, 2022). An adaptive teacher disposition is critical in the provision of appropriate stimuli as well as a constructive response to students to ensure their ongoing learning engagement. Teachers need to monitor students' responses to their initial assessment activity and then use these responses to develop differentiated assessment activities and the needed assessment knowledge and skills. This changes the focus of teacher assessment practices to monitor student responses to enhance their learning. In so doing, they will acknowledge that their students' responses are not always aligned with their intentions when employing assessment activities (Loughland & Alonzo, 2019).

Conclusion

The answer to the title of this chapter, 'When Do We Engage Students in Assessment?', is apparent. We need to engage them in assessment when they

114 Engaging Students in Assessment

have acquired a certain level of assessment knowledge and developed practical skills and positive dispositions. The three case studies provide evidence that student engagement in assessment largely depends on their understanding of assessment principles, processes and practices. However, students are not born with assessment proficiencies, so they need to be supported to develop their assessment literacy. The schools' and teachers' roles in this area are critically important. Also, teachers' implementation of assessment activities should be carefully planned to provide space for students to actively engage in assessment to enhance their learning. Teachers should be mindful of the limiting impact of their approaches on student engagement.

References

Alonzo, D. (2016). *Development and application of a teacher assessment for learning (AfL) literacy tool.* University of New South Wales. http://unsworks.unsw.edu.au/fapi/datastream/unsworks:38345/SOURCE02?view=true

Alonzo, D. (2020). Teacher education and professional development in industry 4.0: The case for building a strong assessment literacy. In J. P. Ashadi, A. T. Basikin, & N. H. P. S. Putro (Eds.), *Teacher education and professional development in industry 4.0.* Taylor & Francis Group.

Alonzo, D., & Loughland, T. (2022). Variability of students' responses to assessment activities: The influence of achievement levels. *International Journal of Instruction, 15*(4), 1071–1090. https://doi.org/10.29333/iji.2022.15457a

ARG. (2002). *Assessment for learning: 10 principles.* https://www.storre.stir.ac.uk/bitstream/1893/32458/1/Assessment%20for%20learning%2010%20principles%202002.pdf

Baird, J.-A., Andrich, D., Hopfenbeck, T. N., & Stobart, G. (2017). Assessment and learning: Fields apart? *Assessment in Education: Principles, Policy & Practice, 24*(3), 317–350. https://doi.org/10.1080/0969594X.2017.1319337

Bird, F. L., & Yucel, R. (2015). Feedback codes and action plans: Building the capacity of first-year students to apply feedback to a scientific report. *Assessment & Evaluation in Higher Education, 40*(4), 508–527. https://doi.org/10.1080/02602938.2014.924476

Black, P., & Wiliam, D. (1998). Assessment and classroom learning. *Assessment in Education: Principles, Policies and Practice, 5*(1), 7–74.

Black, P., & Wiliam, D. (1999). *Assessment for learning: Beyond the black box.* A. R. Group.

Bourke, R., & MacDonald, J. (2016). Creating a space for student voice in an educational evaluation. *International Journal of Research & Method in Education, 41*(2), 156–168. https://doi.org/10.1080/1743727X.2016.1256983

Carless, D., Salter, D., Yang, M., & Lam, J. (2011). Develping sustainable feedback practices. *Studies in Higher Education, 36*(4), 395–407. https://doi.org/a0.1080/03075071003642449

Chan, C. K. Y., & Luo, J. (2021). A four-dimensional conceptual framework for student assessment literacy in holistic competency development. *Assessment & Evaluation in Higher Education, 46*(3), 451–466. https://doi.org/10.1080/02602938.2020.1777388

Chin, C. (2006). Classroom interaction in science: Teacher questioning and feedback to students' responses. *International Journal of Science Education, 28*(11), 1315–1346. https://doi.org/10.1080/09500690600621100

Clark, I. (2011). Formative assessment and motivation: Theories and themes. *Prime Research on Education, 1*(2), 26–36.

Davison, C., & Michell, M. (2014). EAL assessment: What do Australian teachers want? *TESOL in Context, 24*(2), 51–72.

Deeley, S. J., & Bovill, C. (2017). Staff student partnership in assessment: Enhancing assessment literacy through democratic practices. *Assessment & Evaluation in Higher Education, 42*(3), 463–477. https://doi.org/10.1080/02602938.2015.1126551

Doyle, E., Buckley, P., & Whelan, J. (2019). Assessment co-creation: An exploratory analysis of opportunities and challenges based on student and instructor perspectives. *Teaching in Higher Education, 24*(6), 739–754. https://doi.org/10.1080/13562517.2018.1498077

Fastré, G. M. J., van der Klink, M. R., Sluijsmans, D., & van Merriënboer, J. J. G. (2012). Drawing students' attention to relevant assessment criteria: Effects on self-assessment skills and performance. *Journal of Vocational Education & Training, 64*(2), 185–198. https://doi.org/10.1080/13636820.2011.630537

Fitzgerald, J. T., White, C. B., & Gruppen, L. D. (2003). A longitudinal study of self-assessment accuracy. *Medical Education, 37*(7), 645–649. https://doi.org/10.1046/J.1365-2923.2003.01567.X

Fredericksen, J., & Collins, A. (1989). A systems approach to educational testing. *Educational Researcher, 18*(9), 27–32.

Gray, E., & Tall, D. (1994). Duality, ambiguity and flexibility: A proceptual view of simple arithmetic. *Journal for Research in Mathematics Education, 26*(2), 115–141.

Hannigan, C., Alonzo, D., & Oo, C. Z. (2022). Student assessment literacy: Indicators and domains from the literature. *Assessment in Education: Principles, Policy & Practice, 29*(4), 482–504. https://doi.org/10.1080/0969594X.2022.2121911

Harrison, K., O'hara, J., & McNamara, G. (2015). Re-thinking assessment: Self- and peer-assessment as drivers of self-direction in learning. *Eurasian Journal of Educational Research, 60*, 75–88. https://doi.org/10.14689/EJER.2015.60.5

Hattie, J. (2008). *Visible learning: A synthesis of over 800 meta-analyses relating to achievement.* Routledge.

Hill, J., & West, H. (2020). Improving the student learning experience through dialogic feed-forward assessment. *Assessment & Evaluation in Higher Education, 45*(1), 82–97. https://doi.org/10.1080/02602938.2019.1608908

Hounsell, D., McCune, V., Hounsell, J., & Litjens, J. (2008). The quality of guidance and feedback to students. *Higher Education Research & Development, 27*(1), 55–67.

Hovardas, T., Tsivitanidou, O. E., & Zacharia, Z. C. (2014). Peer versus expert feedback: An investigation of the quality of Peer feedback among secondary school students. *Computers & Education, 71*, 133–152. https://doi.org/10.1016/j.compedu.2013.09.019

Kahl, S. R., Hofman, P., & Bryant, S. (2013). Assessment literacy standards and performance measures for teacher candidates and practicing teachers. *A report prepared ofr the Council for Accreditation of Educator Preparation.* Measured Progress.

116 Engaging Students in Assessment

Kalata, L. R., & Abate, M. A. (2013). A mentor-based portfolio program to evaluate pharmacy students' self-assessment skills. *American Journal of Pharmaceutical Education, 77*(4). https://doi.org/10.5688/AJPE77481

Kaufman, J. H., & Schunn, C. D. (2011). Students' perceptions about peer assessment for writing: their origin and impact on revision work. *Instructional Science, 39*(3), 387–406. https://doi.org/10.1007/s11251-010-9133-6

Klenowski, V. (1995). Student self-evaluation processes in student-centred teaching and learning contexts of Australia and England. *Assessment in Education: Principles, Policy & Practice, 2*(2), 145–163. doi: 10.1080/0969594950020203

Klenowski, V. (2011). Assessment for learning in the accountability era: Queensland, Australia. *Studies in Educational Evaluation, 37*(1), 78–83. https://doi.org/10.1016/j.stueduc.2011.03.003

Lew, M. D. N., Alwis, W. A. M., & Schmidt, H. G. (2010). Accuracy of students' self-assessment and their beliefs about its utility. *Assessment & Evaluation in Higher Education, 35*(2), 135–156. https://doi.org/10.1080/02602930802687737

Lorber, P., Rooney, S., & Van Der Enden, M. (2019). Making assessment accessible: A student–staff partnership perspective. *Higher Education Pedagogies, 4*(1), 488–502. https://doi.org/10.1080/23752696.2019.169552

Loughland, T., & Alonzo, D. (2019). Teacher adaptive practices: A key factor in teachers' implementation of assessment for learning. *Australian Journal of Teacher Education, 44*(7). https://doi.org/10.14221/ajte.2019v44n7.2

Nicol, D. (2009). Assessment for learner self-regulation: Enhancing achievement in the first year using learning technologies. *Assessment & Evaluation in Higher Education, 34*(3), 335–352. https://doi.org/10.1080/02602930802255139

Nicol, D. J., & Macfarlane-Dick, D. (2006). Formative assessment and self-regulated learning: A model and seven principles of good feedback practice. *Studies in Higher Education, 31*(2), 199–218.

McMahon, T. (2010). Peer feedback in an undergraduate programme: using action research to overcome students' reluctance to criticise. *Educational Action Research, 18*(2), 273–287. https://doi.org/10.1080/09650791003741814

O'Donovan, B., Price, M., & Rust, C. (2008). Developing student understanding of assessment standards: A nested hierarchy of approaches. *Teaching in Higher Education, 13*(2), 205–217. https://doi.org/10.1080/13562510801923344

Popham, W. J. (2011). Assessment literacy overlooked: A teacher educator's confession. *The Teacher Educator, 46*(4), 265–273. https://doi.org/10.1080/08878730.2011.605048

Price, M., Rust, C., O'Donovan, B., Handley, K., & Bryant, R. (2012). *Assessment literacy: The foundation of improving student learning.* Oxford Centre for Staff and Learning Development.

Rust, C., Price, M., & O'Donovan, B. (2003). Improving students' learning by developing their understanding of assessment criteria and processes. *Assessment and Evaluation in Higher Education, 28*, 147–164.

Sadler, D. R. (1989). Formative assessment and the design of instructional systems. *Instructional Science, 18*, 119–144.

Sadler, D. (2010). Beyond feedback: Developing student capability in complex appraisal. *Assessment & Evaluation in Higher Education, 35*(5), 535–550. https://doi.org/10.1080/02602930903541015

Sardareh, S. A., Saad, M. R. M., Othman, A. J., & Me, R. C. (2014). ESL teachers' questioning technique in an assessment for learning context: Promising or problematic? *International Education Studies*, *7*(9), 161–174. https://pdfs.semanticscholar.org/93a5/d6eda4a77294bc2b960f657ea68a4d5f64b5.pdf

Sluijsmans, D., Brand-Gruwel, S., Van Merriënboer, J. J. G., & Martens, R. L. (2004). Training teachers in peer-assessment skills: Effects on performance and perceptions. *Innovations in Education and Teaching International*, *41*(1), 59–78. https://doi.org/10.1080/1470329032000172720

Smith, C. D., Worsfold, K., Davies, L., Fisher, R., & McPhail, R. (2013). Assessment literacy and student learning: The case for explicitly developing students 'assessment literacy'. *Assessment & Evaluation in Higher Education*, *38*(1), 44–60. https://doi.org/10.1080/02602938.2011.598636

Stiggins, R. J., Arter, J., Chappuis, J., & Chappuis, S. (2007). *Classroom assessment for student learning: Doing it right-using it well*. Pearson Education, Inc.

Sridharan, B., Tai, J., & Boud, D. (2019). Does the use of summative peer assessment in collaborative group work inhibit good judgement? *Higher Education*, *77*(5), 853–870. https://doi.org/10.1007/S10734-018-0305-7/FIGURES/7

Sun, Z. (2012). An empirical study on new teacher-student relationship and questioning strategies in ESL classroom. *English Language Teaching*, *5*(7), 175–183. http://dx.doi.org/10.5539/elt.v5n7p175

To, J., & Liu, Y. (2018). Using peer and teacher-student exemplar dialogues to unpack assessment standards: Challenges and possibilities. *Assessment & Evaluation in Higher Education*, *43*(3), 449–460. https://doi.org/10.1080/02602938.2017.1356907

Van Booven, C. D. (2015). Revisiting the authoritative–dialogic tension in inquiry-based elementary science teacher questioning. *International Journal of Science Education*, *37*(8), 1182–1201. https://doi.org/10.1080/09500693.2015.1023868

Walker, M. (2015). The quality of written peer feedback on undergraduates' draft answers to an assignment, and the use made of the feedback. *Assessment & Evaluation in Higher Education*, *40*(2), 232–247. https://doi.org/10.1080/02602938.2014.898737

Westbroek, H. B., van Rens, L., van den Berg, E., & Janssen, F. (2020). A practical approach to assessment for learning and differentiated instruction. *International Journal of Science Education*, *42*(6), 955–976. https://doi.org/10.1080/09500693.2020.1744044

Wiliam, D., & Thompson, M. (2007). Integrating assessment with instruction: What will it take to make it work. In C. A. Dwyer (Ed.), *The future of assessment*. Lawrence Erlbaum Associates.

Wiliam, D., & Thompson, M. (2008). Integrating assessment with learning: What will it take to make it work? In C.A. Dwyer (Ed.), *The Future of Assessment: Shaping Teaching and Learning*, (pp. 53–82). New York: Erlbaum.

Chapter 7

Are Teacher Assessment Practices Reliable and Valid?

Introduction

One of the major criticisms of teacher assessment is the argument that they have low reliability and validity, which limits utilisation due to their perceived inconsistencies (Baird et al., 2017). Reliability and validity measures are critically important for ensuring consistency and accuracy of assessment and the inferences drawn to inform decisions about learning and teaching. Reliability measures the assessment tools' internal consistency or ability to produce the same results over time. In contrast, validity measures their accuracy, whether the results represent the outcomes measured or their ability to give valid inferences about student learning (Tabachnick & Fidell, 2007). These properties are critical aspects of assessment because any measurement error would significantly affect results (Field, 2009), and assessment results would not reflect students' actual learning. Any errors in assessment will significantly compromise teachers' decision-making and students' learning. Ideally, all assessments used in schools should have high reliability and validity to give users confidence that assessment results are consistent across time and context. Hence, the inferences drawn are useful to support students in their learning and adjust teacher teaching.

Reliability and validity are often associated with the psychometric principles of assessment and are often tied to summative assessments (SAs), including formal tests and high-stake examinations, which allow for the computation of reliability and validity indices. However, these concepts are inappropriate when applied to teacher assessments. Inside the classroom, teachers generally use assessments, including self-assessment, peer assessment, feedback and questioning, with no statistical metrics to establish their psychometric properties. Van der Vleuten and Schuwirth (2005) argue that the overreliance of assessment on psychometric issues limits the utility of other assessment strategies.

To address the limitations of reliability and validity, Brookhart (2003), Moss (2003) and Smith (2003) developed 'classroometric' principles to account for the accuracy and consistency measures of teacher assessment. According to Brookhart, "the classroom assessment environment, the integration of

DOI: 10.4324/9781003396277-7

Ensuring Trustworthiness of Assessment   119

assessment and instruction, and the pervasive formative purpose of classroom assessment" (p. 8) need to be accounted for when discussing the consistency and accuracy issues of assessment. The focus of classroometric principles is on ensuring high-quality assessments that provide rigorous information about students' learning and immediately become part of the learning environment.

In classroometric principles, reliability is ensured through the sufficiency of information (Smith, 2003). Any decisions made by the teacher must be supported by consistent and integrated assessment information drawn from multiple sources, including anecdotal records, observations, interviews, classroom tests and many other informal assessment activities. In the same way, accuracy measures (validity) in these types of assessment position assessment as an integral part of learning and teaching activities. "The inferences made, and actions taken are internal to the measurement processes" (Brookhart, 2003, p. 9), which takes into account the responsibility of the students to understand the role of assessment in their learning, to partner with teachers to understand how their work compares to ideal work and address the gap to further improve their learning. In addition, the validity of classroometric principles highlights that "the measurement context is construct-relevant" (p. 9). The interpretation of assessment information largely depends on several factors, including content knowledge, teacher beliefs, views and practices. The goal of accuracy in classroometric principles is to understand how students' work compares to ideal work.

Parallel to classroometric principles, van der Vleuten and Schuwirth (2005) proposed the concept of programmatic assessment, where a range of assessment strategies should be used to gather information for decision-making. The quality and accuracy of these assessments are established if multiple sources of assessment information reveal similar insights, leading to trustworthy and defensible decisions to support learning and teaching.

The Problem

The strongest criticism of teacher assessment practices relates to reliability and validity, and whether consistency and accuracy measures are enough to argue for the rigour of assessment. As argued in Chapter 2 of this book, all assessments should be used to support learning and teaching. However, decisions should be fair, accurate, consistent and trustworthy. The reliability and validity indices are relatively easy to establish for SAs and high-stake tests. However, for in-class contingent assessment, the concepts of reliability and validity become challenging to apply. Brown (2019) argues that classroom assessments used by teachers to make in-class decisions and provide feedback fail to meet the rigour required for assessment. The interpretations and decisions made by teachers based on these assessments cannot be scrutinised to establish their accuracy and consistency. Hence, in-class contingent assessment cannot provide evidence to inform decisions beyond classroom interactions.

Even with the introduction of the classroometric principles, there are still issues related to their appropriateness in ensuring the consistency and accuracy of assessment when viewed as a continuum of practice where formative assessment (FA) and SA are interacting. In the current conceptualisation of assessment, where every piece of information is used to support student learning and teaching (ARG, 1999, 2002; Baird et al., 2017), psychometrics and 'classroometric' principles are not enough to account for the various factors that contribute to the consistency and accuracy measures of assessment and assessment data (Alonzo, 2016). These measures are not inherent characteristics of assessments and teachers' decision-making processes but are somewhat influenced by many personal and contextual factors (Alonzo et al., 2021; Taylor, 2013; van der Vleuten & Schuwirth, 2005). The psychometric principles do not account for teachers' knowledge of theory, technical skills, principles and concepts, pedagogy, sociocultural values, local practices, personal beliefs and attitudes as necessary requisites for effective assessment and decision-making (Taylor, 2013). In addition, focusing on using 'classroometric' principles will limit the use of SA, which is highly valued by the system.

The three case studies below highlight ways teachers can defend the consistency and accuracy measures of assessment, particularly self and peer assessment, feedback, questioning, observations, interviews and other informal assessments where the computation of reliability and validity indices is impossible.

Case 1: Holistic and analytical judgements for consistency and accuracy of teacher assessment

Description of the Study

Understanding the processes undertaken by teachers to make decisions highlights ways to improve the consistency and accuracy of assessment. The case presented here is drawn from a three-stage study by Phung and Michell (2022) about the nature and dynamics of teacher decision-making. The study explored the variability of teacher-based assessment when using the oral assessment tasks and protocols developed as part of an Australian assessment project, the Tools to Enhance Assessment Literacy for Teachers of English as an Additional Language. A mixed-method research approach was employed with 12 experienced primary and secondary English as an Additional Language teachers. The first stage was a participant project information, consent and assessment training session. During this stage, a questionnaire was used to collect background information from the participating teachers. The second stage was a teacher assessment activity where teachers watched a set of videos of students' performances and assigned scores. The third stage was a retrospective think-aloud activity and follow-up semi-structured interviews to seek explanations of teachers' decisions and justifications.

This chapter concludes that teacher-based language assessment decision-making is largely influenced by teachers' first impressions or 'assessment Gestalts'. It also reveals three different pathways for making these decisions and the factors that shape them. Holistic judgements involve making an overall assessment based on global characteristics such as fluency or accuracy without focusing too much on individual criteria. Analytical judgements focus more closely on specific criteria like grammar or pronunciation to make assessments. The third pathway is a combination of both approaches that allows teachers to switch back and forth between looking at overall features and individual details when forming their opinion about student performance, which can lead to more balanced judgements that are less likely to be influenced by personal biases. The interplay between holistic and analytical judgements is an important factor in teacher assessment decisions.

Problem Being Addressed

While there has been extensive research on factors that affect the variability and consistency of teacher-based assessment, the teacher-thinking processes that affect the trustworthiness of teacher-based assessment are not well understood. Teacher-thinking processes refer to the cognitive processes that teachers use to make assessment decisions. These processes include the use of holistic and analytical thinking, which are two different approaches to making decisions. Holistic thinking involves looking at the overall picture and making decisions based on the context. In contrast, analytical thinking involves breaking down the problem into smaller parts and making decisions based on the individual components.

Factors Influencing the Problem

Several factors influence teachers' thinking process when making judgement of students' work. These include the following:

1 *Physical characteristics such as race and gender.*
   These initial impressions can shape the way a teacher perceives an individual's ability to perform on tasks like language tests, which in turn affects their assessment decisions. When there is insufficient information about a student's performance, teachers infer or speculate on contextual information such as student personality traits and behaviours to

make an assessment judgement. This is because they need to fill in the gaps in the information they have to make a sound decision.

2 *Teacher initial perception of student performance.*

When teachers assess students' performance based on their own perceptions, it leads to inaccurate judgement. The results do not reflect students' actual performance, as their biases and preconceived notions filter their objective judgement. When teachers assess students' performance based on their own experiences, beliefs and values, it leads to inaccurate marking and interpretation of students' outcomes. For example, a teacher may have a preconceived notion that a certain student is incapable of performing well, which may lead to an inaccurate assessment of the student's performance. Similarly, a teacher may have a preconceived notion that a certain student is capable of performing well, which may lead to an overly positive assessment of student performance. Therefore, it is important to be aware of the potential for bias in teacher assessment, as this can lead to inaccurate assessments of student performance.

3 *Process adopted by teachers.*

Teachers need engagement in a robust analysis of task-based assessment criteria to interrogate strong initial 'gut feelings'. This process creates a meta-criterial reframing that enables teachers to arrive at an overall 'on balance' judgement synthesis. If teachers fail to interrogate strong initial Gestalts robustly, it continues as the dominant frame, pushing aside the analytical processes, and resulting in unbalanced assessment judgements. When teachers engage in fragmented analysis of isolated task criteria without strong guiding Gestalt, indecision and conflicted assessment ensue.

4 *Teachers' teacher reflexivity and meta-reflection.*

The two-way interactions between holistic and analytical judgements highlight the critical role teacher reflexivity and meta-reflection play in sound assessment decision-making. 'On balance' judgements may be seen as a 'best fit' appraisal with given assessment information. This decision-making synthesis draws on teachers' latent assessment experiences as well as criterion-related assessment information arising from assessment tool engagement and reflects their meta-criterial interpretations of 'the spirit' of assessment rubrics rather than 'feature by feature' compliance according to 'the letter'.

Implications of the Problem

The usefulness of assessment data lies in its accuracy. Thus, teacher judgement is a critical process in assessment. Teachers should be aware of the factors which shape their decisions, such as first impressions and personal biases. These factors cannot be isolated in the assessment process, but having an awareness of how they influence teachers' decision-making helps to ensure objective judgement of students' learning.

Another implication is that better accuracy of teacher judgement can be achieved if teachers also strive to use analytical thinking when making assessments so that judgements can be based on evidence rather than preconceived notions. Also, it is important to have multiple assessors evaluate students' performance before coming to conclusions about their ability or progress.

More importantly, the findings of this study imply that teachers should be trained in how to mark or score students' output objectively. This training includes designing assessment tasks, interpreting and applying assessment criteria, and evaluating the rigour of their marking, including identifying factors that might have influenced the marking process and the outcomes. This training is particularly helpful for early career teachers to ensure their marking practices are rigorous and accurate and that valid inferences can be drawn to inform other learning and teaching activities.

Case 2: Increasing accuracy of teacher judgement

Description of the Study

Teacher judgement of students' learning is influenced by many factors. This case study illustrates how classroom context plays a significant role in ensuring accuracy of teacher judgement. Kaiser et al. (2017) demonstrate that teachers' judgements of students' academic achievement are affected by more than just the students' achievement per se. They are also affected by characteristics such as ethnicity, gender and minority status. The authors conducted four experimental studies by comparing the average level of teacher judgements for students from different ethnic backgrounds. They expected lower judgements for students from an ethnicity with generally low achievement levels (Turkish students) and higher judgements for students from an ethnicity with generally high achievement levels (Asian students). Also, they examined whether students' ethnicity or their minority status moderated teachers' judgement accuracy. They operationalised judgement accuracy as the relationship between students' achievement and teachers' judgements. Two hypotheses were tested: the ethnicity hypothesis, which suggests that judgement accuracy differs for judgements of students from whom low or high academic achievement is generally expected, and the minority hypothesis, which suggests that not the ethnicity but the minority status itself leads to different teacher judgement accuracy.

Results showed that minority students tended to be judged more accurately than majority students, regardless of their actual achievement. This suggests that classroom characteristics must be considered when researching teachers' judgement accuracy to understand the influence of individual student characteristics and composition effects.

Problem Being Addressed

Teacher assessment practices, particularly their judgement and judgement accuracy, are influenced by many factors, including students' characteristics. As demonstrated by Kaiser et al. (2017), when teachers rely only on student achievement data to make judgements, they will likely make inaccurate judgements. Ensuring consistency and accuracy of teacher judgement is critically important because any decisions about students' learning have learning and social consequences (McNamara & Roever, 2006). Any inaccurate judgement will lead to wrong decisions, compromising students' learning. If teachers' purpose of using assessment and assessment information is to optimise student learning, then there is a need to ensure that their judgement is accurate to make fair, consistent and trustworthy decisions. Teachers using inaccurate assessment information to modify their learning will implement learning and teaching activities that are not meeting the learning needs of students. Teachers using inaccurate information to make high-stake decisions, like admission, promotion or segregation to ability classes, will inappropriately place students. Thus, the accuracy of teacher judgement is critical to make trustworthy decisions.

Factors Influencing the Problem

Kaiser et al.'s (2017) study shows that accuracy of teachers' judgement is influenced by the following factors:

1 *Students' characteristics.*

Fairness of teachers' judgements of students' academic achievement is influenced by student characteristics such as ethnicity, gender and minority status. This phenomenon can be explained by the expectation hypothesis, the ethnicity hypothesis and the minority hypothesis. The expectation hypothesis suggests that teachers' judgements of ethnic minority students are based on the predominant expectation of the group rather than on the student's actual achievement. The ethnicity hypothesis supports states that students' ethnicity influences teachers' judgement accuracy. Further, the minority hypothesis supports that students' minority status influences teachers' judgement accuracy.

2 *Classroom characteristics.*

Understanding classroom characteristics, such as student composition and achievement levels, can help improve the fairness and accuracy of teachers' evaluations. There is a tendency that high-performing students' output is judged by default due to their previous outputs or performance.

In other words, teachers' expectations associated with students' ethnicity influence their judgement. These hypotheses were tested in four separate experiments, with the results suggesting that minority students were judged more accurately than majority students.

Implications of the Problem

As teachers' judgements are the basis for many instructional and placement decisions, can influence students' self-concepts and can play an important role in students' academic careers, accurate judgements are clearly desirable.

For teachers to ensure the consistency of their judgements about their students, they must take into account the context in which their students are learning. This includes not only the school context but also the classroom context. The characteristics of the students in the classroom have an impact on how teachers judge their students. For example, Ready and Wright (2011) found that students from lower socio-economic backgrounds (SES) stand out more in high-SES classrooms and therefore may be judged differently by the teachers. This idea is referred to as the 'reference-group effect' and is the idea that students are judged relative to the performance of their peers in the classroom (Südkamp & Möller, 2009). Additionally, teachers should account for other factors, such as the size of the class and the variance in student achievement, when studying teachers' judgement accuracy. Teachers should be aware of their potential biases in relation to minority students and students from other ethnic groups. Especially for students with learning problems, more accurate judgements might help support their academic career (Hachfeld et al., 2010).

Case 3: Implementing fair and consistent assessment activities

Description of the Study

Fairness is an important aspect of ensuring trustworthiness of teacher assessment practices. This case study highlights some factors that make assessment unfair. The work of Alm and Colnerud (2015) answers the research question, "What aspects of a teacher's grading contribute to the grade being perceived as unfair?" A total of 411 teachers from nine municipalities in Sweden responded to the survey. Findings show that teachers can contribute to the students' perception of unfair grading when they do not follow the guidelines of the grading system, use unreliable information, allow themselves to be influenced by irrelevant factors or are ambiguous in their communication. The study also found that if teachers place too much emphasis on one piece of assessment data, students may perceive this as an unfair practice.

Problem Being Addressed

Students' perception of the fairness of teachers' assessment practices influences their engagement in assessment, which has consequences for their learning outcomes. Teachers' awareness of factors that make their assessment practices unfair is critical to safeguard their assessment practices, particularly in the aspect of grading, against negative perceptions from students. Ensuring that students have positive perception of assessment enhances their motivation, engagement and learning outcomes (Hannigan et al., 2022). In addition, implementing fair and consistent assessment practices ensures that assessment and assessment data are used as intended to support learning and teaching. Any grades awarded to students have social consequences (McNamara & Roever, 2006), especially if the results are used for high-stake decisions like promotion, admission or qualifications. Thus, it is critically important that teacher assessment practices are fair to make trustworthy assessment decisions.

Factors Influencing the Problem

Based on this study, several factors influence the fairness of teachers' grading system. These include the following:

1 *Inadequate application of systems leads to unfair practices.*
   Teachers' incorrect interpretation and application of the grading system may lead to unfair grading of students. For example, there is

Ensuring Trustworthiness of Assessment   127

a misconception about the application of the concept of the normal curve, where teachers think that students' grades must achieve the normal distribution, despite the change of the grading system to a criteria-referenced system. As a result, some students were told that the highest grade was no longer available. Thus, teacher assessment literacy is particularly important to ensure that policies and procedures are accurately and consistently applied, and that students' marks reflect their actual achievement.

2 *Teachers' use of personal rules.*

This refers to "locally or personally construed rules or principles concerning what is or is not possible in terms of grading" (p. 139). Teachers may adjust students' grades without a strong rationale, and this impacts the fairness of assessment. In addition, there is a tendency for teachers to favour one single assessment result. There are cases where teachers use the results of the national assessment as a benchmark for students' grades, and any other assessments, regardless of the results, will not result in marks higher than the national assessment. Consequently, students' grades are adjusted to conform to the national examination results. This is particularly unfair as the national assessment is conducted only once and assesses only limited learning outcomes.

3 *Use of undependable data.*

When teachers fail to use reliable or dependable data when grading their students, this can lead to students feeling that their grades are unfair. This happens when teachers do not gather adequate assessment data to make decisions. Teachers assign grades without conducting actual assessments or allowing students' suggested grades to be their final grades. In addition, teachers' use of incorrect data also causes students to receive an unfairly lower or higher grade than they should have received. This can happen when teachers are unaware of the identities of their students or when they confuse one student with another. It can also happen when teachers take into account the achievements and performances of other students when grading an individual student's work. For example, a teacher may fail an entire group on a group task if one member of the group completely ignores the task, thus grading the students not only on their performance but also on the performance of others. Moreover, teachers may base students' grades on deficient information or misleading information. This means that the information used to decide the student's grade is inaccurate and does not properly reflect their actual ability. The example given in the chapter is of a student who wrote their answers in ink and then realised they had made a mistake. They drew arrows to the correct answers as they could not erase the ink. However, the teacher failed them on the two questions, even though the arrows pointed to the correct answers. The teacher said the student had failed because the test paper was too messy. This reduces the quality of the assessment data and contributes to the student's feeling that they have been incorrectly assessed. The second example is when teachers base their assessment on written examinations only and fail to consider the verbal skills in a language or the ability to play an instrument or read musical notes. This means the teacher lacks important information to assess the student's overall ability.

4 *Students' emotional state during assessment.*

Teachers can base their assessments on an atypical performance that does not reflect the student's actual ability, such as when the student is too nervous or unwell. This results in teachers having insufficient information to accurately assess the actual learning of students.

5 *Inappropriate grade adjustment.*

This happens when a teacher adjusts students' grades as a result of irrelevant factors rather than their performance. Teachers' personal notions and expectations of an individual or group of pupils influence grade adjustments. For example, teachers may adjust a student's grade with reference to an older sibling's performance, which sets teacher expectations.

6 *Demographics' influence.*

Parental influence, social status, gender, students' attitude towards teachers and many other factors are sometimes used by teachers to award students' final grades. This demonstrates a lack of objectivity from teachers, as the students' learning achievement is not judged on its own merits, but rather on external factors.

7 *Ambiguous communication.*

Communications between teachers and students regarding grades can be a source of perceived unfairness and injustice. This occurs when teachers cannot explain or justify a grade or when students are not given the grade they feel they should be given. This is because teachers may not have explained the reasons for why they awarded a certain grade clearly or may not have followed what was previously told to the students about what grade to expect. When teachers do not clearly explain why a certain grade was given, it is difficult for students to understand why they did not receive higher grades. This is demonstrated in the example of a student receiving a lower grade than expected despite achieving the targets set by their teacher. The teacher justified this simply by saying that the student could have done even better.

Implications of the Problem

The perceived fairness of teachers' grading practices contributes to the discourse around the reliability and validity of teacher assessment practices. Thus, teachers should ensure that students perceive their practices to be fair. Teachers should use sufficient quantity and high-quality assessment data. The lack of data, use of incorrect data, use of deficient data and incorrect conclusion about students' learning signify low validity and reliability of teachers' assessment practices. The perception of unfairness is associated with the teacher using deficient data. Teachers' use of a range of assessments to gather sufficient information to make judgements about student learning ensures the reliability of teacher assessment (Smith, 2003). Similarly, the interpretation of students' learning with consideration of the context by which learning and assessment occur, but without the influence of external factors, contributes to the validity measure (Moss, 2003).

Teachers should not make inappropriate grade adjustments without a strong basis to not compromise the validity of assessment. In addition, teachers should follow the guidelines of the current grading system, use undependable information and not be influenced by irrelevant factors to ensure that students will perceive not the grading process as unfair. The perception of unfairness lies in the teacher wholly or partially replacing the legitimate assessment data with irrelevant factors.

There are two aspects of unfair grading that are not captured by the concepts of validity and reliability. These two aspects are the inadequate application of systems and the ambiguous communication. System congruence refers to the extent to which a grading system is applied consistently and fairly, while procedural conciseness is when the rules of the grading system are clearly communicated to students so that they understand the criteria used in grading. Therefore, these two concepts are important to consider when assessing whether a grade is seen as fair. The perception of unfairness lies in the teacher using the grading scale and associated regulations incorrectly in some respect. Adherence to the assessment system is aligned with the context-dependent nature of assessment, where policy influences the whole process of assessment use. The teacher is misleading or giving the student false hopes when communicating the outcome of a comparison between the actual quantity (performance) and symbolic quantity (grading scale). The perception of unfairness lies in the teacher not being able to explain the method used to grade the student in a comprehensible way or the student feeling that the teacher does not keep promises (pp. 144–145).

Proposed Solutions

As demonstrated in the three case studies above, the consistency and accuracy of teacher assessment practices are influenced by many factors, including teachers' knowledge, beliefs and dispositions, students' background and engagement in assessment, school context and policy. These factors should be considered when developing and implementing assessment and when interpreting and using results to inform learning and teaching decisions.

The use of classroometric principles seem appropriate to argue for the consistency and accuracy of teachers' assessment. However, when SA is integrated into teacher assessment results to make decisions, the use of psychometric principles may limit the process. However, the use of two parallel principles, psychometric principles and 'classroometric' (Brookhart, 2003) principles, to measure the quality of assessment tools has had the opposite effect to that intended, widening the perceived dichotomy between FAs and SAs, which was argued to be irrelevant when assessment is conceptualised within a broader pedagogical model (see Chapters 2 and 3 of this book). Competing assessment terminologies slowly become irrelevant as it is acknowledged that all types and forms of assessment can be and should be used to support learning and teaching beyond the accountability requirements of educational systems.

Alonzo and Teng (2023) proposed a new way to argue for the consistency and accuracy of assessment and decision-making using the concept of trustworthiness derived from qualitative research. The application of trustworthiness in assessment is increasingly being adopted to ensure consistency in teachers' decision-making. Trustworthiness refers to various characteristics of assessment, including its quality, design, processes, implementation and quality assurance mechanisms implemented by schools and teachers.

Apart from the sufficiency of information and conceptualising assessment as an integral part of learning and teaching, other elements contribute to the accuracy and consistency measures of teachers' assessment practices. Alonzo and Teng developed the framework for ensuring the trustworthiness of assessment and assessment decisions. The key elements are as follows:

1 The capability and integrity of the people involved. This includes teachers' assessment literacy (Alm & Colnerud, 2015; Klenowski, 2014) (Siegel, 2007), students' assessment literacy to have a deeper understanding of the purpose to engage in any assessment activity (Flores et al., 2015), parents' involvement in assessment activities and other stakeholders' participation in assessment (Klenowski, 2014). Also, the school leadership team contributes trustworthiness of assessment through the strategic development of assessment culture (Alm & Colnerud, 2015; Harlen, 2005).

2 The quality of assessment design, tools and strategies used. This includes the authenticity of assessment (Villarroel et al., 2018) – how it reflects the skills developed and measured (Palmer, 2004) and ensures equity

Ensuring Trustworthiness of Assessment 131

(Driver, 2019; Scott et al., 2014) by adapting assessment to cater to students' diverse backgrounds (Murillo & Hidalgo, 2017; Siegel, 2007), avoids sources of bias (Alm & Colnerud, 2015; Harlen, 2005) and guarantees students' success (Yung & Yung, 2001).

3 The assessment processes used to maximise the use of assessment to support student learning. This includes the pedagogical approaches used by teachers in embedding assessment in learning and teaching (Colbert et al., 2012; Rasooli et al., 2018), the use of explicit criteria and standards (Pepper & Pathak, 2008), modification of assessment activities to account student diverse backgrounds and interactions of teachers and students (Klenowski, 2014).

4 The data management system used by teachers and schools in general. This includes using a recording mechanism that is accurate and accessible (Webb et al., 2003), integrating the range of assessment data from various sources (Bacon et al., 2015; Klenowski, 2014) and locating students in a continuum accurately (Medaille et al., 2019).

5 The decision-making processes. This includes engaging in moderation activity to make a consistent judgement (Colbert et al., 2012), validating the inference drawn from the data (Webb et al., 2003; Wiliam, 1993), using these inferences to identify opportunities to further support student learning (Lantolf & Poehner, 2013), evaluating how assessment data reflect student actual knowledge (Harlen, 2005) and adapting learning and teaching activities to further support students (Murillo & Hidalgo, 2017).

6 The impact of contextual, cultural and personal factors. Teachers need to consider the effect of students' background, learning needs and cultural orientation when engaging in assessment and how they demonstrate their learning (Driver, 2019). Teachers' assessment practices should be strongly underpinned by fairness, equity, access and equality (Cherry et al., 2003; Driver, 2019; Murillo & Hidalgo, 2017; Rasooli et al., 2018).

7 The influences of assessment policies. They shape the assessment culture in schools (Harlen, 2005). Also, teachers need to consider how cultural, structural, political and technical issues influence the effectiveness of assessment (Billing & Thomas, 2000).

Conclusion

The psychometric principles of reliability and validity are inappropriate for establishing the consistency and accuracy of teacher assessment practices. It is not surprising that teacher assessment practices are heavily critiqued for their low reliability and validity because the measures used are not fit for purpose. The introduction of classroometric principles as proxy measures of reliability and validity for other types of assessment, where statistical metrics cannot be calculated, seems to address the issue. However, using two sets of principles

132 Ensuring Trustworthiness of Assessment

has too often reinforced the perceived dichotomy between FA and SA. The concept of trustworthiness is applied as an overarching concept to ensure that all assessments are consistent and accurate. Ensuring trustworthiness considers various factors that influence the accuracy and consistency of assessment, including its quality, design, processes, implementation and quality assurance mechanisms implemented by schools and teachers, teachers' assessment knowledge, skills and dispositions, and student engagement in assessment. By ensuring that all these factors support any assessment, teachers can argue for the accuracy and consistency of their assessment practices, including the use of assessment data for their decision-making.

References

Alm, F., & Colnerud, G. (2015). Teachers' experiences of unfair grading. *Educational Assessment, 20*(2), 132–150. https://doi.org/10.1080/10627197.2015.1028620

Alonzo, D. (2016). *Development and application of a teacher assessment for learning (AfL) literacy tool.* University of New South Wales]. Sydney. http://unsworks.unsw.edu.au/fapi/datastream/unsworks:38345/SOURCE02?view=true

Alonzo, D., Leverett, J., & Obsioma, E. (2021). Leading an assessment reform: Ensuring a whole-school approach for decision-making. *Frontiers in Education, 6*(62). https://doi.org/10.3389/feduc.2021.631857

Alonzo, D., & Teng, S. (2023). Trustworthiness of teacher assessment and decision-making: Reframing the consistency and accuracy measures. *International Journal of Instruction, 16*(3), 1075–1094.

ARG. (2002). *Assessment for learning: 10 principles.* https://www.storre.stir.ac.uk/bitstream/1893/32458/1/Assessment%20for%20learning%2010%20principles%202002.pdf

Bacon, R., Williams, L., Grealish, L., & Jamieson, M. (2015). Credible and defensible assessment of entry-level clinical competence: Insights from a modified Delphi study. *Focus on Health Professional Education, 16*(3), 57–72.

Baird, J.-A., Andrich, D., Hopfenbeck, T. N., & Stobart, G. (2017). Assessment and learning: Fields apart? *Assessment in Education: Principles, Policy & Practice, 24*(3), 317–350. https://doi.org/10.1080/0969594X.2017.1319337

Billing, D., & Thomas, H. (2000). The international transferability of quality assessment systems for higher education: The Turkish experience. *Quality in Higher Education, 6*(1), 31–40. https://doi.org/10.1080/13538320050001054

Brookhart, S. M. (2003). Developing measurement theory for classroom assessment purposes and uses. *Educational Measurement: Issues and Practice, 22*(4), 5–12. https://doi.org/10.1111/j.1745-3992.2003.tb00139.x

Brown, G. T. L. (2019). Is assessment for learning really assessment? [Perspective]. *Frontiers in Education, 4*(64). https://doi.org/10.3389/feduc.2019.00064

Cherry, B., Ordóñez, L. D., & Gilliland, S. W. (2003). Grade expectations: The effects of expectations on fairness and satisfaction perceptions. *Journal of Behavioral Decision Making, 16*(5), 375–395. https://doi.org/10.1002/bdm.452

Colbert, P., Wyatt-Smith, C., & Klenowski, V. (2012). A systems-level approach to building sustainable assessment cultures: Moderation, quality task design and dependability of judgement. *Policy Futures in Education, 10*(4), 386–401. https://doi.org/10.2304/pfie.2012.10.4.386

Driver, M. K. (2019). Understanding equitable assessment: How preservice teachers make meaning of disability. *Journal of Multicultural Affairs, 4*(1). https://scholarworks.sfasu.edu/jma/vol4/iss1/3

Field, A. (2009). *Discovering statistics using SPSS.* Sage.

Flores, M. A., Veiga Simão, A. M., Barros, A., & Pereira, D. (2015). Perceptions of effectiveness, fairness and feedback of assessment methods: A study in higher education. *Studies in Higher Education, 40*(9), 1523–1534. https://doi.org/10.1080/03075079.2014.881348

Hachfeld, A., Anders, Y., Schroeder, S., Stanat, P., & Kunter, M. (2010). Does immigration background matter? How teachers' predictions of students' performance relate to student background. *International Journal of Educational Research, 49*(2), 78–91. https://doi.org/10.1016/j.ijer.2010.09.002

Hannigan, C., Alonzo, D., & Oo, C. Z. (2022). Student assessment literacy: Indicators and domains from the literature. *Assessment in Education: Principles, Policy & Practice, 29*(4), 482–504. https://doi.org/10.1080/0969594X.2022.2121911

Harlen, W. (2005). Trusting teachers' judgement: Research evidence of the reliability and validity of teachers' assessment used for summative purposes. *Research Papers in Education, 20*(3), 245–270. https://doi.org/10.1080/02671520500193744

Kaiser, J., Südkamp, A., & Möller, J. (2017). The effects of student characteristics on teachers' judgment accuracy: Disentangling ethnicity, minority status, and achievement. *Journal of Educational Psychology, 109*(6), 871–888. https://doi.org/10.1037/edu0000156

Klenowski, V. (2014). Towards fairer assessment. *The Australian Educational Researcher, 41*(4), 445–470. https://doi.org/10.1007/s13384-013-0132-x

Lantolf, J. P., & Poehner, M. E. (2013). The unfairness of equal treatment: Objectivity in L2 testing and dynamic assessment. *Educational Research and Evaluation, 19*(2–3), 141–157. https://doi.org/10.1080/13803611.2013.767616

McNamara, T., & Roever, C. (2006). *Language testing: The social dimension.* Blackwell.

Medaille, A., Goldrup, S., & Abernathy, T. (2019). Assessing rigor in teacher education: Do NCTQ's guidelines measure up? *The Teacher Educator, 54*(1), 72–89. https://doi.org/10.1080/08878730.2018.1516260

Moss, P. A. (2003). Reconceptualizing validity for classroom assessment. *Educational Measurement: Issues and Practice, 22*(4), 13–25. https://doi.org/10.1111/j.1745-3992.2003.tb00140.x

Murillo, F. J., & Hidalgo, N. (2017). Students' conceptions about a fair assessment of their learning. *Studies in Educational Evaluation, 53*, 10–16. https://doi.org/10.1016/j.stueduc.2017.01.001

Palmer, S. (2004). Authenticity in assessment: Reflecting undergraduate study and professional practice. *European Journal of Engineering Education, 29*(2), 193–202. https://doi.org/10.1080/03043790310001633179

Pepper, M. B., & Pathak, S. (2008). Classroom contribution: What do students perceive as fair assessment? *Journal of Education for Business, 83*(6), 360–367. https://doi.org/10.3200/JOEB.83.6.360-368

Phung, D. V., & Michell, M. (2022). Inside teacher assessment decision-making: From judgement gestalts to assessment pathways. *Frontiers in Education, 7.* https://doi.org/10.3389/feduc.2022.830311

Rasooli, A., Zandi, H., & DeLuca, C. (2018). Re-conceptualizing classroom assessment fairness: A systematic meta-ethnography of assessment literature and beyond. *Studies in Educational Evaluation, 56,* 164–181. https://doi.org/10.1016/j.stueduc.2017.12.008

Ready, D. D., & Wright, D. L. (2011). Accuracy and inaccuracy in teachers' perceptions of young children's cognitive abilities: The role of child background and classroom context. *American Educational Research Journal, 48*(2), 335–360. https://doi.org/10.3102/0002831210374874

Scott, S., Webber, C. F., Lupart, J. L., Aitken, N., & Scott, D. E. (2014). Fair and equitable assessment practices for all students. *Assessment in Education: Principles, Policy & Practice, 21*(1), 52–70. https://doi.org/10.1080/0969594X.2013.776943

Siegel, M. A. (2007). Striving for equitable classroom assessments for linguistic minorities: Strategies for and effects of revising life science items. *Journal of Research in Science Teaching, 44*(6), 864–881. https://doi.org/10.1002/tea.20176

Smith, J. K. (2003). Reconsidering reliability in classroom assessment and grading. *Educational Measurement: Issues and Practice, 22*(4), 26–33. https://doi.org/10.1111/j.1745-3992.2003.tb00141.x

Südkamp, A., & Möller, J. (2009). Referenzgruppeneffekte im Simulierten Klassenraum. *Zeitschrift für Pädagogische Psychologie, 23*(34), 161–174. https://doi.org/10.1024/1010-0652.23.34.161

Tabachnick, B. G., & Fidell, L. S. (2007). *Using multivariate statistics.* Pearson Education Inc.

Taylor, L. (2013). Communicating the theory, practice and principles of language testing to test stakeholders: Some reflections. *Language Testing, 30*(3), 403–412. https://doi.org/10.1177/0265532213480338

van der Vleuten C.P., Schuwirth L.W. (2005). Assessing professional competence: From methods to programmes. *Medical Education, 39,* 309–317. https://doi.org/10.1111/j.1365-2929.2005.02094.x

Villarroel, V., Bloxham, S., Bruna, D., Bruna, C., & Herrera-Seda, C. (2018). Authentic assessment: Creating a blueprint for course design. *Assessment & Evaluation in Higher Education, 43,* 840–854.

Webb, C., Endacott, R., Gray, M. A., Jasper, M. A., McMullan, M., & Scholes, J. (2003). Evaluating portfolio assessment systems: What are the appropriate criteria? *Nurse Education Today, 23*(8), 600–609. https://doi.org/10.1016/S0260-6917(03)00098-4

Wiliam, D. (1993). Validity, dependability and reliability in National Curriculum assessment. *The Curriculum Journal, 4*(3), 335–350. https://doi.org/10.1080/0958517930040303

Yung, B. H. W., & Yung, B. H. W. (2001). Three views of fairness in a school-based assessment scheme of practical work in biology. *International Journal of Science Education, 23*(10), 985–1005. https://doi.org/10.1080/09500690010017129

Chapter 8

Are Teachers and Students the Only Key Players in Assessment?

Introduction

Assessment literacy is not only a professional competence for teachers but also for other education stakeholders, including school leaders, students, parents and policy-makers (Davison, 2013). This construct, apart from being context-driven, is linked to the key responsibilities of the stakeholders (Popham, 2009). People with different stakes in education have different assessment information needs and responsibilities, and hence, they need a set of assessment knowledge and skills to understand the assessment principles, processes and practices. Davison (2013) found that the most important factor contributing to the failure of assessment reform is misconceptions among policy-makers about what assessment really is, thus impacting the articulation of policy and teachers' assessment practices. Due to the lack of understanding of what it takes to implement assessment reform, policy-makers may think that simply articulating policies that outline principles would achieve the expected outcomes, or just simply changing teachers' assessment practices will make the assessment reform successful. This, however, is not the case because teachers are not autonomous or working in isolation. Their practices are influenced by many social factors, each holds certain expectations and responsibilities that have critical implications or teachers' practices.

For assessment reform to succeed, the establishment of a strong context-driven assessment culture across the system with a common language among stakeholders is required (Alonzo et al., 2021a; Davison & Leung, 2009). A concerted effort and common understanding by all stakeholders are needed to ensure that government policies, curriculum design and parents' expectations support the effective implementation of assessment (Bennett, 2011; Davison, 2013). Assessment operates in a broader educational context; thus, policy-makers play an important role in assessment (Davison, 2013). The policies and guidelines they create may make or break assessment implementation.

Teachers, students and all other stakeholders involved in the educational process, particularly policy-makers and parents, need to have common aims, beliefs and understandings to support teachers for the successful implementation of

DOI: 10.4324/9781003396277-8

assessment (Gleeson et al., 2020; Lee & Louis, 2019; Yan & Brown, 2021). Thus, an agreed definition of teacher assessment literacy is necessary as a guiding principle for supporting teachers. The definition of assessment should not only focus on the roles of teachers, but it should also consider system issues referred to by Bennett (2011). For example, in a high accountability educational culture, implementing other types of assessment apart from tests is impossible even if teachers are experts in all assessment domains. To successfully implement assessment reform, all components of the education system should function coherently.

Alonzo (2016) has redefined teacher assessment literacy as follows:

> (It) accounts for knowledge and skills in making highly contextualised, fair, consistent, and trustworthy assessment decisions to inform learning and teaching to effectively support both students' and teachers' professional learning. The aim of teachers is (to build) students' and other stakeholders' capabilities and confidence to take an active role in assessment, learning and teaching activities to enable and provide the needed support for more effective learning.
>
> (p. 58)

As indicated in this conceptualisation, assessment literacy is no longer confined to teachers, but there is a strong emphasis on the assessment literacy of other stakeholders, which recent research highlights to ensure effective learning and teaching (Davison, 2013; Erickson et al., 2022; Kremmel & Harding, 2020; Ratnam-Lim & Tan, 2015). The roles of teachers are expanded to include providing assessment and assessment information to stakeholders to make them understand the overall assessment culture in schools (Taylor, 2009). This notion of teacher assessment literacy has been shaped by pressures at the system level, where the effectiveness of teacher assessment practices is constrained by external pressures due to the inconsistencies of understanding and expectations of other stakeholders.

This call for stakeholder assessment literacy was first evident in Popham's (2009) view that assessment literacy is directly linked to the responsibilities of people, which means that different stakeholders have different assessment literacy needs. Teacher assessment literacy is critical for addressing the assessment needs of and building the assessment literacy of other stakeholders. In particular, the conceptualisation above emphasises the responsibility of teachers to work with students, colleagues, parents and the community. Assessment literate teachers provide assessment information to various stakeholder groups. Apart from the ability of teachers to communicate assessment results to students, they must also provide assessment information to different stakeholder groups tailored to each group's information needs (Davison, 2013). The dialogue between teachers and stakeholders provides a means to deepen their understanding of assessment principles, processes and practices, which may develop their assessment literacy and draw positive support from them.

The Problem

Implementing assessment reform is often teacher-centric rather than a shared responsibility of all stakeholders. System, school and the wider community put pressure on teachers to implement assessment reforms to increase students' outcomes. However, the misalignment of expectations and provision of inappropriate support from stakeholders limits the effectiveness of teacher assessment practices. The alignment of stakeholders' beliefs, views and practices with teacher assessment practices will enable them to provide enabling and supporting mechanisms for teachers to implement assessment more effectively. Theorising assessment from a socio-cultural lens highlights other stakeholders' shared responsibility in assessment.

Policy-makers articulate assessment policies underpinned by their own stake in education. More often than not, assessment policies put high regard to high-stake examinations for reporting and meeting the accountability information needs of policy-makers. These policies are then handed down to schools for implementation. When teachers' practices are contrary to what the policies require, they tend to lean towards implementing the policies for fear of poor judgement from policy-makers. This top-down approach for articulating and implementing assessment policies detaches it from the actual classroom contexts, thus increasing the disconnect between teachers' assessment practices and the policies they need to enact those practices. In the same way, parents' and community's expectations are often unrealistic and are not aligned to the assessment culture of schools. Even if the policies and teacher assessment practices are well aligned, parents and the community may put pressure on teachers to meet their assessment information needs, particularly in matters relating to students' marks and homework. There is also another problem in terms of parents' understanding of assessment reports. Even how robust the students' assessment report is if parents cannot understand it, it becomes useless from parents' viewpoint, thereby limiting their agency to provide support for their children's learning. It may even create a negative perception towards the school and teachers' assessment practices.

Case 1: Parents' beliefs about assessment

Description of the Study

This case study draws on the work of Ratnam-Lim and Tan (2015) to demonstrate the impact of parents' beliefs about assessment in enacting a national policy. A 'Holistic Assessment' system has been adopted by Singapore's primary education system, which according to the Ministry of Education plan (Ministry of Education Press Release, 2010) should

138 Engaging Other Key Players in Assessment

have been implemented in 183 primary schools by 2014. This system seeks to provide constructive feedback to students in both academic and non-academic aspects of their development to enable meaningful learning for pupils. It is an attempt to shift the focus of assessment from an exam-oriented approach to one that emphasises learning and educational outcomes for all primary pupils. Ratnam-Lim and Tan (2015) surveyed teachers' views from a random sample of 30 (16.4%) schools, ensuring that one teacher represents each school. To ensure that the responses were representative of the various socio-demographic profiles of Singaporean primary schools, they randomly sampled teachers attending in-service courses at the National Institute of Education. In addition, they also approached secondary school teachers attending in-service courses who were parents ($n = 13$) of primary school students who are enrolled in schools implementing 'Holistic Assessment'.

Data analysis revealed the challenges faced in implementing a holistic assessment system, such as resistance from teachers and parents, the difficulty of providing meaningful feedback to young students and the tension between formative assessment and accountability systems. Further, findings show that assessment reform in Singapore was impeded by a dominant belief in the importance of high-stake assessment and that there was a need to broaden the value and meaning of merit in assessment validity. The findings provide insights into the consequent realities of a nationwide shift in assessment purpose and discourse on teachers and parents. One critical finding of this study is that parental beliefs in assessment are one of the factors that influence the success of assessment reform implementation.

Problem Being Addressed

This study addresses the role of parents in implementing a large-scale assessment reform in one country. Previous studies cited by the authors (e.g., (Lim-Ratnam, 2013; Stipek et al., 1992) argue that parents of children in the primary years of schooling (age 6–12) are a major force in the 'underlife' and micropolitics of school. They constitute a significant part of the processes of interpretation, translation and enactment of policy, and they are often very vocal in expressing their views, opinions and feelings. Furthermore, they feel they have more control over their children's education in this age group, making them the 'reality definers' (Spillane et al., 2002) in the policy enactment process. Thus, parents are influential in shaping the reality of the implementation of the policy and its actual effects.

In this study, it is reported that although parents welcomed the policy of holistic assessment as a way of relieving stress in the high-stake

Engaging Other Key Players in Assessment 139

examination culture, the challenges and reality of implementation indicate that there were complex issues and deep, paradigmatic shifts needed. Teachers and parents had different views on what the policy should be and how it should be implemented.

Factors Influencing the Problem

Although parents in this study reported positive impacts of the assessment reform, including children feeling less overwhelmed by the demands of schooling, younger children helped to settle into the rhythm of school and their anxiety about attending school reduced; there were barriers to the effective implementation of the reform. Some factors influenced parental expectations in assessment. These included the following:

1 *Societal norms and expectations.*
   Singaporean society is heavily influenced by meritocracy, a system in which people are rewarded based on their abilities and talents, and people's success is judged based on academic excellence and job performance. This system created a culture where everyone, particularly the political elite or those in positions of power, must have a high level of academic achievement to be successful. As a result, the contest for what qualifies as high-stake merit in Singapore begins in schools, where students are assessed and prepared for national examinations. This societal norm shapes parents' perception that exam preparation is necessary, favouring the use of tests to better prepare students for national examinations.
2 *The dominant use of high-stake tests.*
   To achieve societal norm and expectations, high-stake tests are predominantly used. The system's and schools' assessment culture may have shape parents' expectations because they are used to seeing high-stake test results for the longer time. Thus, they see these assessments as the early and pre-ordinate production of what qualifies as high-stake merit in Singapore. School assessments are seen as the first step in determining who is qualified for higher positions in Singapore. This belief is widely and strongly held by parents, which continues to influence their resistance to other forms of assessment.
3 *Parental understanding of assessment.*
   There is an apparent lack of understanding that high-stake tests are summative by nature, and to better achieve higher achievement in these assessments, other forms of assessments are needed to help identify the individual learning needs of students. Due to societal norms and expectations, and the long tradition of using high-stake

tests to sort out people based on academic achievement, parents have a limited understanding of what makes assessment effective in supporting learning and teaching. They think that tests and examinations are the only valid assessments. Also, they believe that assessments are implemented for their promotion and qualification functions only. This limited understanding of parents influences their beliefs about the use of other types of assessment to gather data to adapt learning and teaching activities.

4 *The actual implementation of the reform.*

The regular use of 'bite-sized' assessments puts stress on parents as they still view these as tests, which add up to the final score of the students. They spend time preparing and coaching their children but feel that despite their hard work, marks do not reflect their effort, as these assessments contribute little to the final mark. The adopted approach for assessment reform is not fully understood by parents, thus negatively impacting their perception of and actual support to their children.

Implications of the Problem

The findings of this study illustrate the challenges in achieving the aims of assessment reform and changing the assessment culture of the system. This type of change requires people not just to do things differently but also to change their beliefs and perceptions. This change is also systemic in nature, as it involves changing expectations, goals, structures, roles and norms. If these changes do not occur, resistance from parents will continue to challenge the policy and teachers' assessment practices. The resistance is linked to the dominant belief in the importance and merit of high-stake assessments, which is reflected in the parents' resistance to the assessment reform, and the conflict between holistic assessment and narrower assessment achievements. A closer look at this belief system is needed to understand the impediment to assessment change. The misalignment of parents' beliefs to the principles of effective assessment practices is a barrier to assessment change. Changing parents' beliefs requires exploring and removing or reconstructing discourses for assessment reform. In the context of Singapore, the notion of meritocracy is identified as a salient discourse that encapsulates the prevailing paradigm, which assessment reform in Singapore needs to contend with.

The researchers suggest that if society is to move beyond this stratified view of merit, then the notion of assessment validity must be broadened. This would involve exploring other forms of assessments that can be used to determine merit. Ultimately, this would involve increasing the assessment literacy of parents to explore a broader range of actions that should be used to change their beliefs, which eventually would create positive dispositions, expectations and actions to support teachers in implementing effective assessment practices to help their children learn more effectively. Parental assessment literacy is critically important to ensure that their beliefs, perceptions and understanding of assessment, including its principles, functions, consequences, merits and value, are aligned with the philosophy of assessment reforms implemented.

Case 2: The role of policy-makers in enacting policy that supports teacher implementation of assessment

Description of the Study

Teachers' implementation of assessment practices is influenced by policy. A policy that outlines only the expected outcomes without clearly acknowledging the support needed by teachers would most likely fail. Van der Kleij et al. (2018) examined the evolving policy expectations and support for teachers' formative assessment practices in the context of two recent Australian education reforms: (1) the introduction of the first national curriculum, and (2) new professional standards for teachers. The reforms, which include the national policy statement, the Melbourne Declaration, the Australian Curriculum, and the Professional Standards for Teachers, are intended to improve teacher quality and student learning. Previous reforms have been described as 'assessment-driven', seeking to increase the use of assessment evidence for formative purposes. The Melbourne Declaration (Ministerial Council on Education, Employment, Training andYouth Affairs [MCEETYA], 2008) focuses on formative assessment as part of a world-class assessment, which has been shown to positively impact student learning. The researchers conclude that while formative assessment is expected to be a critical component of teachers' work in Australia, it is unlikely to be successful under the current conditions. This is because while formative assessment is strongly advocated as a critical component of Australian teachers' work, support for teachers that will lead to effective implementation of formative assessment is inadequate. Further, they also conclude that curriculum reforms that do not integrate and embed assessment with curriculum will not be successful in creating assessment culture that will enhance student learning.

Problem Being Addressed

This study illustrates how policy-makers articulate assessment policies but fail to provide support for teachers to effectively enact them. Van der Kleij et al. (2018) demonstrate that despite the expectations for formative assessment in the Australian Curriculum, Professional Standards (AITSL, 2011) and at the state and territory level, the limited and sometimes inappropriate guidance for teachers provides little to encourage and support them in implementing effective formative assessment practices. Furthermore, they note that formative assessment in the curriculum has been reduced to a formal statement of significance and general principles, a pattern seen in many other policy contexts (Pryor, 2015).

Factors Influencing the Problem

Policy-makers support for the implementation of assessment reform is influenced by several factors:

1 *The symbolism of assessment in the national curriculum.*

As shown in the study, there is a national consensus among the states and territories of Australia about the importance of formative assessment practices for students' learning. However, the removal of formative assessment from the Australian Curriculum Framework has resulted in unequal support from the states and territories for the principles of formative assessment as well as its implementation. This leads to diverse approaches towards the implementation of the Australian Curriculum, with some states putting less emphasis on the use of formative assessment.

2 *Limited understanding of policy-makers.*

When policy-makers lack understanding of the theoretical and empirical basis for using a range of assessment strategies, this leads to the lack of strong and structured support for teachers, professional development and time to develop effective implementation strategies. The lack of clear assessment guidance and support for teachers and limited professional learning opportunities about assessment in conjunction with curriculum change are major causes of curriculum reform failure. Policy-makers can only provide support for teachers if they have understood the challenges in embedding a range of assessment strategies in learning and teaching activities. Understanding how to implement effective assessment that supports students' learning requires a deeper understanding of the intersections of assessment, curriculum and pedagogy.

Engaging Other Key Players in Assessment   143

3 *Misalignment of policy-makers expectations and the actual policy.*

The increased emphasis of policy-makers on accountability testing is counter-productive to the goals of the reform, which is to emphasise the use of assessment that will inform learning and teaching. Their prioritisation of external and summative assessments is narrowing the focus of teachers' teaching and assessment practices and constraining the potential for curriculum innovation rather than broadening learning outcomes. This leads teachers to follow a convergent summative assessment approach rather than a formative one, which influences their assessment practices. The increased pressure from summative assessments and preparation for these necessarily absorb the time needed to effectively carry out formative assessments. This reduces the system support and commitment needed to promote quality formative assessment.

4 *The inappropriate articulation of policy.*

The expectations for graduate teachers are relatively low compared to proficient teachers, as articulated in the Australian Teaching Standards. Graduate teachers are expected to only understand and provide feedback on formative assessment, while proficient teachers are expected to be able to use effective formative strategies to assess student learning. This differentiation is contrary to what research evidence research suggest that formative assessment should occupy in the repertoire of skills of beginning teachers. These low expectations for new teachers lead to a lack of exposure to quality formative assessment approaches in the initial teacher education curriculum.

Implications of the Problem

To ensure that policy is well articulated and aligned with research evidence and practical skills of teachers, policy-makers should have a higher level of assessment literacy, including knowledge of curriculum, pedagogy and effective learning. The common understanding of curriculum theories, pedagogy and assessment across the system will ensure that assessment policies are developed, support for teachers is articulated and provided, and the curriculum is designed to allow teachers to implement effective assessment practices. Unless policy-makers understand learning, teaching and assessment processes in the classroom, their approach to articulating policies is centred on meeting their political agenda and information need to justify school spending.

In addition, policy-makers' understanding of the demands of teachers' work and nature of students' learning will help them set realistic expectations, including the time frame to expect key changes in teachers'

144 Engaging Other Key Players in Assessment

assessment practices and actual impact on students' learning. When expectations are too high, there is an overwhelming pressure for teachers to meet those expectations at the risk of narrowing down practices and target only specific outcomes to provide evidence of their effectiveness. This is an unsustainable approach because teachers are under constant pressure to perform. Once they reach capacity-sealing, they will get burnt out and revert to their old practices.

Moreover, policy-makers' nuanced understanding of the complexities of learning, teaching and assessment will make them find the balance between accountability and teacher autonomy. Teachers should be supported to creatively solve learning issues because they have contextual understanding of these issues that policy-makers do not have. A rigid and overly simplistic policy will not provide solutions, let alone the risk for constraining teachers' capacity to adapt their pedagogical and assessment approaches to the emerging landscape of learning and teaching. Polices should provide avenue for teachers to account and reflect on emerging research evidence and use them in their practice.

Case 3: The influence of leadership in assessment culture change

Description of the Study

This case study builds on the work of Adie et al. (2021) to argue for the critical role of school leaders in assessment reforms. They illustrate that introducing a new assessment policy can have a ripple effect throughout all levels of schooling. They looked at one Australian school's reaction to introducing a new assessment system in the senior years. Six school leaders, academic directors of Mathematics, Science, Humanities and English faculties, the curriculum director and a deputy principal were interviewed at the beginning and end of the project. The project was implemented for two years with 12 meetings to promote collaborative thinking about effective assessment and evidence of improved student learning. During the meetings, teachers shared their planning, teaching strategies and resources for collecting evidence of learning and promoting student agency. The data collected from these meetings included meeting notes, artefacts used in the meetings and an audio recording from the final meeting.

Findings reveal the practices required to make critical changes to the assessment culture and related assessment systems for the school within a context of national assessment accountabilities and high community expectations. These practices include the collaboration of school leaders with teachers, students and parents to drive change while maintaining high performance and external pressures of national assessment accountabilities and high community expectations. To do this, schools must focus on assessments that support learning and teaching rather than summative assessment and develop strategies to combine formative and summative assessment. This research also highlights the importance of understanding the different perspectives of all stakeholders and recognising the difficulty of disrupting established practices regarding assessment.

Problem Being Addressed

Implementing an assessment reform is a complex process. There are epistemological, conceptual, structural and paradigmatic changes needed for its successful implementation. The role of school leadership has been argued in many research articles, suggesting that they are one of the key players in changing teachers' assessment practices and creating a strong assessment culture that supports learning and teaching while maintaining accountability requirements. The role of school leaders in building the school assessment culture points to their assessment literacy that requires both instructional leadership role and assessment knowledge and skills. It is not enough that school leaders should develop strategies to translate the system-level reform to their school context. They need to provide an expert advice for teachers how to effectively enact the schools' strategic agenda into actual classroom practices.

Factors Influencing the Problem

Shifting an assessment culture from an examination-driven to a more learning-driven assessment requires strong leadership that drives the reform. Some factors that influence school leadership are as follows:

1 *Clear understanding of the nuances of assessment.*
   School leaders make critical decisions in the process of building a strong assessment culture. Their understanding of the multifaceted aspects of assessment and many factor including its implementation, including the need for discipline-specific assessment skills, will allow them to provide targeted support and resources for individual teachers. This means that the school leaders should recognise the need for different assessment skills for different teachers, disciplines and year

levels. Their assessment literacy will allow them to work with teachers to develop units of work and lesson plans that align with school assessment culture.

2 *School leaders' intent.*

If school leaders' intent is to reduce the reliance on summative grades and focus on formative practices, teachers will be most likely to follow suit. The clear communication with this intent should be coupled with support for teachers to shift their attention and practices from grades which measure students' performance at the end of the course, to formative practices, which provide feedback to students on their learning throughout the course. This shift is not easily realised when there is no strong instructional support provided by school leaders.

3 *Clear communication with students.*

School leaders' intent should also be communicated to students and parents. In this study, the intent is implemented through the English faculty, where students were given direct instructions to submit their written presentations for the oral assessment several days before the presentation. This is done to reduce the anxiety surrounding the oral assessments.

4 *Working with parents.*

School leaders should work with parents to prioritise learning. This can be done by providing support for parents to focus their attention on enabling students to understand themselves as learners. In addition, school leaders can ask ongoing feedback from parents about their children's learning needs, assessment experience and their specific information needs to better support their children. The dialogue with and feedback from parents can be a valuable input for the school.

5 *School leaders' instructional leadership.*

Part of the responsibility of school leaders is to provide not only support in terms of social-emotional and resources but also professional support. They should work closely with teachers to design and implement a range of assessment strategies and provide feedback to teachers for any areas needing improvement. This process will enhance the credibility of school leaders because teachers will see them that they understand effective assessment principles and practices. In this study, the Curriculum Director identified the skills that students need to self-assess their work. These skills include focusing on what they still need to learn, breaking down topics into smaller components, structuring their time and looking at themselves to see how they feel about things. These strategies help students develop their assessment skills, have ownership of their learning and manage assessment stress and anxiety.

Implications of the Problem

Disrupting the established assessment practices in schools is challenging. Thus, implementing school assessment reform requires school leaders to acknowledge the complex interplay between competing epistemologies of curriculum, assessment and learning. Shifting the focus of assessment from accountability to supporting learning and teaching and developing self-regulated learners who can successfully navigate formal summative assessment in later years requires visionary leadership and a school community willing to trial new practices. School leaders should examine how the social and cultural characteristics of a school can support risk-taking to trial assessment innovations.

One conceptual change that school leaders need to articulate is to reconcile the tension between formative and summative assessment in an environment of high test-based accountability, risk management and aversion, while still maintaining market competitiveness and considering student well-being. The solution to this issue is to fully understand the complementary roles of FA and SA in supporting learning and meeting accountability requirements. This is extensively discussed in Chapter 4.

Additionally, school leaders should acknowledge the importance of understanding the different perspectives of all stakeholders to make successful changes to the assessment culture and system. School leaders need to work with teachers, parents and students to build their assessment literacy to increase their responsibilisation of and engagement in assessment. The alignment of teachers' practices, parents' understanding of assessment and support to their children, and students' accountability of their learning ensures the successful implementation of assessment reforms, leading to meaningful learning experiences and improved student outcomes.

Furthermore, school leaders and the whole school community need to establish a specific timeline for the reform implementation. This chapter allotted a period of 2 years for shifting the assessment culture of the school. Changing or realigning teachers' assessment practices to the reform agenda requires time for learning and unlearning. Targeted professional development activities are needed to support teachers and other key stakeholders in developing their assessment literacy.

Proposed Solutions

Implementing effective assessment practices is a shared responsibility of all stakeholders. Although assessment is planned, designed, implemented and analysed by teachers, the end users of assessment results include students, parents,

148 Engaging Other Key Players in Assessment

community and policy-makers. Also, assessment is not a teacher-centric approach, but individual stakeholders have responsibility and accountability in the overall implementation of assessment (Davison, 2021). However, the responsibility of stakeholders can only be performed if they have the required assessment literacy, which has similarities across but has specific knowledge and skills to each stakeholder group.

To support teachers in implementing effective assessment practices to enhance learning and teaching, policy-makers should develop and implement an assessment framework that will develop a common language across the system. This framework should clearly articulate the intersections of learning, teaching and assessment and shape the curriculum structure and content to allow teachers to implement effective assessment practices. School-level and classroom-level support for teachers should be explicitly articulated within the policy. In this regard, the assessment literacy of policy-makers is critical for articulating a policy that is underpinned by research evidence on effective assessment practices. Without the appropriate assessment knowledge and skills, policy-makers will implement a policy that is not evidence-informed, compromising the positive impact of assessment on learning and teaching. The nature and principles of assessment should be clearly understood to facilitate the legislation of some prerequisites for institutionalising assessment implementation. Once policy-makers clearly understand assessment principles, processes and practices, they can also strategically provide the support needed by schools, teachers, students, parents and the broader community.

The implementation of policy at the school level is largely influenced by school leaders. They interpret the policy, and their views, perceptions, knowledge and skills influence their understanding, consequently shaping their implementation in their respective schools. They filter the provisions in the policy which they think are effective that suit their leadership agenda. Thus, their assessment literacy is needed to understand the policy and develop a whole school approach to develop an assessment culture that supports learning and teaching (Alonzo et al., 2021b). In addition, school leaders need to provide instructional leadership to teachers to guide them in planning and implementing assessment and, later on, evaluating the effectiveness of their practices. Their high level of understanding of effective assessment practices will also positively impact the implementation of policy that ill-defined effective assessment practices. They can develop approaches to implementing the policy without compromising students' learning.

Part of the assessment responsibility of teachers is to work closely with other stakeholders, including students, parents and the community to develop their assessment literacy to perform their individual responsibilities in assessment. This is highlighted in one of the dimensions of teachers' assessment literacy, teachers as stakeholder partners (Alonzo, 2020).

This dimension covers the ability of teachers to work closely with stakeholders to improve their assessment literacy to ensure that their expectations and beliefs are aligned with the school's assessment culture. This is described by Davison (2013) as a critical component for assessment reform within and across school systems. Every assessment reform should have a shared understanding and a common belief system among all stakeholders from the school level, including students, parents and school heads, and across all levels of the education bureaucracy. Indeed, the existence of this factor reinforces the early work of Taylor (2009), who emphasises that part of a teacher's assessment literacy is developing other stakeholders' assessment literacy.

The ability of teachers to work with stakeholders has tremendous impact on supporting students in their learning. Effective communication and ongoing dialogue with stakeholders should be an integral part of teachers' assessment practices. School leaders should provide an avenue for teachers to reach out to stakeholders to understand their responsibility in supporting students and to address their information needs. The continuing dialogue and interactions of teachers with school leaders, parents and the community related to student learning and assessment practices provide avenues for building shared understanding among them. Stakeholders' understanding of the rationale and the theoretical and empirical support for teacher assessment practices ensures that they would support teachers' practices. Also, as part of this dimension, teachers need to consider that each group of stakeholders has different assessment literacy needs because they have different assessment knowledge, assumptions and responsibilities (Popham, 2009). While preparing reports for various stakeholders, teachers need to consider the trustworthiness of the report. All stakeholders need to understand the quality of the information provided and how the report addresses their information needs to build their trust in teachers (Alonzo, 2020; Knight, 2002).

Conclusion

The answer to the title of this chapter is a resounding 'no'. This chapter highlights the critical importance of various stakeholders' assessment literacy in supporting teachers in ensuring effective learning and teaching. Using assessment to support learning and teaching is a shared responsibility and a concerted effort of all stakeholders within schools and across the system. The teacher-centric responsibilisation of assessment is ineffective because individual stakeholders' understanding of assessment, including its principles, processes, practices, and functions, influences teachers' assessment practices that can either support or constrain teacher implementation of assessment. Also, the assessment information needs of stakeholders influence teachers' assessment practices. Teachers' assessment literacy alone is not sufficient to effect effective learning when all other stakeholders are not taking responsibility for their roles. A common assessment language articulated in the policy will guide all stakeholders to develop a shared understanding and beliefs and to guide professional development for policy-makers, school leaders, teachers, parents, students and the broader school community.

150 Engaging Other Key Players in Assessment

References

Adie, L., Addison, B., & Lingard, B. (2021). Assessment and learning: An in-depth analysis of change in one school's assessment culture. *Oxford Review of Education*, *47*(3), 404–422. https://doi.org/10.1080/03054985.2020.1850436

Alonzo, D. (2016). *Development and application of a teacher assessment for learning (AfL) literacy tool*. University of New South Wales]. Sydney. http://unsworks.unsw.edu.au/fapi/datastream/unsworks:38345/SOURCE02?view=true

Alonzo, D. (2020). Teacher education and professional development in industry 4.0: The case for building a strong assessment literacy. In J. P. Ashadi, A. T. Basikin, & N. H. P. S. Putro (Eds.), *Teacher education and professional development in industry 4.0*. Taylor & Francis Group.

Alonzo, D., Labad, V., Bejano, J., & Guerra, F. (2021a). The policy-driven dimensions of teacher beliefs about assessment. *Australian Journal of Teacher Education*, *46*(3). https://ro.ecu.edu.au/cgi/viewcontent.cgi?article=4761&context=ajte

Alonzo, D., Leverett, J., & Obsioma, E. (2021b). Leading an assessment reform: Ensuring a whole-school approach for decision-making. *Frontiers in Education*, *6*(62). https://doi.org/10.3389/feduc.2021.631857

Australian Institute for Teaching and School Leadership. (2011). National professional standards for teachers. https://www.aitsl.edu.au/docs/default-source/default-document-library/aitsl_national_professional_standards_for_teachers

Bennett, R. E. (2011). Formative assessment: A critical review. *Assessment in Education: Principles Policy and Practice*, *18*(1), 5–25.

Davison, C. (2013). Innovation in assessment: Common misconceptions and problems. In K. Hyland & L. Wong (Eds.), *Innovation and change in English language education* (pp. 263–275). Routledge.

Davison, C. (2021). Enhancing teacher assessment literacy: One approach to improving teacher knowledge and skills in Australia. In X. Zhu & H. Song (Eds.), *Envisioning teaching and learning of teachers for excellence and equity in education* (pp. 33–43). Springer. https://doi.org/10.1007/978-981-16-2802-3_3

Davison, C., & Leung, C. (2009). Current issues in English language teacher-based assessment. *TESOL Quarterly*, *43*(3), 393–415.

Erickson, G., Borger, L., & Olsson, E. (2022). National assessment of foreign languages in Sweden: A multifaceted and collaborative venture. *Language Testing*, *39*(3), 474–493. https://doi.org/10.1177/02655322221075067

Gleeson, J., Klenowski, V., & Looney, A. (2020). Curriculum change in Australia and Ireland: A comparative study of recent reforms. *Journal of Curriculum Studies*, *52*(4), 478–497. https://doi.org/10.1080/00220272.2019.1704064

Knight, P. (2002). Summative assessment in higher education: Practices in disarray. *Studies in Higher Education*, *27*(3), 275–286.

Kremmel, B., & Harding, L. (2020). Towards a comprehensive, empirical model of language assessment literacy across stakeholder groups: Developing the language assessment literacy survey. *Language Assessment Quarterly*, *17*(1), 100–120. https://doi.org/10.1080/15434303.2019.1674855

Lee, M., & Louis, K. S. (2019). Mapping a strong school culture and linking it to sustainable school improvement. *Teaching and Teacher Education*, *81*, 84–96. https://doi.org/10.1016/j.tate.2019.02.001

Lim-Ratnam, C. (2013). Tensions in defining quality pre-school education: The Singapore context. *Educational Review, 65*(4), 416–431. https://doi.org/10.1080/00131911.2012.707641

Ministerial Council on Education, Employment, Training and Youth Affairs. (2008). Melbourne declaration on educational goals for young Australians. https://www.curriculum.edu.au/verve/_resources/National_Declaration_on_the_Educational_Goals_for_Young_Australians.pdf

Ministry of Education Press Release. (2010). PERI Holistic Assessment seminar 2010 – 16 schools share Holistic Assessment practices and resources. http://www.moe.gov.sg/media/press/2010/07/peri-holistic-assessment-seminar.php

Popham, W. J. (2009). Assessment literacy for teachers: Faddish or fundamental? *Theory Into Practice, 48*(1), 4–11. https://doi.org/10.1080/00405840802577536

Pryor, J. (2015). Formative assessment: A success story? In D. Scott & D. Hargreaves (Eds.), *The SAGE handbook of learning* (pp. 207–217). SAGE.

Ratnam-Lim, C. T. L., & Tan, K. H. K. (2015). Large-scale implementation of formative assessment practices in an examination-oriented culture. *Assessment in Education: Principles, Policy & Practice, 22*(1), 61–78. https://doi.org/10.1080/0969594X.2014.1001319

Spillane, J. P., Diamond, J. B., Burch, P., Hallett, T., Jita, L., & Zoltners, J. (2002). Managing in the middle: School leaders and the enactment of accountability policy. *Educational Policy, 16*(5), 731–762. https://doi.org/10.1177/089590402237311

Stipek, D., Milburn, S., Clements, D., & Daniels, D. H. (1992). Parents' beliefs about appropriate education for young children. *Journal of Applied Developmental Psychology, 13*(3), 293–310. https://doi.org/10.1016/0193-3973(92)90034-F

Taylor, L. (2009). Developing assessment literacy. *Annual Review of Applied Linguistics, 29*, 21–36.

Van der Kleij, F. M., Cumming, J. J., & Looney, A. (2018). Policy expectations and support for teacher formative assessment in Australian education reform. *Assessment in Education: Principles, Policy & Practice, 25*(6), 620–637. https://doi.org/10.1080/0969594X.2017.1374924

Yan, Z., & Brown, G. T. L. (2021). Assessment for learning in the Hong Kong assessment reform: A case of policy borrowing. *Studies in Educational Evaluation, 68*, 100985. https://doi.org/10.1016/j.stueduc.2021.100985

Chapter 9

How Do We Decide If Students Are Improving?

Introduction

As already established in the previous chapters, learning is a complex process with multiple outcomes. The relationships between learning and teaching activities and student achievement are not always linear. Thus, there are multiple indirect outcomes (i.e., social-emotional otucomes), which eventually influence student achievement. However, due to the accountability-driven culture, teachers are forced to measure and report students' learning by almost exclusively using test scores or marks. Disregarding other outcomes in the reporting scheme shapes and is shaped by this narrow view of outcomes pertaining only to test cores or marks referred to as 'performance'. Teachers are expected to produce high scores in limited learning and teaching time, at the expense of other positive outcomes. This view is underpinned by a narrow understanding of outcomes that only positions the achievement of knowledge and skills.

Increases in students' scores are often considered as evidence for the effectiveness of any classroom intervention. Often, the desired increased test scores do not manifest after a learning and teaching episode, and the failure to increase the test scores at a certain level suggests that learning and teaching is ineffective. This perception puts pressure on teachers to narrow the focus of the curriculum to teaching discrete knowledge and skills that can easily be learned and measured, with the intention of showing the effectiveness of their teaching. This is one of the backwash effects of assessment due to the limited conceptualisation and error in implementation.

Teachers' use of assessment and assessment data does not always directly impact student achievement. Evidence points out other outcome measures, including an increase in engagement (Alonzo et al., 2023; Hughes, 2014) and motivation (Clark, 2011; Leenknecht et al., 2021), as well as a reduction of classroom management issues (Andrade & Brookhart, 2020). Studies suggest that an increase in these other outcomes will eventually increase student achievement (Hughes, 2014; Martin & Pickett, 2013; Vaessen et al., 2017). While teachers recognise these assessment outcomes as important in the classroom context, these are often ignored at the system level. Recognising these

DOI: 10.4324/9781003396277-9

measures as direct outcomes of using assessment would broaden our understanding of the impacts of assessment, thus limiting the risk of judging the ineffectiveness of learning and teaching when the desired achievement scores are not achieved.

The Problem

In educational discourse, particularly in the context of learning, student outcomes are often used synonymously with student achievement. Thus, when we say an increase in student outcomes, it is often understood as an increase in student scores. However, this is a limited understanding of student outcomes. When using assessment to improve learning and teaching, assessment has direct and indirect effects on students' achievement. More often than not, these indirect effects are mediated by other outcomes that have an impact on improving students' achievement.

Although teachers, school heads and policy-makers are familiar with these 'other' outcomes, they are often ignored in reporting within schools and across the bureaucracy. If these outcomes are not given equal importance to student achievement scores, there is a greater risk of inappropriately using and reporting the outcomes of assessment to support learning and teaching. More broadly, the failure to account for these 'other' outcomes will continue to narrow the understanding of the impact of assessment, shaping the school assessment culture to use summative assessment (SA) to find evidence of increased students' achievement.

The three case studies presented below demonstrate these 'other' outcomes as a result of using assessment and how they subsequently improved students' learning. These outcomes include increased independence and self-regulation, motivation and positive perception of learning, and self-efficacy. The list of outcomes in this chapter is not exhaustive. These outcomes are used only to illustrate that using assessment to support learning and teaching brings about 'other' outcomes apart from academic achievement.

Case 1: Increased independence and self-regulation as outcomes of assessment

Description of the Study

One of the principles of effective assessment practices is an emphasis on developing students' independent learning skills and self-regulation (ARG, 2022). The impact of using assessment on students' independence and self-regulation is demonstrated by the work of DeLuca et al. (2020). The study explored how kindergarten teachers use assessment practices, particularly Assessment as Learning (AaL), to support students' learning within play-based classrooms. As defined, AaL is a form of assessment that focuses on the student's ability to self-regulate and take ownership of their learning. It is based on the idea that assessment should help students understand their learning and progress, rather than simply measure their performance. Implementing AaL approaches requires training students to take responsibility for their learning and to use assessment to inform their subsequent learning decisions and actions.

Data were drawn from 20 kindergarten classrooms through interviews to explore their beliefs on self-regulated learning and assessment in play-based learning contexts. Classroom observations were conducted to see how these beliefs are enacted in their actual practice. Then, video elicitation interviews were conducted with half of the participating teachers. Data analyses show that kindergarten teachers are successfully leveraging assessment practices to support students' learning within play-based classrooms. Teachers demonstrate how they promote students' self-regulation and independence to meet early school success. A focus on AaL and self-regulation is the key factor in bridging the gap between standards-based education and assessment mandates with play pedagogies, helping diminish any divide between these two priorities. Another notable finding is the impact of teachers' views of students on their assessment practices. Teachers who view their students as active agents in their classroom have an open conversation with them about their learning and how they can develop their skills further. They provide the space for dialogue and give explicit feedback, helping students achieve better outcomes.

Problem Being Addressed

The two main priorities of kindergarten education are perceived to be counter-related. The first priority is recognising that early learning must maintain a developmental orientation and support socio-personal growth. Kindergarten education should focus on helping children develop their skills and abilities and their social and personal growth. The second priority is a growing emphasis on standards-based curriculum and the use of assessment to support students' learning. This means that kindergarten education should focus on teaching younger students the skills and knowledge they need to meet certain standards and using assessment to measure their progress. Some researchers argue that these two priorities are in opposition to each other due to the influence of accountability-driven culture. The greater emphasis on students' academic achievement narrows teaching practices to teaching prescribed learning outcomes focused on increasing their academic knowledge and skills. The value placed on these outcomes ignores the social and personal growth of kindergarten. The work of DeLuca et al. (2020) demonstrates how these two main priorities can be met using play-based activities to teach children the skills and knowledge they need to meet certain standards while also helping them develop their skills and abilities and their social and personal growth.

Factors Influencing the Problem

There are factors identified that influence the use of assessment in kindergarten to meet the two priorities:

1 *Teachers' practices.*
   The research found that many teachers maintained a level of distance between their students and their assessment practices, collecting data but refraining from discussing it directly with students. Also, some teachers explicitly expressed their discomfort at the idea of sharing an assessment process with students, which may explain the broader tendency towards assessment privacy.
2 *Teacher prioritisation of assessment processes.*
   The authors found that more than half of the teachers felt overwhelmed by the amount of digital data they had to collect and analyse. They are spending a lot of time collecting and analysing data, which was taking away from the time they could spend having conversations, connecting with students and helping them learn. Teachers had to analyse data outside of instructional time, which had substantial workload implications.
3 *Data analysis skills.*
   In addition to the overabundance of assessment data, teachers' capacity to meaningfully analyse all the data to make timely adjustments to instruction influences the effectiveness of assessment. Teachers prioritise collecting data primarily for reporting purposes to justify the learning occurring in the classroom during formal reporting cycles. This priority is understandable given the increased emphasis on evidence-based decision-making and reporting, which is a characteristic of the standards-based and accountability paradigm of public education. This paradigm is believed to ensure that students meet the educational system's standards.
4 *Tensions between formative and SAs.*
   The emphasis on evidence-based decision-making and reporting displaces some teachers' primary focus in ongoing assessment, from

working directly with students to externally assessing students. The accountability-driven assessment culture shapes teachers' assessment practices, using more SAs and external tests to measure students' learning to meet the information needs of policy-makers.

5 *The teacher perceived inappropriateness of assessment.*

Some teachers expressed their concerns regarding the effectiveness of a developmental approach to assessment in producing adequate academic skills. The teachers were apprehensive about parents' perception, as they felt that parents were more concerned with whether their children were ready for Grade 1 than with the developmental approach. This tug-of-war between academic preparation and a developmental approach led to challenging assessment situations for the teachers. The developmental approach to assessment, focusing on the development of the student's skills and abilities rather than on academic performance, is often used in early childhood education, as it is believed to be more beneficial for the child's overall development. Teachers were concerned that this approach might not be sufficient to prepare the students for Grade 1 to meet parents' expectations.

6 *Teachers' inappropriate use of assessment.*

Some assessment practices, such as digital recording, can reduce the opportunity for students to develop self-regulated learning. When teachers focus on documentation to the exclusion of their interactions with students, the assessment can reduce the opportunity for the development of self-regulated learning. This happens because the teacher cannot share eye contact, sustained attention or conversation with students. Additionally, digital recording can reduce students' opportunities for reflection and use of language.

7 *Insufficient time for assessment.*

When teachers are especially busy, trying to move a student quickly towards accomplishing a task, or when faced with complex undesired behaviour, they sometimes engage in feedback designed to yield quick results rather than work towards a more self-regulated response. This type of feedback can be seen to replace that which notices and names evidence of desired performance, thus distancing students from the information they might use in subsequent self-regulation. It de-emphasises student agency and replaces it with an emphasis on teachers' questions, thinking and priorities.

8 *The use of appropriate assessment practices.*

Teachers' use of AaL as a pedagogical approach involves them sharing an understanding of learning with students and helping them to develop their metacognitive awareness and self-regulated learning. Teachers discussed the importance of helping students to know themselves and the importance of student reflection. This suggests that AaL can be used to bridge the divide between the two priorities of kindergarten education: a developmental orientation and socio-personal growth and standards-based curriculum and assessment.

Implications of the Problem

The study highlights that assessment can be used to develop students' self-regulation while increasing their academic achievement. The appropriate use and implementation of assessment can potentially bridge the divide between developmental orientation and standards-based curriculum in early childhood education.

The findings from this study could be used to inform teacher training programs. School leaders should explore teachers' assessment literacy and identify their specific professional development needs. Ensuring that teachers have positive dispositions, assessment knowledge and skills would result in the proper implementation of assessment to support learning and teaching. Teachers' assessment literacy helps them achieve the balance between the accountability and developmental functions of assessment.

Also, teachers with a deeper understanding and positive beliefs about how assessment can be an important resources. They can be asked to support other teachers to implement assessment activities that support the development of students' self-regulation and independence to achieve outcomes.

In addition, the results of this study can be used to inform policy initiatives related to using assessment to improve educational outcomes for younger students. Many researchers highlight the role of policy in shaping teachers' assessment practices. When the policy constrains their practices, teachers tend to adhere to practices that meet the policy requirement even if those practices are known by them to impact students' learning negatively. This study demonstrated that the prominence of the accountability system in the policy continues to leverage the tensions between the use of formative and SAs, and teachers have a strong inclination to implement SAs and high-stake tests to gather evidence for reporting and accountability.

Moreover, there is a need to review teachers' workload when a new assessment reform is implemented. Teachers will continue to resist using effective assessment strategies if they need to spend more time outside their allocated work time to achieve the desired outcomes. Policy articulation should account for the hours teachers need to implement any intervention. In addition, there is a need to review the curriculum structure and content. When the curriculum is rigid, and teachers are expected to complete the specified content, they tend to rush the process to complete the prescribed content at the risk of missing learning gains. Teachers must also be supported in implementing curriculum content against the backdrop of new assessment reform. A change in policy without changing the fundamental structure and content of the curriculum and providing support for teachers to enact the curriculum within the policy context will not result in a change in practice. Thus, limited positive outcomes may be observed.

Furthermore, there is also a conceptual change that needs to happen. Unless the tension between FA and SA is resolved, teachers will continue to prioritise the use of SA to gather evidence and report student learning (see Chapter 3 for SA and FA debate). SA produces numerical values denoting student outcomes, whereas some FAs do not produce 'numbers' that the system values. The high importance given to achieving learning outcomes, understood as marks, narrows teachers' assessment practice. It intensifies the view that SA gives a more accurate and consistent measure of students' learning, which undermines teachers' assessment practices. They lose their confidence in their ability and efficacy in implementing assessment practices that they know would support students in their learning.

Thus, we need a holistic approach to building a strong assessment culture in schools. The policy, practice, curriculum, workload, teacher skills and parents' expectations should be aligned with the principles of effective assessment practices which require a holistic understanding of learning outcomes.

Case 2: Increased student positive perception of learning as an outcome of assessment

Description of the Study

This case study shows how assessment helps students to increase their motivation and perception of learning as well as achieve the learning outcomes. Tapingkae et al. (2020) integrate digital game-based learning and formative assessment (FA) to help students understand the importance of digital citizenship and make better decisions when using computer and communication technologies. The study was conducted in northern Thailand with 115 seventh and eighth graders (12–14-year-old). The students were divided into two groups: the experimental group received digital citizenship learning activities with an FA-based contextual digital gaming approach. In contrast, the control group completed the digital citizenship learning activities with the conventional learning approach. Students completed a 10-minute pre-digital citizenship questionnaire to evaluate prior practices of digital citizenship. Then, over 10 minutes, the teacher introduced the basic knowledge of digital citizenship and the overall learning goals and activities. Afterwards, over four days (a total of 160 minutes), students in the experimental group learned digital citizenship with the FA-based contextual digital gaming approach as the in-class learning activity with the teacher as facilitator. In contrast, those in the control group learned digital citizenship with the conventional learning approach, with the teacher providing a chalk-and-talk learning activity and feedback. Both groups of students completed a similar worksheet after the learning activities. Students then took a post-digital citizenship questionnaire to evaluate their score of digital citizenship and filled out the learning motivation and perception questionnaires. The score of digital citizenship of the two groups was compared based on their pre- and post-digital citizenship behaviours. Learning motivations and perceptions of the learning approach were also analysed and compared. The results of this chapter indicate that the FA-based contextual gaming approach was effective in enhancing students' digital citizenship behaviours, as well as enhancing their motivations and perceptions.

Problem Being Addressed

Previous studies have indicated that students face problems in digital situations and lack opportunities to make decisions. In the conventional-lecture strategy, teachers directly deliver content to students and ask them to discuss the situations concerning behaviour using computer and communication technologies. During the discussion, teachers provide students with feedback. However, scholars have pointed out several problems with this approach, including low learning motivation and interest and the lack of sufficient opportunities and guidance to promote students' higher order thinking. This lack of opportunities and guidance makes it difficult to provide digital citizenship learning activities that empower students to think critically, practice good decision-making, behave safely and participate responsibly in daily digital life situations. This has posed a challenge in promoting digital citizenship.

Factors Influencing the Problem

There are several factors influencing the problem. These include:

1 *Authenticity and interactivity.*

The importance of providing students with authentic and interactive contexts to help them link what they have learned to what they are experiencing. This means that students should be given the opportunity to apply their knowledge in real-world situations, as this will help them to understand better the concepts they have learned and to make connections between them. This is particularly important when it comes to digital citizenship because it is essential for students to make informed decisions and understand the implications of their actions.

2 *The challenge for providing immediate feedback during interactive activities.*

It is important to provide students with guidance to assist and monitor their learning. In a constrained learning environment, providing individual feedback to students is impossible, particularly in large classes. Feedback is valued by students and the lack thereof misses the opportunity to further support students in their learning.

3 *Assessment design.*

Designing an assessment activity should not only focus on achieving the pre-determined learning outcomes, the knowledge and skills valued by the system. Assessment design should tap on how to enhance students' interest and motivation to engage in their learning. Due to the emotional impact of assessment, there is a higher tendency for students to dislike assessment activities if they find them irrelevant.

4 *The overall learning and teaching design.*

In the study above, the relationships between learning, assessment and technology produce the learning pathways that produced the desired outcomes. Designing digital learning and teaching activities with embedded assessment activities requires a high technical expertise. Most often, this is outside the capability of teachers, and hence, computer programmers are needed to help teachers build such system. This case highlights the need for teacher support in designing assessment activities that support teacher enactment of their pedagogical content knowledge.

Implications of the Problem

This study demonstrates that the intersections between assessment and learning, gamification, and teaching design improve student behaviour, motivation and perception towards digital citizenship, which consequently increased student knowledge and skills. What is shown is that assessment activities directly enhanced the social-emotional attributes of students, which positively influenced their learning gains. Thus, the pathway for increasing student learning is not always straightforward but takes a complex system of direct and indirect effects, following multiple paths. One way that is uncertain is how long the indirect effects of assessment to student outcomes can be observed. This uncertainty has an implication in terms of measuring student achievement and using the data to evaluate learning and teaching effectiveness. The students' achievement may just be a fraction of the actual outcomes of assessment.

The results of this study imply that assessment and learning and teaching activities should be designed to enhance the social-emotional attributes. As shown, tapping on the social-emotional attributes of students increased their learning gains as compared to those students with no FA embedded in the learning unit. It was demonstrated that the assessment design leveraged the effectiveness of the intersections between content knowledge and pedagogical content knowledge in meeting the desired outcomes. Thus, teachers should be supported in designing effective learning, teaching and assessment activities. But more importantly, other outcomes for using assessment should be acknowledged and used to report the effectiveness of assessment.

Case 3: Increased student academic achievement and self-efficacy as outcomes of assessment

Description of the Study

Student' ability to engage with assessment task with minimal supervision is a critical factor for their success. One of the outcomes of assessment is increased student self-efficacy. Yan et al. (2020) used self-assessment diaries as a low-cost intervention to help students improve their learning in Hong Kong. The study examined the effects of such an intervention on students' academic achievement (M_{age} = 12.2 years), self-regulation and motivation by comparing two groups: one with access to a standardised diary system for assessing progress in studies or homework assignments (experimental group) and another without it (control group). Difference-in-differences analyses were used to measure any changes between these two groups before and after implementing the interventions.

Results show that self-assessment diaries increased students' self-efficacy and intrinsic value among students. The researchers argued that this assessment activity might have increased students' mastery experience and influenced their self-efficacy. In addition, they have argued that the increase in student intrinsic value will subsequently enhance their competence and self-awareness. Engaging students in self-assessment activities enables them to monitor their learning progress. This self-awareness of progress may also enhance their engagement and enjoyment of learning. They also noted that students with lower past achievements benefit more from this intervention. Overall, this study shows that engaging students in self-assessment directly enhances their motivational and affective processes, indirectly influencing their learning achievement. The researchers concluded that this result was consistent with the findings of Sitzmann et al. (2010) that self-assessment is strongly linked to improved motivational outcomes than cognitive outcomes.

Problem Being Addressed

As argued, the use of assessment should enhance student outcomes. Any assessment activity that does not bring any significant improvement must not be used. Also, there is an issue regarding the time required to complete some assessment tasks. Given that the curriculum is highly constrained with targets to complete specified content, teachers can hardly use a range of assessment activities within class time to optimise student learning.

This study demonstrated the use of self-assessment diaries after completing each homework assignment designed to help students reflect on their work and identify any weaknesses or areas for improvement. Teachers encouraged students to act on the self-assessment information to close the self-feedback loop. This could include addressing any weaknesses identified in the self-assessment diary or implementing strategies proposed from the previous assignment. The process of self-assessment has multiple social-emotional outcomes that have eventually increased student performance.

Factors Influencing the Problem

The effectiveness of using self-assessment is influenced by many factors. In this study, the following factors influence it:

1 *Time required for engaging students in self-assessment.*
   Teacher-led student self-assessment requires time for students to complete it in the classroom. This deters teachers from engaging

students in self-assessment, particularly if they have to cover a large amount of content within the specified teaching term.

2 *Teacher preparation and effort.*

Teachers should set up the classroom for self-assessment and monitor students while engaging in the process. With the competing workload, the amount of preparation and effort is overwhelming for some teachers.

3 *Design of self-assessment.*

The lack of explicit instruction and support for self-assessment does not increase students' effort regulation. With the intent to minimise teachers' workload, the use of rubrics and teacher feedback are not included as part of the self-assessment process. Many studies show that the effectiveness of self-assessment is enhanced when the results of students' assessments are validated by teachers' feedback.

4 *Student motivation.*

Students have varying levels of motivation and hence engagement in self-assessment. Some students have positive views on using self-assessment, while others are bored with it. This implies the need for a differentiated approach for using self-assessment.

5 *Influence of knowledge tradition.*

Students perceived self-assessment activities as useful for some key learning areas but not others. However, there is no consensus on which subjects the self-assessment is useful.

6 *Students' knowledge of self-assessment.*

They need to understand the principles, purpose, process and benefits of self-assessment to develop a positive disposition, leading to their active engagement.

Implications of the Problem

This study shows that engaging students in self-assessment directly enhances their motivational and affective processes, indirectly influencing their learning achievement. Teachers' broader understanding of the indirect outcomes of self-assessment may help them to develop positive dispositions to design and implement a more realistic and manageable approach. When the implementation of assessment activity is focused on raising student achievement, other outcomes are seen as negligible when, in fact, they are mediating the effects of assessment on student achievement.

Besides recognising these outcomes, teachers should also explore ways to measure them and monitor if students' motivational and affective processes are increasing. There are readily available tools that have been established to be reliable and valid. The use of these tools can help teachers monitor students' overall learning. When motivational and affective factors are developed, students will have better engagement, motivation and self-efficacy, which are all linked to positive student outcomes.

Proposed Solutions

As shown in the three case studies, using and engaging students in assessment results in other outcomes apart from increased achievement. There are non-cognitive outcomes that have direct or indirect effects on increasing students' learning. There is strong theoretical and empirical support for the link between social-emotional outcomes and students' achievement (Bostwick et al., 2019; Collie, 2022; Holliman et al., 2019). These outcomes are an integral part of the educative process and, thus, should be recognised as learning gains.

In the context of assessment, evaluating the effectiveness of teacher assessment activities and reporting student outcomes should include these other outcomes. Apart from those outcomes reported in the three case studies presented, there are other outcomes reported in many studies. Assessment activities, for example, eliciting and giving feedback, could increase student educational resilience and belongingness and can reduce academic procrastination (Dong & Izadpanah, 2022). Also, using different assessment strategies is positively linked to a growth mindset, and the synergy of both enhances academic achievement (Yan et al., 2021). In addition, group-dynamic assessment can increase students' intrinsic motivation, which causes students to deeply engage in learning and teaching activities and develop a sustained passion for learning (Azizi & Farid Khafaga, 2023; Ting-Chia et al., 2023). In addition, assessment activities, like peer assessment, have been shown to increase students' engagement and well-being, reducing their stress while increasing their motivation and critical thinking, resulting to higher performance (Chien et al., 2020).

Given the importance of these other outcomes and the way assessment influences them, they should be clearly part of the discourse on using assessment to increase student achievement. At the system level, a more explicit definition of learning outcomes would formalise these 'other' outcomes of using assessment to support learning. When clearly articulated in the policy, these outcomes would broaden the focus of teachers' assessment practices, promoting a more balanced and comprehensive approach to learning, teaching and assessment. The broad representation of outcomes in the policy will shape discourses around effectiveness of assessment and teacher practices. Recognising these social-emotional outcomes as a result of using assessment will shape policy support and the overall system-level expectations on student improvement. Consequently, teachers will not be forced to 'teach to the test' in an attempt to increase students' achievement scores. Rather, their emphasis on

Recognising Other Outcomes of Assessment   165

using assessment would be to achieve broader learning outcomes, leading to increased students' achievement.

A review of the principles of effective assessment practices will highlight the intersections between assessment and social-emotional and behavioural attributes. The Assessment Reform Group (ARG, 2002) clearly articulates two principles that relate to this:

1 *Assessment should take account of the importance of learner motivation.*

Assessment that encourages learning fosters motivation by emphasising progress and achievement rather than failure. Comparison with others who have been more successful is unlikely to motivate learners. It can also lead to their withdrawing from the learning process in areas where they have been made to feel they are 'no good'. Motivation can be preserved and enhanced by assessment methods which protect the learner's autonomy, provide some choice and constructive feedback and create opportunity for self-direction.

2 *Assessment for learning should be sensitive and constructive because any assessment has an emotional impact.*

Teachers should be aware of the impact that comments, marks and grades can have on learners' confidence and enthusiasm and should be as constructive as possible in the feedbacks that they give. Comments that focus on the work rather than the person are more constructive for both learning and motivation (p. 2).

These two principles highlight that assessment can influence students' dispositions of their learning, which can shape their ability to learn and the belief that they can succeed even with challenging assessment tasks. The recognition of the influence of assessment on students' motivation can help them to embrace the complex nature of learning, including the recognition of mistakes as art of the learning journey, the role of trial-and-error and the importance of managing their emotional response to assessment.

The clarity and recognition of these outcomes are aligned with the true purpose of education, which is the holistic development of every student. As argued in DeLuca et al. (2020), education must maintain a developmental orientation and support socio-personal growth. This is true across stages of schooling, including university students (Elmi, 2020; Martin et al., 2023), and is not exclusive to younger students. Supporting students to develop their social and personal growth is also linked to increased resilience (Herbers et al., 2021), reduced dropout rates (Reschly, 2020; Samuel & Burger, 2020), improved classroom behaviour (Fredrick et al., 2022; Trigueros et al., 2020) and positive self-concept (Casino-García et al., 2021; Papadopoulos, 2021). Given these positive impacts, the 'other' outcomes of using assessment should be recognised and given equal importance and value in academic discussion and reporting student outcomes.

Thus, given the research evidence highlighting the various outcomes of engaging students in assessment, we can propose a broader definition of assessment outcomes to refer to increased student achievement and other social-emotional and behavioural outcomes that have direct effects or indirect effects on increasing students' learning. This definition does not put primacy to student's scores or marks as the most important measure of the effectiveness of assessment in supporting learning and teaching.

Conclusion

This chapter presents an answer to the question of how we decide if students are improving. As argued, one of the common criticisms of assessment is its narrow focus on measuring discrete content knowledge and skills without putting equal importance on other outcomes, particularly social-emotional and behavioural outcomes. The three case studies highlighted that engaging students in assessment enhances their social-emotional outcomes. These outcomes include increased motivation, engagement, autonomy, growth mindset, reduction in classroom management issues, positive self-concept and many others. These social-emotional and behavioural outcomes are strongly linked to increased student achievement. Thus, it is important to expand our understanding of assessment outcomes to recognise research evidence relating to the relationships of many factors that improve students' achievement. This holistic understanding of assessment outcomes will build an assessment culture that promotes the holistic development of students.

References

Alonzo, D., Oo, C. Z., Wijarwadi, W., & Hannigan, C. (2023). Using social media for assessment purposes: Practices and future directions. *Frontiers in Psychology, 13.* https://doi.org/10.3389/fpsyg.2022.1075818

Andrade, H. L., & Brookhart, S. M. (2020). Classroom assessment as the co-regulation of learning. *Assessment in Education: Principles, Policy & Practice, 27*(4), 350–372. https://doi.org/10.1080/0969594X.2019.1571992

ARG. (2002). *Assessment for learning: 10 principles.* https://www.storre.stir.ac.uk/bitstream/1893/32458/1/Assessment%20for%20learning%2010%20principles%202002.pdf

Azizi, Z., & Farid Khafaga, A. (2023). Scaffolding via group-dynamic assessment to positively affect motivation, learning anxiety, and willingness to communicate: A case study of high school students. *Journal of Psycholinguistic Research, 52*(3), 831–851. https://doi.org/10.1007/s10936-023-09935-6

Bostwick, K. C. P., Martin, A. J., Collie, R. J., & Durksen, T. L. (2019). Growth orientation predicts gains in middle and high school students' mathematics outcomes over time. *Contemporary Educational Psychology, 58,* 213–227. https://doi.org/10.1016/j.cedpsych.2019.03.010

Casino-García, A. M., Llopis-Bueno, M. J., & Llinares-Insa, L. I. (2021). Emotional intelligence profiles and self-esteem/self-concept: An analysis of relationships in gifted students. *International Journal of Environmental Research and Public Health*, *18*(3), 1006. https://www.mdpi.com/1660-4601/18/3/1006

Chien, S.-Y., Hwang, G.-J., & Jong, M. S.-Y. (2020). Effects of peer assessment within the context of spherical video-based virtual reality on EFL students' English-speaking performance and learning perceptions. *Computers & Education*, *146*, 103751. https://doi.org/10.1016/j.compedu.2019.103751

Clark, I. (2011). Formative assessment and motivation: Theories and themes. *Prime Research on Education*, *1*(2), 26–36.

Collie, R. J. (2022). Instructional support, perceived social-emotional competence, and students' behavioral and emotional well-being outcomes. *Educational Psychology*, *42*(1), 4–22. https://doi.org/10.1080/01443410.2021.1994127

DeLuca, C., Pyle, A., Braund, H., & Faith, L. (2020). Leveraging assessment to promote kindergarten learners' independence and self-regulation within play-based classrooms. *Assessment in Education: Principles, Policy & Practice*, *27*(4), 394–415. https://doi.org/10.1080/0969594X.2020.1719033

Dong, Y., & Izadpanah, S. (2022). The effect of corrective feedback from female teachers on formative assessments: Educational resilience, Educational belongingness, and academic procrastination in an English language course. *Current Psychology*. https://doi.org/10.1007/s12144-022-03825-1

Elmi, C. (2020). Integrating social emotional learning strategies in higher education. *European Journal of Investigation in Health, Psychology and Education*, *10*(3), 848–858. https://www.mdpi.com/2254-9625/10/3/61

Fredrick, S. S., Traudt, S., & Nickerson, A. B. (2022). *Social emotional learning practices in schools and bullying prevention*. Routledge. https://doi.org/10.4324/9781138609877-REE171-1

Herbers, J. E., Hayes, K. R., & Cutuli, J. J. (2021). Adaptive systems for student resilience in the context of COVID-19. *School Psychology*, *36*, 422–426. https://doi.org/10.1037/spq0000471

Holliman, A. J., Sheriston, L., Martin, A. J., Collie, R. J., & Sayer, D. (2019). Adaptability: Does students' adjustment to university predict their mid-course academic achievement and satisfaction? *Journal of Further and Higher Education*, *43*(10), 1444–1455. https://doi.org/10.1080/0309877X.2018.1491957

Hughes, C. (2014). Improving student engagement and development through assessment: Theory and practice in higher education. *Higher Education Research & Development*, *33*(1), 176–177. https://doi.org/10.1080/07294360.2013.783954

Leenknecht, M., Wijnia, L., Köhlen, M., Fryer, L., Rikers, R., & Loyens, S. (2021). Formative assessment as practice: The role of students' motivation. *Assessment & Evaluation in Higher Education*, *46*(2), 236–255. https://doi.org/10.1080/02602938.2020.1765228

Martin, M. R., & Pickett, M. T. (2013). *The effects of differentiated instruction on motivation and engagement in fifth-grade gifted math and music students*. Saint Xavier University.

Martin, A. J., Ginns, P., & Collie, R. J. (2023). University students in COVID-19 lockdown: The role of adaptability and fluid reasoning in supporting their academic motivation and engagement. *Learning and Instruction*, *83*, 101712. https://doi.org/10.1016/j.learninstruc.2022.101712

Papadopoulos, D. (2021). Examining the relationships among cognitive ability, domain-specific self-concept, and behavioral self-esteem of gifted children aged 5–6 years: A cross-sectional study. *Behavioral Sciences*, *11*(7), 93. https://www.mdpi.com/2076-328X/11/7/93

Reschly, A. L. (2020). Dropout prevention and student engagement. In A. L. Reschly, A. J. Pohl, & S. L. Christenson (Eds.), *Student engagement: Effective academic, behavioral, cognitive, and affective interventions at school* (pp. 31–54). Springer International Publishing. https://doi.org/10.1007/978-3-030-37285-9_2

Samuel, R., & Burger, K. (2020). Negative life events, self-efficacy, and social support: Risk and protective factors for school dropout intentions and dropout. *Journal of Educational Psychology*, *112*, 973–986. https://doi.org/10.1037/edu0000406

Sitzmann, T., Ely, K., Brown, K. G., & Bauer, K. N. (2010). Self-assessment of knowledge: A cognitive learning or affective measure? *Academy of Management Learning & Education*, *9*(2), 169–191. http://www.jstor.org/stable/25682447

Tapingkae, P., Panjaburee, P., Hwang, G.-J., & Srisawasdi, N. (2020). Effects of a formative assessment-based contextual gaming approach on students' digital citizenship behaviours, learning motivations, and perceptions. *Computers & Education*, *159*, 103998. https://doi.org/10.1016/j.compedu.2020.103998

Ting-Chia, H., Wen-Li, C., & Hwang, G.-J. (2023). Impacts of interactions between peer assessment and learning styles on students' mobile learning achievements and motivations in vocational design certification courses. *Interactive Learning Environments*, *31*(3), 1351–1363. https://doi.org/10.1080/10494820.2020.1833351

Trigueros, R., Sanchez-Sanchez, E., Mercader, I., Aguilar-Parra, J. M., López-Liria, R., Morales-Gázquez, M. J., Fernández-Campoy, J. M., & Rocamora, P. (2020). Relationship between emotional intelligence, social skills and Peer harassment. A study with high school students. *International Journal of Environmental Research and Public Health*, *17*(12), 4208. https://www.mdpi.com/1660-4601/17/12/4208

Vaessen, B. E., van den Beemt, A., van de Watering, G., van Meeuwen, L. W., Lemmens, L., & den Brok, P. (2017). Students' perception of frequent assessments and its relation to motivation and grades in A statistics course: A pilot study. *Assessment & Evaluation in Higher Education*, *42*(6), 872–886. https://doi.org/10.1080/02602938.2016.1204532

Yan, Z., Chiu, M. M., & Ko, P. Y. (2020). Effects of self-assessment diaries on academic achievement, self-regulation, and motivation. *Assessment in Education: Principles, Policy & Practice*, *27*(5), 562–583. https://doi.org/10.1080/0969594X.2020.1827221

Yan, Z., King, R. B., & Haw, J. Y. (2021). Formative assessment, growth mindset, and achievement: Examining their relations in the East and the West. *Assessment in Education: Principles, Policy & Practice*, *28*(5–6), 676–702. https://doi.org/10.1080/0969594X.2021.1988510

Chapter 10

How Do We Know When Teachers Are Doing It Right?

Introduction

Researchers and educators argue that to support teachers in developing a high level of assessment literacy, an assessment literacy program should be congruent with the philosophy of effective assessment practices (Davison, 2013). It must begin with describing individual teachers' current assessment literacy levels and then identifying their specific training and support needs. To perform these processes, a teacher assessment literacy framework should be used both as a performance evaluation and professional development tool. There have been numerous attempts to develop and use tests, rating scales and other forms of assessments to evaluate teacher assessment literacy. The problem with existing teacher assessment frameworks is that they are not aligned with the principles of effective assessment practices and are detached from the school context. Due to misalignment with assessment principles, there is a need to develop a teacher assessment literacy tool underpinned by a strong theoretical rationale and robust empirical evidence. The assessment literacy framework should give confidence to the users, particularly teachers in their self-assessment and school leaders in their periodic monitoring of teacher performance so that meaningful information about individual teachers' level of assessment literacy can be provided across the stages of their professional development. Furthermore, the same should be used to identify individual teachers' assessment literacy needs to develop a needs-based professional development program to further support and advance their assessment literacy.

Many frameworks are recommended for building teachers' assessment literacy, but a context-driven framework for evaluating assessment literacy is needed (Alonzo et al., 2021a). A useful framework considers policy and contextual factors to support teachers in building their assessment literacy effectively. Just like students' learning, teachers' assessment practices need to be assessed to gain significant insights into what knowledge and skills they need to further develop and what support they need. Several frameworks or models for teacher assessment literacy have been developed and recommended for use by several authors, either for mainstream education or specific fields. These models can

DOI: 10.4324/9781003396277-10

be categorically identified based on their uses and application. Some are descriptive and are useful guides for teachers' classroom practices (e.g. Brookhart et al., 2006; Cowie & Bell, 1999; Harlen, 2007), while others are prescriptive and more suitable for the evaluation of teacher assessment literacy for professional development (Harlen, 2007); and one is a specific framework for researching teacher assessment practices (Hill & McNamara, 2012).

Descriptive Frameworks and Models

Descriptive frameworks and models not only describe the assessment knowledge and skills that teachers need but they describe different kinds of practices. For example, the model presented by Cowie and Bell (1999), which was generated from their two-year study of science classrooms involving 10 teachers of students in Years 7–10, revealed from their 128 classroom observations throughout the research period that teachers were using two types of formative assessment. Teachers engage in either planned or interactive formative assessment. The former happens when teachers use pre-planned assessment tasks to elicit students' performances. Teachers then interpret these performances and act according to the purpose of the assessment. On the other hand, interactive formative assessment is what Davison (2007) calls 'in-class contingent formative assessment', which happens when teachers respond to assessment opportunities during learning interactions. Although the model presented by Cowie and Bell (1999) is useful in accounting for two different types of formative assessment, this model is insufficient to describe all assessment activities that have the potential to further support student learning.

The typology of teacher assessment practices developed by Davison (2007) adds to Cowie and Bell's model by incorporating two types of more formal assessments that teachers might use for classroom assessment, that is, (1) more formal mock or trial assessment modelled on summative assessments but used for formative purposes that are focused to determining the gap between students' current performance and the desired performance; and (2) prescribed summative assessments, but where the results are also used formatively to guide future teaching and learning focused mainly on determining what the students have achieved in relation to the standards and what the students need to do in their future learning. In Davison's model, all four assessment types are placed on a continuum rather than taking the formative and summative assessment as a dichotomy of practice.

Another model, which is descriptive by nature, is the time dimension framework of Harlen (2007). This model clearly shows the interaction between formative and summative assessments, supporting the conceptualisation that the distinction between formative and summative assessments becomes irrelevant when conceptualised within a broader model of pedagogy. In this model, Harlen argues that a cycle of formative assessment occurs in every episode of learning and teaching activity across the entire course duration. The range of evidence collected is used to help students achieve the specific lesson goals of the following learning episode. In addition, this collected evidence can be used to report the overall achievement of the students to satisfy the summative report. This model looks at the longitudinal relationship between formative and summative assessments and puts summative assessment at the end. This shows only the linear relationship between formative and summative assessments, where summative assessment is at the terminal end of the spectrum of assessment activities. However, in reality, summative assessment can be administered at any period of learning and teaching. It has been widely argued that the results gathered in summative assessment can also be used for formative purposes (Davison, 2007; Taras, 2009). In fact, according to Biggs (1999), formative assessment starts with a summative assessment where feedback given to students is based on the assessment conducted by the teacher, which is summative by nature.

Prescriptive Frameworks and Models

Prescriptive frameworks and models provide more details about the 'what and how' of teacher assessment practices, which teachers can use to reflect on their practices and provide dialogic feedback between school leaders and teachers. For example, the model of Wiliam and Thompson (2008), which captures both Cowie and Bell and Harlen models described above, uses the three key purposes of instructional processes embedded in the definition of assessment for learning (AfL) by the Assessment Reform Group (2002).

This model shows the roles of teacher and students in ensuring the achievement of learning outcomes. The model provides clarity and ways to operationalise the definition of AfL. However, just like the previous models described, it does not account for other factors that affect assessment and student learning. This is similar to the framework developed by Harlen (2007), which specifies seven components and their corresponding key concepts and describes the assessment system by which teachers operate. Although this model covers a wide range of assessment knowledge and skills, the interactions of various assessment skills are not established. It appears that teachers' individual assessment skills operate in isolation.

Other models view teacher assessment practices within the broader context in which assessment occurs. For example, the model proposed by Brookhart et al. (2006), founded on Brookhart (1997) earlier model of classroom assessment, is relatively comprehensive. It retains the original components of the older model, such as the causal relationship amongst teacher assessment practices, student effort and student learning. However, it adds the function of student motivation (the desire to do something) as directly affecting the level of students' effort exerted to complete the task. Another feature of this model, as opposed to the earlier version, is the expansion of teacher assessment practices to what it refers to as the unique 'classroom assessment environment'. Hence, every assessment experience is different from the rest because of the

172 Knowing When Teachers Are Doing It Right

concept of context-dependent assessment experiences. This classroom assessment framework explains the multifaceted nature of student learning, where several interrelated factors drive students to either engage or withdraw from their learning. These factors could either result from assessment activities or drive the assessment activities per se.

A more comprehensive prescriptive model is developed by Davison (2008) and adopted in Singapore schools. The model demonstrates a step-by-step process from planning assessment, collecting information and making a professional judgement to provide appropriate feedback or advice to help students achieve the learning outcomes. Each stage in Davison's model has suggested assessment strategies or activities. This model can be used either to guide teachers' assessment practices or as a tool for professional development. However, the ability of teachers to reflect on their assessment and teaching experiences and identify their professional needs both in terms of content and assessment skills is not included in this model, even though it is widely acknowledged that it is the most effective method to increase levels of teacher assessment literacy. In turn, the increase in teacher assessment literacy brought about by engagement in professional development, either formal or informal, contributes significantly to improving student learning.

A Research-based Model

One specific model of AfL literacy was intentionally developed to guide researching classroom assessment. The framework proposed by Hill and McNamara (2012) can be used to evaluate existing assessment practices. It covers the various aspects of assessment practices, including planning and actual assessment conduct, the assessment constructs (enterprises, qualities and standards) available, the theoretical and epistemological bases for teacher assessment practices, and students' beliefs and understanding of assessment processes. The questions provided in the framework are useful guides for eliciting responses to gather detailed information about assessment practices in the classroom. Apart from its use in researching assessment practices, the framework can be used as a checklist for teachers to reflect on their assessment practices. However, the framework lacks the other factors that are described by Brookhart et al. (2006) that affect student engagement in their learning. The model of Hill and McNamara, if used to guide practices and for professional development, may make teachers think that assessment can be isolated from other factors affecting student learning.

Although the frameworks and models described above have limitations in terms of their functions and scope, they are useful in understanding, describing or guiding teacher assessment practices. However, to support teachers to implement effective assessment practices, individual schools should develop their own teacher assessment literacy model that captures not only the knowledge, skills and dispositions but the contextual and policy contexts. The misalignment of teacher assessment literacy and these factors would create tensions between what teachers can do and are expected to do within the policy and context of their schools.

The Problem

The continuous publication of teacher assessment literacy tools and frameworks implies that there is no universal conceptualisation of this construct. This is because teachers' assessment literacy is context-dependent and largely shaped by policy and contextual factors. The context-driven nature of assessment calls for a context-driven teacher assessment literacy framework to define, shape, assess and evaluate teachers' assessment practices. As discussed throughout this book, personal, social, paradigmatic, contextual and policy factors influence teachers' assessment practices. The factors should be considered in assessing teachers' assessment literacy; hence, they should be an integral part of the framework for assessing teachers' assessment literacy.

Case 1:   The conceptual, praxeological and socio-emotional dimensions of teacher assessment literacy

Description of the Study

Pastore and Andrade (2019) used a critical literature review to examine existing studies on teacher assessment literacy to develop a theoretical model. Following a literature review, a Delphi inquiry method was used to engage international experts to provide feedback on the proposed model. The first round of questionnaire proposed a version of teacher assessment literacy and asked expert participants to express their level of agreement (on a Likert-type scale of 1–6) concerning three dimensions of the assessment literacy construct: conceptual, praxeological and socio-emotional. Participants were also asked to suggest revisions to the model and the components identified for each dimension. In line with the assumptions of the proposed model, experts were not asked to express their level of agreement for individual elements of the three components but to focus on the dimensions overall. This led to the opportunity to replace standard definitions of assessment literacy as a set (or list) of knowledge and skills with an enriched, conceptual idea of assessment literacy. The second round of questionnaire asked participants ($n = 27$ of the previous 35 participants) to indicate their agreement (on a Likert-type scale of 1–6) with changes made to the previous Delphi round's proposal of teacher assessment literacy. Data analysis used both quantitative and qualitative methods. The experts' agreement was evaluated using Kendall's coefficient of concordance (W). A cross-checking procedure of independently coded data was also used.

The researchers conclude that teacher assessment literacy is a complex concept with three dimensions:

1 *Conceptual knowledge dimension.*
This refers to teachers' understanding of assessment using different models and methods. This understanding is based on teachers' conceptions of what assessment is, why, what and how to assess, how to analyse assessment data and how to effectively communicate assessment results to students, parents, other teachers and other stakeholders.

2 *Praxeological dimension.*
This is the ability of a teacher to integrate the assessment process with other teaching practices to monitor, judge and manage the teaching-learning process. This involves the teacher taking on multiple, and sometimes competing, assessment demands.

- Define learning targets and assessment criteria and align them with the assessment aims.
- Select and differentiate strategies and tools to gather data on student learning.
- Collect and interpret evidence of student learning.
- Use data on learning to adjust instruction and adapt the curriculum.
- Communicate feedback to students (for both formative and summative purposes).
- Engage with other stakeholders (e.g. parents, other teachers, administrators) about assessment information.
- Teach and support students in using assessment information to regulate their learning.

  - Manage student-involved assessment practices within the classroom context.
  - Scaffold student understanding of self- and peer assessment practice.

- Report and communicate assessment results to students, parents, administrators and other major users (pp. 135–136).

3 *Socio-emotional dimension.*
This means that assessment is not just a technical process but also a social process involving people. Teachers who are assessment literate can manage the social and emotional aspects of assessment, especially but not exclusively within the context of the classroom. This means that they can understand

the social and emotional implications of assessment and manage them in a way that is beneficial to the students and the classroom environment.

- Are effective in working with colleagues, parents and other stakeholders to create a shared sense-making of assessment practices and enhance assessment systems in the service of student learning
- Are conscious of their own role as assessor and of issues of trust, responsibilities and rights (e.g. protecting the privacy of student data that results from assessment)
- Attend to ethical aspects such as

  - Unintended consequences (consequential validity)
  - Cheating, teaching to the test and other assessment malpractices
  - Fairness and equity

- Have awareness of power, and the impact assessment has on

  - Students' involvement/engagement
  - Teacher-student relationships (p. 136)

Problem Being Addressed

Previous models for describing teacher assessment literacy focus on listing discrete behaviours, knowledge and skills, emphasising applying measurement theory and practice. With the more recent development of the conceptualisation of assessment as an integral part of learning and teaching activities, there has been an emphasis on other knowledge and skills, including how teachers use assessment and assessment data to support individual students. In addition, there is now an agreement that knowledge and skills dimensions of teacher assessment literacy are not enough to capture the construct holistically. Teachers' dispositions are often neglected in the conceptualisation of their assessment literacy. Teachers' beliefs, perceptions and other socio-emotional skills are part of the larger picture of knowledge and skills. Teachers' dispositions shape their assessment knowledge, skills and their actual practices to support individual students in their learning.

Factors Influencing the Problem

The different models of teacher assessment literacy are influenced by various factors:

1 *The conceptualisation of the construct.*
   Earlier research on teacher assessment literacy focused more on teachers' understanding of measurement principles and practices as

influenced by the value placed by the system on summative assessment. The aim during this time is to ensure that assessment data are reliable and valid based on the measurement principles. More recent works account for the range of assessments, from teacher assessment practices to high-stake tests. This changes the focus of teacher assessment literacy from more examination-driven knowledge and skills to ensure the use of a range of assessment activities and data to inform learning and teaching activities. Thus, in schools, it is important to clearly develop a shared understanding of assessment principles, purposes and practices to have a common conceptual understanding of assessment and their intended outcomes.

2 *Their intended use.*

As discussed in the introduction of this chapter, the frameworks for teacher assessment literacy have three intended uses. Assessment experts developed mostly those frameworks based on their needs rather than on the needs of teachers to use assessment more effectively. Thus, school leaders and teachers often view these frameworks as irrelevant to their needs in building a strong assessment culture. The motivation behind developing a framework or model is to support teachers, and thus, the frameworks or models should describe the contextual their knowledge, skills and dispositions against the backdrop of policy and contextual factors.

3 *The inputs.*

In this three-dimensional model proposed by Pastore and Andrade (2019), the first draft was informed by the literature review. International experts in assessment and teacher education validated and provided feedback to the model. This model is theoretically driven and expert-driven. However, the model does not reflect the views of teachers, policy makers and other stakeholders. Although some stakeholders might have informed the inputs used by the extant literature used in the earlier part of the study to develop the theoretical model, the final stage of refining it is a completely assessment expert-driven process. This raises the issue of the face validity of the framework: Is the framework acceptable from the viewpoint of teachers being the end-users of such? Let alone be its acceptability and relevance from the viewpoint of school leaders who set the direction of school assessment culture.

Implications of the Problem

The three-dimensional model of assessment literacy describes the knowledge, skills, dispositions and attitudes related to assessment that teachers need to effectively integrate assessment into their daily teaching practice. This emphasis has resulted in professional standards that cover a broad and more detailed range of activities in the assessment domain. These activities include meeting higher expectations for students' learning, choosing and developing assessment methods, administering and scoring tests, interpreting and communicating assessment results, and grading ethically. These activities provide the foundational discrete assessment knowledge and skills of teachers, which are useful to define and describe teacher assessment literacy. However, caution should be taken if this framework should be adopted by schools. School leaders and teachers should be guided how these knowledge and skills operate within specific policy and contextual factors. Some of these might need to be contextualised for effective enactment and meeting the school and system-level expectations while putting student learning at the centre of building teacher assessment literacy.

One notable contribution of this study described above is the integration of socio-emotional dimension in the conceptualisation of teachers' assessment literacy. Inclusion of this dimension expands the view on what comprises teachers' effective assessment practices. This treats teachers and students as human being, and their practices and engagement in assessment are influenced by their emotions, relationships and social factors. Teachers who acknowledge the social and emotional dynamics involved in the assessment process can build a positive classroom environment because stakeholders, particularly parents and students, would see that their emotions are acknowledged, valued and integrated in the system, thus increasing their motivation to enact their responsibilities in the learning and assessment processes. Similarly, when teachers can manage their emotional responses when faced with setbacks during their implementation of assessment activity, they can better reflect on what went wrong and what went well and revise their approach for the next iteration.

Furthermore, as many factors influence the concept of teacher assessment literacy, and these factors are constantly evolving, there should be an ongoing exploration of the conceptualisation of this construct. The evolving landscape of educational effectiveness, the constantly changing policy, the unprecedented rise in the use of advanced educational technologies, the dynamics of educational discourse, the various needs of students and among others should influence the ongoing investigation of this construct. Even for schools with a strong assessment culture that supports learning and teaching, there is a need for ongoing experimentation to develop new practical assessment knowledge and skills.

Case 2: Teacher assessment literacy as a context-driven construct

Description of the Study

While many assessment practices seem generic (i.e. sharing learning outcomes, use of rubrics, self and peer assessment, feedback, questioning), teacher assessment literacy is context-driven. This case study uses the work of Lam (2019) that explored teacher assessment literacy in second language (L2) writing. He investigated what Hong Kong secondary school teachers know and think about and how they practice classroom-based writing assessments through a questionnaire, telephone interviews and classroom observations. The study qualitatively examined the extent to which 66 teachers achieved teacher assessment literacy from their perspectives. Also, he identified aspects that needed further consolidation.

The main approaches discussed in this research paper are assessment of learning (AoL), AfL and assessment as learning (AaL). As defined, AoL is a process that evaluates student performance against predetermined criteria. It usually occurs at the end of an educational program or course, with results used to determine grades or other forms of recognition, such as diplomas. In contrast, AfL focuses on providing feedback during instruction so students can adjust their understanding and improve their skills while they learn. Finally, AaL involves using assessments to help learners become more aware of how they think and what strategies work best when solving problems related to the subject matter being studied.

Results show that most respondents had pertinent assessment knowledge and positive conceptions about alternative writing assessments. However, observation data indicate that some respondents only had a partial understanding of AoL and AfL but not AaL. Additionally, when attempting to use AaL, the respondents could merely mimic its 'procedures' rather than internalise its 'essence'. This is a classic example of 'ticking the box' approach in implementing an assessment reform.

Problem Being Addressed

Lam pointed out the range of research done on assessment literacy and how it equips language teachers with knowledge and skills to effectively design and implement classroom-based assessment. Previous studies on teacher assessment literacy inform how training supports the development of assessment literacy and what practices teachers adopt to evaluate students. However, it is still unknown whether secondary school teachers have the competence necessary to deal with standardised testing and classroom-based assessment, whether they can experiment with various assessment practices such as AfL and AaL, or whether they know how to make their teaching benefit from alternative assessments. There are reports that teachers' views and understanding of assessment are not often translated into their actual practices.

Factors Influencing the Problem

The apparent discrepancy between the teachers' perceived levels of their assessment literacy and their professional training can be due to several factors:

1 *Sources of their assessment knowledge and skills.*
   The inputs received by teachers influence their understanding and practice. In this study, teachers acquire their knowledge and understanding of assessment through self-study, pre-service training, experience and professional training. The quality of the input, including its rigour, use of evidence-informed assessment knowledge and skills, the overall messaging of what assessment literacy is and how it should be enacted in various contexts, is critical for shaping teachers' assessment literacy.
2 *Lacking pedagogical practice.*
   The study shows that when introducing alternative assessments such as self-reflection in writing, teacher participants still adopted a teacher-centred rather than a student-centred pedagogical approach. This means that teachers were more focused on teaching the students rather than allowing them to take ownership of their learning. A paradigmatic change necessitates the implementation of assessment to support learning and teaching. The 'ticking the box' approach is ineffective in using assessment to increase student outcomes.
3 *Lacking awareness to shift their mindsets and philosophies.*
   Teachers did not understand that AaL, like AfL, involves students playing a proactive role in learning and requires learners to self-assess their writing critically and independently. Without making students notice their new roles as self-regulated learners, implementing AaL remains a challenge. A deeper understanding of effective assessment principles, practices and processes is needed to ensure that teachers enact their assessment literacy underpinned by these principles.

Implications of the Problem

The discrepancy between teachers' perceived levels of assessment literacy and their professional training implies that even with the policy support for enhancing assessment practices, teachers should have more strategic professional development training to align their practices to the complementary facets of different types of assessment. To facilitate the development of teacher assessment literacy, Lam suggests three actionable recommendations. First, school leaders can provide teachers with support for attempting alternative assessments, such as self-reflection in portfolio works, interactive use of exemplars and applications of feedback dialogues in writing. All these initiatives need extra funding, teaching relief and professional training. Without creating space, support and autonomy, teachers may find it challenging to develop their TAL in a fuller sense. When teachers are not provided with support, they will tend to revert to their old practices, thinking that those practices work well within the constrained of the current resources and context. The ability of the school leaders to modify the school context to some extent will make it more favourable for teachers to implement alternative assessments. The business-as-usual approach will not help teachers to build and their assessment literacy.

Second, as suggested by the findings, sharing assessment strategies as a community of practice would be a way forward. Through building sustained professional dialogues, teachers can develop expert assessment judgements when evaluating writing and disseminate good assessment practices to colleagues. As such, enhanced teacher professionalism in writing assessment is likely to contribute to achieving teacher assessment literacy. A structural and social changes need to happen. For example, school leaders can create a platform (i.e. whole-school collaboration, stage meeting, cross-disciplinary team, subject-area meetings) for teachers' exchange of best practices and discussion of new assessment knowledge or issues impacting their practices. In addition, school leaders can draw from the expertise of more experienced teachers to support the developing teachers. They can implement various collaborative activities (i.e. instructional rounds, mentoring or coaching, peer feedback) to observe classes and provide feedback and engage in a dialogue what areas needing further improvement. These structural and social changes provide the mechanisms for teachers within school to develop a shared understanding of the principles, processes and practices of assessment, which consequently builds their assessment literacy.

Third, the inclusion of teacher assessment literacy as a mandated component of teacher training qualifications would create a positive washback effect on learning and teaching in teacher preparation programmes. In teaching standards of most educational bureaucracies, TAL is a major component, and thus, a dedicated unit on pre-service teacher curriculum should be in place. The same is needed for in-service teachers' professional development, where the key focus is on building teacher assessment literacy. Adding teacher assessment literacy as part of pedagogical content knowledge would make its measurement legitimate in both coursework and teaching practicum. There should be a continuous attention to assessing individual teachers' assessment literacy and identifying areas needing improvement. The original definition of AfL can be applied for teacher learning, that is, "the process of collecting and interpreting evidence for use by [school leaders and teachers] to decide where they are in their learning, where they need to go, and how best to get there." The phrase 'where they are' refers to the current assessment literacy of teachers, whereas the phrase 'where they need to go' refers to the acceptable benchmark or the goal of teacher training and development. The third phrase, 'how best to get there', requires analysing the gap between teachers' current level and the desired level and develop mechanism to support teachers.

Case 3: Needs-based professional development in assessment

Description of the Study

This case study demonstrates that approach to be used to building teachers' assessment literacy should be carefully selected. The study by Christoforidou and Kyriakides (2021) investigated the extent to which the dynamic approach (DA) to teacher professional development can help teachers develop their assessment skills and contribute to improving student learning outcomes. To achieve this aim, a multi-treatment group randomisation study was conducted to compare the impact of the DA with the impact of the competency-based approach (CBA) on developing assessment skills and promoting student learning outcomes. Data from 178 teachers and the achievement of their students ($n = 2358$) were collected before and after the intervention to compare the impact of each approach on developing teacher assessment skills and promoting student learning outcomes. Results show that DA has a more significant impact on teacher assessment skills and student learning outcomes than CBA. Additionally, differences in the effectiveness of each approach were only identified for teachers who already possessed higher levels of assessment skills. These findings suggest that providing ongoing support to teachers effectively improves their teaching practices and ultimately enhances students' academic performance.

Problem Being Addressed

Christoforidou and Kyriakides (2021) point out that many professional development interventions focus on improving teachers' knowledge base and skill sets but do not provide teachers with the opportunity to practice what they have learned and incorporate new ideas into their assessment practices. There is no mechanism that supports and monitors teachers to apply their knowledge and skills in meaningful ways. Consequently, regardless of the quality of professional development undertaken, there is an apparent lack of improvement in their assessment skills and student learning outcomes.

The CBA has been recognised as one of the most dominant approaches to teacher professional development, and the use of both CBA and DA acknowledges the importance of developing teachers' competencies and recognises a stage notion of skill development. However, these approaches have significant differences regarding how professional development is organised and offered in terms of content and mode of delivery. The DA is based on findings that skills can be grouped into stages with differences in complexity and difficulty. The content of professional development is therefore adjusted to address not a single skill each time but specific groups of skills. In addition, DA requires an initial evaluation of teacher skills before their engagement. The results of this initial evaluation are used to highlight specific areas of improvement for each group of teachers that correspond to the grouping of skills identified, and the professional development content is adjusted to address these improvement priorities. Therefore, not all teachers receive the same training, and not all skills are covered by all teachers. Furthermore, the DA suggests that for professional development to be effective, it needs to focus on the development of competence, as the CBA acknowledges, but at the same time, it also requires the engagement of participants in critical reflection. Participants are encouraged to take ownership of and critically reflect on their learning throughout the course. Reflection is done with specific reference to the skills under focus.

Factors Influencing the Problem

Shifting teacher practices from summative assessment to formative assessment is influenced by several factors:

1 *Design of professional development program.*

The progression of knowledge and skills and the processes adopted for teacher learning is critically important for enhancing teacher assessment practices. When the content and design of PD correspond to the needs of teachers, it is more effective in helping teachers develop their assessment literacy, which has consequential validity in promoting student learning outcomes.

2 *Support from school leaders.*

Implementing new assessment knowledge and developing practical skills requires support from school leaders. This support includes realistic expectations, expert advice, workload allocation, physical space to explore the implementation of assessment, resources and many others. It was demonstrated in many studies that school leaders' assessment literacy greatly influences teachers' assessment literacy (Anderson et al., 2010; Cosner, 2011; Lasater et al., 2020).

Implications of the Problem

Enhancing teacher assessment literacy requires a proper progression of skills based on their difficulty and complexities. The study found that teacher assessment skills can be grouped into different stages and that the developmental scale was consistently identified in both measurement periods. It was also observed that in cases where a change occurred, it was towards the next demanding level. This implies that the improvement of assessment skills took place gradually, in a stepwise manner (i.e. from stage 1 to stage 2, from stage 2 to stage 3). However, no movement from stage 4 teachers was identified, which might imply that progress is possible, but upward movement from stage 4 is more difficult to be achieved than the upward movement from stages 1, 2 and 3.

Findings of this study suggest ways to help teachers enhance their assessment literacy. Teachers can improve their assessment literacy by undertaking appropriate interventions and participating in effective professional development programs. This is supported by the fact that teachers of the control group did not improve their assessment skills, and all of them remained at the same stage that they were found to be situated at the beginning of the school year. Thus, not all professional development programs can improve teachers' assessment literacy.

It is important to design and implement PD programs that have positive impacts on teachers' practices and student learning.

What is highlighted in this study is that the training initiatives are more effective when structured to correspond to the professional needs of teachers. A mismatch between teachers' perceived PD needs and the actual PD content would result to teachers' negative perception of the effectiveness of PD. The match between the PD program and teachers' needs would increase their motivation to participate and invest their time to meet their PD needs. In addition, teachers would feel a more personalised PD experience, leading to more meaningful and fulfilling engagement. Consequently, teachers would develop a more positive attitude in implementing the new knowledge and skills they have acquired because they can link the PD content to their practices.

More importantly, teachers should be provided with realistic and differentiated professional development that allows them to build on their existing personal and professional strengths. DA was more effective than the CBA in this regard, as it focused not only on competency development but also on systematic and guided critical reflection on assessment practices. This suggests that a focus on both competence and reflection is necessary to achieve effective professional development. The processes adopted for PD implementation influence the actual enactment of teachers in their classroom. When teachers are given time to reflect on their practices, they can identify specific areas to improve.

Proposed Solutions

Supporting teachers to develop their assessment literacy requires the interplay of many policies, personal, social, organisational and contextual factors (Alonzo et al., 2021b). Various processes should be implemented to determine if teachers are doing it right in using assessment to support learning and teaching.

First, a teacher assessment literacy framework is needed to clearly define and describe teacher assessment literacy. This will outline the dispositions, knowledge and skills expected by the system for teachers to demonstrate. This framework must be theoretically and empirically supported to ensure that the conceptualisation of teacher assessment practices to support learning and teaching is evidence-informed. This conceptualisation must be context-driven against the backdrop of the policy and other personal, social, personal and organisational factors. The framework must be rigorously developed, making sure of its consequential validity in improving learning and teaching. The use of a specific framework within school will establish a shared understanding of teachers expected roles and responsibilities in assessment.

Second, this framework should inform school-level policy that outlines support needed by teachers, parents, students and other stakeholders. The resources, time, workload and socio-emotional support must be clearly outlined for teachers and students. More often than not, the enactment of policies becomes problematic across different levels due to the lack of supporting and enabling mechanisms. School leadership is critical for the success of using assessment to support learning and teaching (see Chapter 11).

Third, the framework should become the basis for evaluating teachers' assessment literacy. Evaluating teachers' assessment literacy should become an integral part of performance evaluation. A developmental approach to the evaluation should be adopted to develop a culture of reflection and continuous improvement. The focus of evaluating teacher assessment literacy is on identifying areas needing support and improvement and not to make judgement about their effectiveness. This approach to evaluation may lead to more strategic actions in implementing professional development and providing support for individual teachers (Davison, 2023).

Fourth, the framework and the results of teachers' evaluation should inform the development and implementation of professional development programs. As shown in the study by Christoforidou and Kyriakides (2021), a professional development program linked to teachers' needs has a higher impact on enhancing teachers' assessment literacy, leading to improved student outcomes. The results of teacher assessment literacy evaluation should inform PD content, design and implementation approach.

Fifth, teachers' agency must be developed and should be given autonomy to design and implement assessment strategies. Teachers know their classroom context, students, curriculum content and targets; hence, the system needs to trust their professional competence. They can draw on their professional and practical assessment knowledge and pedagogical content knowledge to implement assessment strategies to support learning and teaching activities. When teachers are being told what to do, they lost their creativity, innovativeness and responsiveness, and there is a higher tendency that prescribed assessment activities are not aligned to students' needs. Teachers' agency and autonomy enables them to take active role in exploring ways to better assess their students and use the results to inform learning and teaching activities.

Conclusion

This chapter answers the issue of how do we know when teachers are doing it right? Many frameworks are recommended to build teachers' assessment literacy, but a context-driven framework for evaluating assessment literacy is

References

Alonzo, D., Labad, V., Bejano, J., & Guerra, F. (2021a). The policy-driven dimensions of teacher beliefs about assessment. *Australian Journal of Teacher Education*, *46*(3). https://ro.ecu.edu.au/cgi/viewcontent.cgi?article=4761&context=ajte

Alonzo, D., Leverett, J., & Obsioma, E. (2021b). Leading an assessment reform: Ensuring a whole-school approach for decision-making. *Frontiers in Education*, *6*(62). https://doi.org/10.3389/feduc.2021.631857

Anderson, S., Leithwood, K., & Strauss, T. (2010). Leading data use in schools: Organizational conditions and practices at the school and district levels. *Leadership and Policy in Schools*, *9*(3), 292–327. https://doi.org/10.1080/1570076100 3731492

ARG. (2002). *Assessment for learning: 10 principles*. https://www.storre.stir.ac.uk/bitstream/1893/32458/1/Assessment%20for%20learning%2010%20principles%202002.pdf

Biggs, J. (1999). What the student does: Teaching for enhanced learning. *Higher Education Research & Development*, *18*(1), 57–75. https://doi.org/10.1080/0729436990180105

Brookhart, S. M. (1997). A theoretical framework for the role of classroom assessment in motivating student effort and achievement. *Applied Measurement in Education*, *10*(2), 161–180. https://doi.org/10.1207/s15324818ame1002_4

Brookhart, S. M., Walsh, J. M., & Zientarski, W. A. (2006). The dynamics of motivation and effort for classroom assessments in middle school science and social studies. *Applied Measurement in Education*, *19*(2), 151–184. https://doi.org/10.1207/s15324818ame1902_5

Christoforidou, M., & Kyriakides, L. (2021). Developing teacher assessment skills: The impact of the dynamic approach to teacher professional development. *Studies in Educational Evaluation*, *70*, 101051. https://doi.org/10.1016/j.stueduc.2021.101051

Cosner, S. (2011). Teacher learning, instructional considerations and principal communication: Lessons from a longitudinal study of collaborative data use by teachers. *Educational Management Administration & Leadership*, *39*(5), 568–589. https://doi.org/10.1177/1741143211408453

Cowie, B., & Bell, B. (1999). A model of formative assessment in science education. *Assessment in Education: Principles, Policy & Practice*, *6*(1), 101–116. https://doi.org/10.1080/09695949993026

Davison, C. (2007). Views from the chalkface: English language school based assessment in Hong Kong. *Language Assessment Quarterly, 4*(1), 37–68. https://doi.org/10.1080/15434300701348359

Davison, C. (2008). Assessment for learning: Building inquiry-oriented assessment communities. 42nd Annual TESOL Convention and Exhibit. New York, NY.

Davison, C. (2013). Innovation in assessment: Common misconceptions and problems. In K. Hyland & L. Wong (Eds.), *Innovation and change in English language education* (pp. 263–275). Oxon: ROutledge.

Davison, C. (2023). Assessment literacy: Changing cultures, enculturing change in Hong Kong. *Chinese Journal of Applied Linguistics, 46*(2), 180–197. https://doi.org/doi:10.1515/CJAL-2023-0203

Harlen, W. (2007). *Assessment for learning.* SAGE.

Hill, K., & McNamara, T. (2012). Developing a comprehensive, empirically based research framework for classroom-based assessment. *Language Testing, 29*(3), 395–420. https://doi.org/10.1177/0265532211428317

Lam, R. (2019). Teacher assessment literacy: Surveying knowledge, conceptions and practices of classroom-based writing assessment in Hong Kong. *System, 81*, 78–89. https://doi.org/10.1016/j.system.2019.01.006

Lasater, K., Albiladi, W. S., Davis, W. S., & Bengtson, E. (2020). The data culture continuum: An examination of school data cultures. *Educational Administration Quarterly, 56*(4), 533–569. https://doi.org/10.1177/0013161X19873034

Pastore, S., & Andrade, H. L. (2019). Teacher assessment literacy: A three-dimensional model. *Teaching and Teacher Education, 84*, 128–138. https://doi.org/10.1016/j.tate.2019.05.003

Taras, M. (2009). Summative assessment: The missing link for formative assessment. *Journal of Further and Higher Education, 33*(1), 57–69.

Wiliam, D., & Thompson, M. (2008). Integrating assessment with learning: What will it take to make it work? In C. A. Dwyer (Ed.), *The future of assessment: Shaping teaching and learning.* Erlbaum.

Chapter 11

How Do We Know When Schools Are Doing It Right?

Introduction

Building a strong assessment culture is a fundamental step to support teachers to enact assessment practices that support learning and teaching and meet accountability requirements. Schools use different approaches, including teacher-led initiatives (Adie et al., 2021), school-led whole-school approach to building teacher capacity (Hopfenbeck et al., 2015), development and implementation of assessment framework or tools (Prytula et al., 2013) and enactment of the system-level policy (Verhoeven & Devos, 2005). Although research evidence suggests that the school-led approach to building assessment culture is the most effective one, this approach is not often the preferred choice. School assessment reforms are often top-down, being dictated by the department regarding what to do and how to implement the reform. A range of literature suggests that a top-down approach to educational reforms is less effective than school-initiated reform (Honkimäki et al., 2022; Maass et al., 2019; Skedsmo & Huber, 2019). This is because policies are often prescriptive by nature and often devoid of the classroom context, where students' diverse backgrounds, resources and contextual factors are not fully considered. School leaders and teachers are better placed to initiate a reform to build an assessment culture because they clearly understand their needs and the context of their schools and classrooms, including students' learning characteristics and needs, where learning and teaching occur.

Similarly, a top-down approach to educational reforms does not tap into school leaders' and teachers' motivation (Nazari & Molana, 2022), resulting in resistance, lack of buy-in and missed opportunities to benefit from richly contextualised expertise. This reduced motivation to implement the assessment reform is usual, particularly when school leaders, teachers and other stakeholders are not part of the development of the assessment reform. Their exclusion in the process does not give them a sense of ownership of the reform, thus reducing the likelihood for meaningful change to happen.

DOI: 10.4324/9781003396277-11

In addition, due to the detached nature of assessment reforms to the school and classroom contexts, the expectations set with regards to timeline and outcomes can be unrealistic, without giving sufficient time for teachers to understand the assessment policy, reflect on the alignment of their teaching philosophy and recalibrate it when necessary, develop approaches and strategies to enact the policy and experiment new practices and develop new practical assessment skills (Christoforidou & Kyriakides, 2021). Due to this top-down approach to assessment reform, the implementation of assessment policy becomes tokenistic, focusing on compliance and control rather than meeting students' needs and helping them learn more effectively. This accountability-focused nature of assessment will always have negative effects on learning and teaching.

The overall approach and underpinning principle of any assessment reform should adhere to the principles of effective assessment to support learning and teaching (Davison, 2013). As such, schools' engagement in continuous evaluation to identify areas needing improvement is necessary. The clarity of outcomes and expectations for building a strong assessment culture that supports learning and teaching must be understood and agreed upon by all stakeholders. The effectiveness of a school assessment reform starts with stakeholders' clear understanding of the basic principles of assessment to support learning and teaching, re-engineering the educational culture and re-aligning educational practices to effective assessment principles to provide teachers with an environment that models assessment culture, providing the necessary support services to teachers, students and parents.

The Problem

Many reports highlight the enactment of assessment policy as a reform strategy to change the assessment practices of teachers. The effectiveness of these reforms is often measured in terms of changes in teacher beliefs, views and practices and improvement in student learning. However, these changes do not often occur, and if they do, they are not aligned to the principles of effective assessment practices. This is because assessment reforms are often top-down and prescriptive by nature. This approach to reform positions school leaders, teachers and students only as passive implementers rather than active participants of the reforms. A school-based assessment reform provides a better mechanism to enhancing the use of assessment to support learning and teaching. Given the sustained interest in developing a school assessment culture that supports learning and teaching, we need to respond to the question: how do we know when schools are doing it right?

Knowing When Schools Are Doing It Right

Case 1: Balancing tensions in educational reforms

Description of the Study

Enactment of a new assessment policy is not always straightforward. There are positive and negative perceptions among stakeholders, which impact teachers' assessment practices. This case study illustrates how tensions among stakeholders can be resolve using a dialogic approach in policy enactment. Hopfenbeck et al. (2015) investigated how different stakeholders in Norway experienced a government-initiated, large-scale policy implementation programme on Assessment for Learning (AfL). Norway's educational system has fewer accountability mechanisms compared to countries such as the USA and England. It has less focus on testing and data collection than other countries but is in a transition period, with an increasing focus on tests and the use of data. The AfL programme in Norway was a national four-year initiative developed and steered by the Norwegian Directorate of Education and Training (DET). It was inspired by the Assessment Reform Group and the experiences in Scotland. At the time of the data collection, the AfL programme involved more than 240 of the 428 municipalities and counties in Norway, which were in charge of almost a thousand schools. The implementation was designed in four phases, with the first group of participants starting an 18-month programme in September 2010 and the fourth group finishing in June 2014.

The researchers interviewed 58 stakeholders, including ministers of education, members of the DET, municipality leaders, teachers, school leaders and students involved in the policy implementation. Results show that dialogue and trust among the municipal leaders, school leaders, teachers and students support the successful implementation of assessment processes. This finding highlights how governments can design education policy reforms and supporting school leaders and teachers to enact them. A bottom-up approach to implementing assessment reform could reduce the tensions among stakeholders. It was seen that when the policy was interpreted as a way of controlling schools instead of improving learning outcomes, its implementation faced challenges. Teachers' resistance to this reform stems from their fear of extra work and the required documentation, which will add to their workload. There is also a negative perception of the reform due to their past experiences when municipal leaders visited their schools when they performed poorly in the national tests. Teachers strongly expressed their need for autonomy to be motivated and not the high-level accountability approach, which often puts too much pressure on them. This lack of autonomy will lead teachers to disengage in the actual assessment reform implementation. The tension between DET and researchers and teacher educators is the lack of credibility of implementation. Researchers do not see the effectiveness of the approach adopted and implemented by DET. The one-size-fits-all approach disregards the contextual differences of schools, including the current practices of schools and the diverse and unique needs of students.

Problem Being Addressed

Implementing a large-scale assessment reform has been challenging for many countries. There is often tension between policy makers' agenda, researchers' perspectives and schools' and teachers' practices. This tension arises when policy makers' expectations are not aligned with the principles of effective assessment practices and research evidence or when the policy demands more than what the schools and teachers can do and achieve. The top-down approach to implementing assessment reforms and the exclusion of various stakeholders in the process, from policy articulation to implementation and evaluation, would often result in a lack of ownership of the reform, thereby creating more issues than positive outcomes. More broadly, there is an apparent gap in the field of educational policy reform regarding the extent to which ideal support conditions of small pilot AfL programmes can be replicated when the approach is scaled up to the national level.

Factors Influencing the Problem

Based on the reported study, there are factors identified that influence the problem:

1 *Teacher understanding of the AfL principles.*
   Teachers should have a deep understanding of AfL principles to develop their confidence and skills in implementing assessment practices that are aligned with these principles. In addition, these principles will help teachers to engage and contribute to the discussions around implementing the assessment reform. They are also better positioned to effectively reflect on and adopt their practices to meet the goals of the reform.
2 *Teachers' resistance to reforms.*
   Teachers feared extra work, the need to document assessment practices and extra workload. When the assessment reform is not well communicated with the schools, school leaders and teachers

might have difficulty figuring out the extent to which the reform will impact their current work, which consequently will develop negative perceptions. To encourage acceptance of the reform, the school and classroom contexts, including the amount of work required and the expectations to implement the reform, must be clearly discussed.

3   *Accountability-driven culture.*

Teachers have negative conceptions about assessment and assessment data due to the long-standing culture of using them for meeting accountability requirements and for evaluating school and teaching effectives. School leaders and teachers mentioned the accountability system in the capital of Norway as a scenario for what they feared could happen. Teachers with work experience from this city commented on how the leader from the municipality level had visited their schools after the school had performed poorer than expected on national tests, and the leader had urged the school to work harder.

4   *Teachers' autonomy.*

Teachers assert that they need autonomy to be motivated to implement the assessment reform. Knowing their classroom context, they can develop a more strategic approach to enact the reform. Also, they do not believe in using accountability tools to monitor the profession. Even how AfL reform is communicated to improve student learning and teachers have autonomy to design classroom-based assessment but when the results are used for accountability purposes, teachers will most likely not use AfL activities.

5   *The credibility of programme implementers.*

The researchers interviewed expressed concern about the implementation strategy decided by Norway's DET. They did not believe that DET had enough knowledge about the local differences in the municipalities, and thus, offering the AfL programme as a one-size-fits-all solution would not work. The researchers commented on the variety of expertise in the municipalities, with some big municipalities having much expertise while other small municipalities not having anyone working there at all. This difference in capacity and expertise was seen as a significant challenge from the researchers' perspectives. The researchers also mentioned that the top-down approach, with DET leading the programme, does not work well with the ideas behind the AfL programme. They feared that the programme could turn into slogans, techniques and quick fixes instead of professional development (PD) for teachers. The researchers also questioned whether AfL could be introduced by law, as it is more about PD.

Implications of the Problem

A bottom-up approach is ideal for the successful implementation of education policy reforms like AfL programmes. However, for enacting system-level policies, ongoing dialogue and trust between stakeholders such as municipality leaders, teachers, school leaders and students will ensure successful enactment of these policies. Engaging all stakeholders in policy articulation creates buy-in and trust and gives everyone a sense of ownership. The shared ownership will consequently create shared responsibility and accountability for the reform. In addition, the engagement of stakeholders provides the avenue for knowledge sharing and co-creating knowledge concerning the reform. Thus, for any assessment reform to happen in schools, everyone involved in the implementation, including school leaders, teachers, students, parents and the wider community, should be part of the whole process, from the initial conversation of policy development to the final impact evaluation of the reform (Davison, 2021), more importantly, in the ongoing monitoring of how teachers are enacting the reform.

It is also important to ensure that these policies are adapted according to the local contexts for them to effectively impact student learning outcomes. The unique and diverse needs of individual classrooms, schools, teachers, students and parents provide challenges for implementing a generic policy. Schools should be given autonomy to operationalise the policy to meet their needs. Respecting schools' autonomy to implement the policy creates a deep sense of trust in the system, putting high regard on the capacity of the school community. School leaders and teachers would feel that their profession and expertise are valued, thus enhancing their motivation and increasing the likelihood that the assessment reform will be implemented as planned.

Furthermore, researchers should also be included in the process so their expertise can help improve educational reform initiatives at the national level. Although school leaders and teachers have practical assessment knowledge and skills, and policy makers have leadership skills, the theoretical and empirical knowledge of researchers are invaluable for decision-making. Researchers could provide empirically driven insights that would influence the whole system and processes to use evidence-based practices. The misalignment between theory and practice is detrimental to the success of any reform. Thus, the practical knowledge and skills of school leaders and teachers must be informed by research evidence and theoretical and empirical knowledge of the researchers must be shaped by practical knowledge. This will ensure that school leaders and teachers are using leading assessment practices that are contextualised for their classroom needs.

Finally, part of implementing an assessment policy is the establishment of learning communities (Leahy et al., 2012). The ongoing situated PD provides opportunities for stakeholders to share their experiences. When PD is tailored to the needs of the schools, teachers will find it more relevant and more likely to implement the knowledge and skills they have gained to ensure effective learning and teaching. Also, engaging teachers in learning communities allows them to work together within and across schools to develop their practice. They can share best practices, insights, successes and challenges in a safe and supportive environment without the fear of judgement of their effectiveness.

Case 2: Structural, organisational, social and behavioural factors influencing school-based assessment reform

Description of the Study

This case study shows the many factors that influence the enactment of a school-based assessment reform and the importance of addressing these factors. Alonzo et al. (2021) used an auto-ethnography to reflect on their experiences in leading a whole-school approach to assessment reform. They combined personal experience with cultural analysis and reflection. Activity theory was used as a lens for understanding how different structural, organisational, social and behavioural factors contribute to the success of the programme.

An assessment literacy programme was implemented in one public primary school in Australia. The school is part of a wider learning community with four other schools, comprising 283 teachers and 4521 students. The programme has been the focus of PD for the last three years, with the goal of building a stronger assessment culture, aimed to build a shared understanding of the principles of AfL amongst school leaders, teachers, students and parents/carers. Five assessment leaders were appointed to work collaboratively with a university partner. Every term, they engage in PD and then develop an action plan to support other teachers with their assessment literacy. Resources and advice are co-developed to support the individual school activity. In the past, teachers at the school participated in a number of professional learning programmes on assessment, but there was no common understanding or collective approach to assessment.

The results of the study identified various structural, organisational, social and behavioural factors which contribute to the success of a school-wide assessment reform programme. Also, they have found that creating partnerships with external stakeholders can help support schools in their efforts to build an effective assessment culture. Finally, they have highlighted the importance of having key players within the school who have clear roles and responsibilities for leading such initiatives. These findings provide valuable insights into how teachers can be supported in using data effectively for decision-making related to learning and teaching practices across different stages at a whole-school level.

Problem Being Addressed

Alonzo et al. (2021) pointed out that building a strong assessment culture with a strong focus on implementing teacher data-driven decision-making is relatively problematic due to the many changes that need to happen in the school. The business-as-usual of the school needs to change to address the issues that the reform is built for. The lack of a shared understanding of effective assessment principles creates confusion and negative assessment practices. The presence of competing principles may result in different views about the role of assessment in learning and teaching. Thus, there is a need to ensure that all teachers across the school are supported to engage in a whole-school approach to ensure that all students across different stages are supported. This requires providing necessary resources and support, including structural, organisational and expert, to implement the school's reform.

Factors Influencing the Problem

Several issues influence the implementation of assessment reform in schools. These include the following:

1 *Conceptual understanding of assessment.*

Teachers may have different understanding of assessment and decision-making. It has been argued in the literature (Davison, 2013) that the presence of multiple and competing views and understandings of assessment in schools poses resistance for teachers to change their practices. A shared understanding of assessment and decision-making is necessary to support teachers towards a common goal. Teachers can realign their beliefs, views, knowledge and skills to the aims of the reform. They can also engage in a more meaningful collaboration due to clarity of expectations and focus on their responsibility. A shared understanding minimises confusion by bridging the conceptual and practical, including values and perspectives of the school community.

2 *Lack of focus of PD.*

A more strategic approach to PD is needed to enhance teachers' assessment knowledge and skills, and decision-making. It has been found that teachers attending several PDs may struggle to see the coherence of the skills taught from each PD activity. A needs-based PD programme is needed to ensure that there is coherence between PD content and teachers' needs. The schools are in the best position to identify their needs and develop an ongoing PD programme.

3 *No central repository of school data.*

The lack of systematic process and infrastructure illustrates that the school has no collective aspiration regarding what assessment culture the school wants to establish. When individual teachers store data, it is difficult to see the overall picture of individual students' learning and the school's overall performance. A holistic view of individual students' data and the collective data of schools and an ability to understand what these data are telling them is critically important for informed action relating to improving learning and teaching and the school in general.

4 *Organisational structure.*

The appointment of assessment leaders in school is a critical factor that provides support for teachers. They work closely with the principal to provide ongoing support for individual teachers, developing and implementing assessment activities, analysing data and identifying insights to inform their decision-making. Assessment leaders provide expert advice and feedback to teachers in a supportive environment. One benefit of the presence of assessment leaders is the accessibility of help and support when teachers need it. Assessment leaders can visit their classroom and support them when they are faced with challenges in implementing assessment activities.

5 *Lack of external support.*

The strong partnership between schools and universities ensures a strong link between theory and practice. The collaborative nature of partnership builds an avenue for knowledge exchange between the university and the school. Academics can provide empirically driven assessment knowledge and skills to enhance teachers' professional and practical knowledge. This ensures that teachers are well informed of research evidence, thereby ensuring that their practices are empirically supported to enhance students' learning.

Implications of the Problem

The results of Alonzo et al. (2021) provide valuable insights into how schools can build an effective assessment culture that supports teachers in using data effectively for decision-making for effective learning and teaching. The structural, organisational, social and behavioural factors pointed in this chapter provide significant insights for other schools to inform their strategies to build an assessment culture. If these factors are not accounted for building a school assessment culture, teachers will not be effectively supported to change their beliefs and practices.

The assessment culture of schools should be shaped by research evidence, and thus, a university-school partnership is critical for ongoing knowledge exchange. The partnership facilitates the development of needs-based PD programmes tailored to addressing the knowledge gaps of teachers. Apart from mentoring provided by the university, the partnership would build the confidence of school leaders and teachers that their practices are the leading practices without the risk of implementing irrelevant and ineffective assessment practices. Through the empirical knowledge provided by the university, teachers can develop innovative assessment practices to drive student learning.

In addition, the structural change sustains the implementation of the reform. Having key players within the school who have clear roles and responsibilities for leading the reform is invaluable. The school could not solely rely on academics providing feedback and support for teachers. What they need is an ongoing support and feedback when they need it. The assessment leaders who are trained as instructional leaders and assessment experts play substantial role in supporting teachers to enact the aims of the reform. Their support and feedback are more relevant to what the university could provide because they know the context of the school and classrooms by which teachers are operating.

Overall, schools need a system approach to implement an assessment reform. The dependencies of all components of the school should underpin the thinking process on how to better support teachers to enact the curriculum. A guiding principle should be, if something needs to happen, how do other components of the school influence it, and how must these components be adapted or modified for it to happen? Are there missing components that may influence the existing components to better perform and support the reform?

Case 3: Contextual barriers for assessment reform implementation

Description of the Study

The context-driven nature of assessment presents another layer of complexities in enacting assessment policy. The study of Arsyad Arrafii (2023) that reports the contextual factors that shape teachers' use of AfL is an excellent example for this case. They use a micro-, meso- and macro-level contextual framework to analyse data collected through semi-structured interviews and three group discussions. Content analysis of teachers' propositions suggests that internal and external factors influence teachers' use of assessment. Internal factors, including insufficient school resources and support for teachers, student/teacher readiness regarding innovative ideas, lack of assessment literacy among students and an absence of reliable placement tests, can act as barriers to the successful implementation of AfL. On the other hand, external-to-school factors were also identified, including the lack of involvement or support from the government and parents. The study concluded that the evidence for implementation barriers outweighed potential opportunities, leading to teachers' perception that reform was difficult to carry out. Due to these factors, teachers adopt more superficial approaches when implementing assessment reforms. The author recommends that the incremental approach to reform implementation and sustainable PD should be promoted to address the implementation barriers.

Problem Being Addressed

The curriculum reform (K13) in Indonesia expects teachers to change their assessment practices from a content-based approach to an interactive, participative and competence-based approach to assessment. Teachers are expected to focus on assessing students' ability to apply their knowledge and skills in a real-world context rather than just assessing their content knowledge. This approach also involves the active participation of students in assessment, as well as the involvement of the wider school community. However, despite the emphasis on students' involvement in the curriculum reform, students' active involvement in assessment is often neglected in the classroom. Teachers do not provide opportunities for individual students to actively take responsibility in the assessment process.

Factors Influencing the Problem

There are several factors influencing teacher implementation of assessment.

1 Internal to school influences include the following:

 a Limited learning resources (e.g., textbooks, audio and video teaching aids, access to the internet). Learning resources support learning and teaching activities, and most often, when new reforms are implemented, new resources are needed to support teachers and students.

 b Equitable access to PD programmes. PD programmes are important supports for teachers to acquire the relevant knowledge and skills to effectively enact the reform. Availability of PD programmes is important but equitable access is another issue. Teachers should be provided with equal opportunities to participate in PD programmes. When only selected teachers are sent to PD programmes, this inequitable approach will demotivate other teachers.

 c Student readiness in terms of their learning motivation, confidence and curiosity, and level of content knowledge and skills. Assessment requires students' ability to participate in the assessment process actively and independently. Teachers' practices are impacted when their students are unprepared to assess their learning and regulate their progress. This is an important part of the assessment process as it encourages students to take ownership of their learning and become more self-directed.

 d Teacher readiness is associated with a lack of content, pedagogical knowledge and assessment literacy. This lack of knowledge and skills limits their ability to change their established pedagogical practices to assessment. In addition, teacher commitment to supporting individual students for effective learning is a critical factor. This perceived incompetency and lack of commitment may be intensified by inadequate learning resources at school, such as materials and funding, and limited support for teachers in terms of opportunities to attend effective PD programmes.

 e Classroom context, including class size and student composition. Large class sizes and mixed-ability classes present a challenge for teachers to implement new assessment practices. This was seen as a barrier to innovation in the classroom, as the resources available in the school were not sufficient to support the development of assessment-driven learning and teaching.

2 External to school influences include the following:

a Paradigmatic inconsistencies. The PD implementers held conflicting views of the curriculum and assessment, thereby confusing teachers. This is where a shared understanding of the assessment reform, including its principles, aims, key processes and expected outcomes are needed across the schools and the system. The competing views communicated to school leaders and teachers compromise the integrity of the reform.

b Misalignment between PD content and teachers' perceived needs. If teachers find the content redundant and irrelevant, they will develop a negative perception of the PD. Consequently, they will not apply the PD content to their practice. The PD content should be aligned to the aims of the reforms and should address the gaps in teachers' knowledge and skills.

c Monitoring of teachers' assessment practices. If the monitoring and providing support of classroom practices is not in place, teachers may continue to revert to their old practices. The ongoing monitoring of teachers' assessment implementation should be done in a supportive environment. The goal is to identify areas needing improvement and to provide support rather than to make evaluative judgements of teachers' effectiveness in raising student outcomes.

d Parental support. Parents are key stakeholders in assessment. Their expectations influence teachers' assessment practices, and their involvement impacts students' learning. Parents with financial or time constraints may find it more difficult to be involved.

Implications of the Problem

To strengthen the assessment reform implementation in educational bureaucracies and in schools, programme implementers should consider the system's readiness. Apart from building a shared understanding across the schools, increasing responsibilisation of parents and students and providing support and resources, a realistic timeline for implementation needs to be considered. An incremental approach to reform implementation can be adopted. This approach is a gradual process of introducing changes over time, avoiding the overwhelming effect of making all necessary changes at once. A realistic timeline and expectations in implementing assessment reforms in schools give sufficient time for teachers to experiment with changing their assessment practices to develop a plethora of assessment skills. When teachers perceive that the expectations for achieving the outcomes of the reform are unrealistic within the specified timeline, they will develop a tokenistic approach to assessment, which limits their effectiveness.

An incremental approach to reform implementation would need to be supplemented by accountable and sustainable PD, preceded by a precise needs analysis of teachers and students and consideration for contextual influences. School leaders should lead in identifying the needs of their teachers and set strategic PD plan to ensure that teachers' needs are addressed, and everyone has access to new knowledge and skills. More importantly, accountability and sustainability should underpin the PD programmes, so teachers can effectively implement these reforms without superficiality or patchiness. Everyone involved in the PD programmes, including implementers, school leaders and teachers, should be accountable of the outcomes of the PD programmes. In addition, PD programmes should be sustainable both its implementation and impacts. A school-based mechanism for ongoing PD and monitoring how teachers are using the new knowledge and skills in the classroom should be part of the reform process. This mechanism will ensure that emerging needs of teachers are identified and addressed, and small successes are celebrated.

Furthermore, it is important for education stakeholders, such as the government or parents, to provide ongoing involvement and support so these reform initiatives can succeed. Schools should clearly community to parents about the reform initiative and its aspirations. Parents' understanding of the reform can leverage their support to their children. They can provide home activities that will complement school and classroom activities. In addition, parents' understanding of and involvement in the assessment reform enable them to provide useful feedback about their observed impacts to their children that are otherwise not captured in schools. Also, well-informed parents can advocate for the assessment reforms to the wider community, communicating effectively accurate information about the reform.

Proposed Solutions

The three case studies demonstrate the challenges of implementing assessment reforms in schools. Overall, building a strong assessment culture in schools requires paradigmatic, conceptual, personal and cultural changes. Effective implementation of school-level reforms may take the following steps.

First, recognition of existing practices, expertise and policies. A thorough analysis of the existing school assessment culture is needed to identify strengths and weaknesses to inform the direction of the reform. This analysis involves exploring stakeholders' dispositions, knowledge, skills and expectations, including school leaders, teachers, students, parents and the community (Alonzo, 2020; Pastore & Andrade, 2019). This information will provide insights for school leaders regarding how to communicate the reform strategy and expected outcomes to all stakeholders, tapping into their existing dispositions, knowledge and skills. All this information must be re-aligned with the system-level policy against the backdrop of contextual factors.

Second, the development of shared organisational assessment culture. A clear vision and goals aligned with students' broader educational objectives and needs must be clearly co-created by all stakeholders to give them a sense of ownership. This process of creating shared decision-making will encourage open dialogue and build consensus on the desired assessment culture, consequently increasing the likelihood that everyone involved will take responsibility for the reform. Also, this process will develop a shared understanding of the vision and goals of the reform. This will establish a common assessment language within the school community. Part of this assessment culture is fostering open communication and transparency. Every stakeholder must be informed of the purpose, objectives and progress of the reform initiative. Any changes in the reform, successes and positive outcomes must be communicated clearly, and any issues or concerns raised must be fully addressed.

Third, the implementation of ongoing PD has been found to increase teachers' assessment literacy (Davison, 2023). Teachers should be fully supported to recalibrate their assessment literacy, ensuring that their dispositions, practical knowledge and skills are aligned with the assessment reform (Tolo et al., 2020). A critical component of this PD is in-school support through mentoring, where expert support is readily available (Alonzo et al., 2021). This mentoring approach will create a supportive environment that encourages continuous learning. Also, part of this PD is giving time for teachers to experiment with implementing new assessment practices. The space provided for teachers to experiment will provide them with the opportunity to translate their theoretical knowledge into practical skills (Lam, 2019). In addition, part of PD is the culture of sharing best practices, collaborating among teachers and creating opportunities for professional dialogue and reflection. Teachers are an invaluable resource for each other. When they are provided with a platform to openly communicate, they can learn from the success of others and can discuss similar issues they have encountered (Davison, 2023). Other teachers can provide feedback and their perspective on the issues, leading to the development of a strategy to solve the issues.

Fourth, the availability of resources and tools supports teachers in enhancing their assessment literacy and enacting assessment practices. Research evidence must be accessible for teachers to continuously update their assessment knowledge to make informed decisions about learning, teaching and assessment practices (Hiebert & Morris, 2012). Also, teachers who are familiar with research evidence can engage in informed discussions with colleagues and

Knowing When Schools Are Doing It Right 203

contribute significantly to professional collaboration. They can meaningfully discuss their best practices or those reported in the literature and contribute to their school's collective knowledge and expertise. Also, they need to be supported to redesign their learning and teaching activities to effectively embed assessment strategies. Implementing an assessment reform may require additional staffing and time allocation for teachers. In addition, developing learning resources (i.e., rubrics, checklists, feedback sheet) for students should be part of the reform strategy. Teachers should be supported to develop or acquire these resources. This is an important aspect of implementing assessment reform in schools to develop tailored-fit resources that are aligned with the reform implementation. When teachers create their own resources, they feel empowered due to their sense of ownership of the reform, leading to higher levels of motivation and commitment to enacting the assessment reform.

Fifth, implementing assessment reform should have a strong focus on building students' capacity to engage in assessment. School leaders and teachers should provide various opportunities for students to develop positive dispositions, knowledge and skills in assessment (Davari Torshizi & Bahraman, 2019). Students were not born with assessment knowledge and skills. Thus, a key requisite for engaging students in assessment is to provide them with explicit training to understand the purpose, process and principles of effective assessment practices, thereby increasing the likelihood that they will engage in assessment (Hannigan et al., 2022). Their assessment literacy will make them understand and fulfil their responsibilities in implementing assessment reform (see Chapter 7 for a detailed discussion of this).

Sixth, the implementation of a monitoring scheme should be part of the reform strategy (Arsyad Arrafii, 2023). A culture of ongoing improvement requires ongoing monitoring of how the reform is implemented. The focus of monitoring is on identifying factors that impact teachers' practices. This focus should be clearly communicated to teachers to provide them with a safe psychological space without the fear of being judged to be effective or ineffective in enacting the reform. Also, school data, teacher data, student data and other data sources must be systematically analysed to identify key insights to inform decisions on further improving the school assessment culture (Alonzo et al., 2021). Moreover, school leaders must continuously seek feedback from all stakeholders to refine their approaches, make necessary adjustments and respond to the emerging needs of students and teachers.

Conclusion

The answer to the title of this chapter is that we know when schools are doing it right when they build a context-based assessment culture. This involves articulating school-level policies underpinned by the system-level assessment policy, which will drive the development of a shared vison for the school to meet the reform's aspirations. In addition, supporting teachers

204 Knowing When Schools Are Doing It Right

to have equitable access to PD programmes is helpful to change their beliefs and practices. They need to be supported to develop contextual assessment resources to ensure the alignment of their practices to the needs of the students.

Overall, when schools implement an assessment reform, school leaders should clearly develop and communicate an assessment culture strategy to all stakeholders. The increased transparency and effective communication will build stakeholders' trust and buy-in, mitigating resistance and misunderstanding. Stakeholders will also become aware of their roles and responsibilities and can actively participate in discussion and decision-making relating to the assessment reform. Thus, the effectiveness and quality of the enactment of the assessment reforms largely depend on the culture of trust, shared understanding and collective commitment created by school leaders.

References

Adie, L., Addison, B., & Lingard, B. (2021). Assessment and learning: An in-depth analysis of change in one school's assessment culture. *Oxford Review of Education, 47*(3), 404–422. https://doi.org/10.1080/03054985.2020.1850436

Alonzo, D. (2020). Teacher education and professional development in industry 4.0: The case for building a strong assessment literacy. In J. P. Ashadi, A. T. Basikin, & N. H. P. S. Putro (Eds.), *Teacher education and professional development in industry 4.0.* Taylor & Francis Group.

Alonzo, D., Leverett, J., & Obsioma, E. (2021). Leading an assessment reform: Ensuring a whole-school approach for decision-making. *Frontiers in Education, 6*(62). https://doi.org/10.3389/feduc.2021.631857

Arsyad Arrafii, M. (2023). Assessment reform in Indonesia: Contextual barriers and opportunities for implementation. *Asia Pacific Journal of Education, 43*(1), 79–94. https://doi.org/10.1080/02188791.2021.1898931

Christoforidou, M., & Kyriakides, L. (2021). Developing teacher assessment skills: The impact of the dynamic approach to teacher professional development. *Studies in Educational Evaluation, 70*, 101051. https://doi.org/10.1016/j.stueduc.2021.101051

Davari Torshizi, M., & Bahraman, M. (2019). I explain, therefore I learn: Improving students' assessment literacy and deep learning by teaching. *Studies in Educational Evaluation, 61*, 66–73. https://doi.org/10.1016/j.stueduc.2019.03.002

Davison, C. (2013). Innovation in assessment: Common misconceptions and problems. In K. Hyland, & L. Wong (Eds.), *Innovation and change in English language education* (pp. 263–275). Routledge.

Davison, C. (2021). Enhancing teacher assessment literacy: One approach to improving teacher knowledge and skills in Australia. In X. Zhu & H. Song (Eds.), *Envisioning teaching and learning of teachers for excellence and equity in education* (pp. 33–43). Springer. https://doi.org/10.1007/978-981-16-2802-3_3

Davison, C. (2023). Assessment literacy: Changing cultures, enculturing change in Hong Kong. *Chinese Journal of Applied Linguistics, 46*(2), 180–197. https://doi.org/doi:10.1515/CJAL-2023-0203

Hannigan, C., Alonzo, D., & Oo, C. Z. (2022). Student assessment literacy: Indicators and domains from the literature. *Assessment in Education: Principles, Policy & Practice*, 1–23. https://doi.org/10.1080/0969594X.2022.2121911

Hiebert, J., & Morris, A. K. (2012). Teaching, rather than teachers, as a path toward improving classroom instruction. *Journal of Teacher Education*, 63(2), 92–102. https://doi.org/10.1177/0022487111428328

Honkimäki, S., Jääskelä, P., Kratochvil, J., & Tynjälä, P. (2022). University-wide, top-down curriculum reform at a Finnish university: Perceptions of the academic staff. *European Journal of Higher Education*, 12(2), 153–170. https://doi.org/10.1080/21568235.2021.1906727

Hopfenbeck, T. N., Flórez Petour, M. T., & Tolo, A. (2015). Balancing tensions in educational policy reforms: Large-scale implementation of assessment for learning in Norway. *Assessment in Education: Principles, Policy & Practice*, 22(1), 44–60. https://doi.org/10.1080/0969594X.2014.996524

Lam, R. (2019). Teacher assessment literacy: Surveying knowledge, conceptions and practices of classroom-based writing assessment in Hong Kong. *System*, 81, 78–89. https://doi.org/10.1016/j.system.2019.01.006

Leahy, S., & Wiliam, D. (2012). From teachers to schools: Scaling up professional development for formative assessment. In J. Gardner (Ed.), *Assessment and learning* (2nd ed., pp. 49–72). SAGE. https://doi.org/10.4135/9781446250808.n4

Maass, K., Cobb, P., Krainer, K., & Potari, D. (2019). Different ways to implement innovative teaching approaches at scale. *Educational Studies in Mathematics*, 102(3), 303–318. https://doi.org/10.1007/s10649-019-09920-8

Nazari, M., & Molana, K. (2022). "Predators of emotions": The role of school assessment policies in English language teachers' emotion labor. *TESOL Quarterly*. https://doi.org/10.1002/tesq.3188

Pastore, S., & Andrade, H. L. (2019). Teacher assessment literacy: A three-dimensional model. *Teaching and Teacher Education*, 84, 128–138. https://doi.org/10.1016/j.tate.2019.05.003

Prytula, M., Noonan, B., & Hellsten, L. (2013). Toward instructional leadership: Principals' perceptions of large-scale assessment in schools. *Canadian Journal of Educational Administration and Policy*, (140). https://cjc-rcc.ucalgary.ca/index.php/cjeap/article/view/42840

Skedsmo, G., & Huber, S. G. (2019). Top-down and bottom-up approaches to improve educational quality: Their intended and unintended consequences. *Educational Assessment, Evaluation and Accountability*, 31(1), 1–4. https://doi.org/10.1007/s11092-019-09294-8

Tolo, A., Lillejord, S., Flórez Petour, M. T., & Hopfenbeck, T. N. (2020). Intelligent accountability in schools: A study of how school leaders work with the implementation of assessment for learning. *Journal of Educational Change*, 21(1), 59–82. https://doi.org/10.1007/s10833-019-09359-x

Verhoeven, J. C., & Devos, G. (2005). School assessment policy and practice in Belgian secondary education with specific reference to vocational education and training. *Assessment in Education: Principles, Policy & Practice*, 12(3), 255–274. https://doi.org/10.1080/09695940500337231

Chapter 12

The Key Elements of Implementing Effective Assessment Reform

Introduction

Since the publication of the seminal paper of Black and Wiliam in 1998, commissioned by the Assessment Reform Group, which later on informed the principles and practices of assessment *for* learning (AfL), many educational bureaucracies have implemented this philosophical framework as part of their national education reform. Such reforms provide the impetus for making assessment the centrepiece of effective learning and teaching. However, after more than three decades of researching assessments, there are reports that assessment reform has still not gained significant traction. There are several reasons cited, including lack of focus on pre-service (Oo et al., 2022) and professional development (PD) programmes (Christoforidou & Kyriakides, 2021), inappropriate tools to guide teachers (Davison, 2013), competing definitions and conceptualisations of effective assessment practices (Alonzo, 2016) and a disconnect between learning theories and assessment (Baird et al., 2017), among others. These issues have been explored in this book through a range of case studies, using extant literature as illustrative examples. Possible solutions are articulated to address these issues.

From a synthesis of the preceding 11 chapters, the following sections present the key elements of assessment reforms, and the key implications for theory, practice and policy, and for future research.

Changes Needed to Build a Strong Assessment Culture

Building a strong assessment culture that supports learning and teaching requires shifting many ideological, conceptual, social, cultural, organisational, structural and practical beliefs and practices. Some of the necessary changes are outlined below.

Personal Change

The personal views and beliefs of all stakeholders about assessment should be aligned with supporting learning and teaching (Taylor, 2013). Their dispositions

DOI: 10.4324/9781003396277-12

influence the enactment of their responsibilities in assessment. For example, the dispositions of policy-makers shape the policy. Their dominant views about the functions of assessment, either for accountability or for improving learning, are reflected in the policy. Similarly, school leaders' view about the purpose of assessment influences their leadership support for teachers. More importantly, teachers' assessment practices are influenced by their dispositions about assessment. They need to realign their views and beliefs with the empirical evidence relating to using assessment to ensure effective learning and teaching (Flórez Petour, 2015).

Social Change

Most approaches used in using assessment to support learning and teaching are teacher-centric. Teachers are perceived to have the biggest responsibility and are accountable for the implementation and outcomes of assessment. However, research evidence points to the increased responsibilisation of other stakeholders as one of the key factors in the success of using assessment to support learning and teaching (Alonzo, 2020). As shown in many studies (Davison, 2021; Hopfenbeck et al., 2015; Pastore & Andrade, 2019), a co-designed and co-implemented approach to assessment reform ensures success in building a strong assessment culture. The interactions and dialogues between policymakers, school leaders, teachers, students, parents and the wider school community develop a shared understanding of assessment principles, processes and practices (Arsyad Arrafii, 2021). These shared understanding will shape common expectations in the system, and through ongoing dialogues, they can support teachers to experiment with new practices and develop practical skills (Christoforidou & Kyriakides, 2021). Also, the interactions among teachers enable them to co-construct solutions to common issues and challenges they face in implementing assessment in their classrooms.

Conceptual Change

The dichotomy between formative assessment (FA) and summative assessment (SA) is still pervasive across schools and within the system. This dichotomy shapes assessment discourses, practices and even research activities. FA is often perceived to be unreliable and thus less useful for decision-making (Brown, 2019). In contrast, SA is perceived to provide more reliable data and thus valued by the system for reporting and accountability requirements. These perceptions undermine the potential use of SA to inform learning and teaching activities and the potential use of FA results to meet accountability requirements (Black, 2017). This dichotomy is further intensified by policies, highlighting the use of SA for reporting students' achievement and schools' performances. Also, SA results are often used to evaluate teaching effectiveness. Similarly, much of the media reports about learning and school effectiveness are drawn heavily from the results of high-stake tests, and school leaders and teachers are judged based on these reports (Thompson, 2013). Across the system, a conceptual change needs to happen where assessment types must be seen as a continuum of practice (Davison, 2007), from in-class contingent FA to the most formal SA where all the results are used for both pedagogical and accountability purposes. This view is supported by Black and Wiliam (2018) where they clearly argue that the distinction between FA and SA becomes irrelevant when assessment is conceptualised within a broader pedagogical mode.

Paradigmatic Change

Assessment, learning and teaching are interconnected, and one cannot function effectively without the other. Despite this understanding, assessment activities remain isolated from learning and teaching activities. Baird et al. (2017) extensively argue that learning and teaching are fields apart. In most cases, assessment activities are implemented without a clear understanding how they can support learning and teaching; thus, the limited use of assessment data to identify students' learning needs and support needed. To optimise the impact of assessment to increasing students' learning, the assessment and learning theories and practices need to be conceptualised and practised coherently, underpinned by a strong belief that assessment is an integral part of effective learning and teaching, and not an activity that happens at a specific episode of learning. Teachers should theorise assessment from the lens of learning theories to establish their mutually inclusive nature to increase student outcomes (Fleer, 2015). Teachers' understanding of learning theories is paramount to understanding the functions of assessment in supporting students' learning. When assessment is conceptualised outside educational theories, it will always be viewed as a discrete episode rather than an integral part of learning and teaching activities.

Curriculum Change

The implementation of effective assessment strategies requires teachers to establish the intersections between assessment and curriculum. Thus, a re-calibration of the curriculum is needed to provide opportunities for teachers and students to effectively engage in assessment. Some assessment strategies require extended time for engagement between teachers and students and for completing the assessment tasks. A rigidly structured curriculum does not support meaningful assessment activities (DeLuca et al., 2020), and by default, the teachers' primary goal becomes to complete the prescribed content with less regard to individual students' learning capacity and the time required for more difficult curriculum content. Thus, using assessment to support learning and teaching requires a fundamental change in curriculum structure, content and processes to provide space for teachers' and students' active engagement.

Key Elements of Implementing Reform   209

Knowledge and Skills Change

Implementing assessment reforms requires assessment knowledge, skills and positive dispositions of all stakeholders. Policy-makers need to have a clear understanding of the intersections of assessment. learning and teaching to articulate policies that support schools leaders and teachers implement assessment reforms. In addition, school leaders should have both assessment literacy and instructional leadership capabilities to develop a strong vision for schools and to support teachers to enact assessment reforms (Christoforidou & Kyriakides, 2021). More importantly, teachers need to have the necessary assessment literacy to effectively use assessment to support student learning (Alonzo, 2016). There are many frameworks and tools that define and describe the specific knowledge, skills and dispositions needed by teachers, but there is no universal set of assessment literacies. Teacher assessment literacy is context-based (Alonzo et al., 2021; Lam, 2019). Thus, educational institutions should define and describe the discrete assessment knowledge, skills and depositions needed by teachers and other stakeholders to implement effective assessment practices underpinned by policy and contextual factors. In addition, the role of teacher education institutions is critically important for developing a pre-service teacher education curriculum that prepares pre-service teachers to use assessment to support learning and teaching. Enhancing teachers' assessment literacy begins in pre-service teacher education (Oo et al., 2022; Oo et al., 2023) and requires ongoing engagement in PD.

Part of this change is a strong focus on building students' assessment literacy, their knowledge and skills required to effectively engage in assessment. Students' engagement in assessment is theoretically and empirically supported (Hannigan et al., 2022). Students should have a strong sense of autonomy to develop the skills and capacity for reflective judgment to activate these roles. Effective engagement in assessment requires students to think critically, reflect on their learning and develop learning strategies to meet the learning outcomes.

Practical Change

Implementing new practices requires time for exploration and experimentation. Thus, part of the changes that need to happen include workload allocation for teachers (DeLuca et al., 2020). To attain automaticity in implementing assessment that supports learning and teaching, teachers need to engage in trial and error activities to sort out which assessment activities best support their students. When teachers need to spend more time outside their allocated worktime to plan, design and implement assessment activities, they tend to resist implementing assessment reform. They will develop a strong negative perception that implementing assessment activities intensifies their work. Also, the classroom set-up should be recalibrated to allow for the processes required for effective assessment implementation. For example, implementing peer assessment requires students' interaction. When classroom set-up does not provide the space for interactions, students may not engage in eliciting and giving feedback to their peers. Moreover, some assessment activities require extended time. Thus, careful planning is needed to ensure that the number of assessment activities implemented is reasonable within the allocated time.

Structural and Organisational Change

Many studies show that implementing an assessment reform requires structural and organisational change. A strong school leadership is needed to establish a vision and common assessment language across and within schools (Alonzo et al., 2021). The assessment literacy of school leaders and their instructional leadership roles are critical for the success of building a strong assessment culture. The alignment of school culture to the principles of effective assessment that supports learning and teaching is a major factor in shaping teachers' assessment practices. School leaders need to find a balance between the accountability function and learning development function of assessment (Hopfenbeck et al., 2015). The designation of assessment leaders who provide support and mentoring for other teachers might help to have focal persons that lead the assessment reform and provide support for other teachers (Alonzo et al., 2021). These assessment leaders can work closely with teachers to design, implement and evaluate the effectiveness of assessment activities. Their interactions with teachers will enable to understand the specific contextual factors affecting assessment in the classroom. They can then support teachers to design highly contextualised assessment activities.

Policy Change

Building a strong assessment culture that supports learning and teaching requires articulating and implementing system-level and school-level policies that support teachers' adoption of effective assessment practices. Policies strongly shape the school assessment culture and teachers' assessment practices, and more often than not, when policies contradict to the principles of effective assessment practices, teachers tend to lean towards following the policies. Thus, assessment policies should clearly acknowledge and support the dual functions of assessments for pedagogical and accountability. There should be neither apparent dichotomisation of assessment nor a strong symbolism of assessment that matters in the bureaucracy. This means that the policy should encourage teachers to use all types of assessment and assessment data to make informed learning and teaching decisions to support individual students and to meet the accountability requirements.

Part of policy change is the recognition of the multiple outcomes of using assessment to improve learning and teaching. The dominant view is the use of student achievement indicators such as scores and marks to evaluate teaching effectiveness and report student outcomes. However, this is a narrow view of outcomes. The impact of assessment on student learning is not always a direct and immediate increase in academic achievement. Assessment can increase student engagement (Alonzo et al., 2023; Hughes, 2014), self-regulation (De-Luca et al., 2020), self-efficacy (Yan et al., 2020) and motivation (Clark, 2011; Leenknecht et al., 2021) and reduce classroom management issues (Andrade & Brookhart, 2020), which are important factors in raising student achievement over the long term. There are multiple pathways, direct and indirect, by which assessment can significantly impact student achievement. Thus, it is important to acknowledge these multiple outcomes of assessment to broaden our understanding of how assessment improves students' learning.

Key Elements in Implementing Assessment Reforms

As argued in this book, implementing assessment reforms, both at system and school levels, require personal, social-emotional, conceptual, paradigmatic, practical, contextual, structural, organisational and policy changes. A holistic and systemic approach to assessment reform should be carefully planned, implemented, monitored and evaluated. Collectively, the following elements should underpin assessment reforms.

Shared Organisational Assessment Culture

Clearly defined assessment culture supported by policy and enabling mechanisms will provide an overarching framework for enacting an assessment reform. At the system level, the goals and vision of assessment reform must be clearly established, and the schools should be given an autonomy to translate it into a school assessment culture. It is particularly important that system's and schools' assessment cultures are focused on improving learning and teaching because these influence teachers' assessment practices (Nortvedt et al., 2016). Thus, it is important that the assessment reform and the policy supporting it must be informed by research evidence to include those practices that have both theoretical and empirical support in improving student outcomes. The policy should enable teachers to design and implement assessment practices that support learning and teaching within the constraints of the curriculum and resources. Also, the policy should support students to meaningfully engage in assessment and learning activities.

Clear Responsibilities of Stakeholders

Responsibilisation of stakeholders through building their assessment literacy. The teacher-centric approach to implementing assessment reform is ineffective because other stakeholders play important roles in building a strong assessment culture that supports learning and teaching. The key to increasing the responsibilisation of stakeholders is to build their assessment literacy. The policymakers have to engage in the literature to explore research evidence for both content and approach of the policy. They should use research evidence to articulate assessment policy and to develop an approach for implementing an assessment reform. School leaders must build their assessment leadership to effectively contextualise the national or state policy to their respective schools. Part of this assessment leadership is to provide professional and social-emotional support for teachers, including the provision of resources for the effective implementation of assessment practices. Teachers should be provided with ongoing PD opportunities focused on building their assessment knowledge and skills aligned to the assessment reform. At the classroom level, teachers need to become student partners (Alonzo, 2020) to build students' assessment literacy. Student engagement in assessment is influenced by their understanding of assessment principles, purposes and processes (Hannigan et al., 2022). Teachers should ensure that they provide opportunities for students to build their assessment knowledge and skills for them to understand the responsibilities they have not only in assessment but in learning and teaching more broadly.

Recognition of Existing Practice, Expertise and Policies

Developing and implementing a new assessment reform requires a thorough analysis of the historical and ideological dimensions of the system (Petour & Teresa, 2015). Having a clear understanding of the historical perspective of the reforms will provide insights how the new reforms are influenced by previous policies, practices, discourses and political figures. In addition, exploring stakeholders' ideologies, knowledge, skills and dispositions will provide insights about the dominant views and beliefs across the system. These understanding can inform the reform's implementation strategy by realigning practices, expertise and policies to its overall aims.

Curriculum Review and Re-alignment

The curriculum content and structure influence teachers' use of assessment (Nortvedt et al., 2016). A rigid curriculum does not allow for teachers to implement empirically driven assessment practices. Given the large number of contents to cover within a short period of time, their main goal is to complete teaching all the content without strong regard to actual student learning. Teachers will use a one-size approach to assessment due to curriculum constraint, which is proven ineffective (Wiliam, 2013). The adaptive disposition of teachers (Loughland & Alonzo, 2019) is needed to develop differentiated assessment practices (Alonzo & Loughland, 2022). Thus, it is critically important that the existing curriculum of educational system must be reviewed with assessment as the central feature of learning and teaching.

Establishing the Intersections of Theories of Assessment, Curriculum and Pedagogy

Across the system, part of the shared understanding is how assessment can be conceptualised within the broader educational theories. Effective embedding of assessment to learning and teaching activities happens when teachers clearly understand that assessment is the central feature of what they do, and all other activities are informed by the assessment data gathered by teachers to design differentiated learning and assessment activities. From the policy makers' viewpoint, their understanding of the complex interactions of assessment with curriculum and pedagogy will help them understand the nuances of assessment. As a result of this understanding, they can develop policies and provide support for teachers' enactment of assessment reforms (Van der Kleij et al., 2018).

Cultural and Linguistic Adaptation of Assessment

The dynamic and emerging nature of FA requires a constant exploration and configuration of approaches and practices. This is compounded by classroom contexts that significantly influence the effectiveness of assessment. Culturally, most assessment activities like dialogic feedback and peer assessment are uncommon for students. Hence, teachers need to develop a classroom climate where students are encouraged to talk about their learning. Teachers should develop a strong partnership with students to engage them in assessment effectively (Hannigan et al., 2022). Linguistically, some assessment activities require higher level of language proficiencies (Black & Wiliam, 2018). For example, peer assessment requires students to clearly articulate their feedback to their classmates. Also, in dialogic feedback, students should interrogate the feedback given teachers. Effective communication of students with their peers and teachers requires higher level of language proficiencies.

School Leaders and Teachers' Agency to Build a Strong Assessment Culture

Implementing assessment reforms should adopt a bottom-up approach (Skedsmo & Huber, 2019). A national assessment policy should only guide school leaders and teachers to develop their school-based approach to implementing the reform. This approach is proven more effective as it taps to and values the agency, motivation and expertise of school leaders and teachers (Nazari & Molana, 2022). Their knowledge about the school context, students' learning characteristics and needs and their practical knowledge better position them to effectively enact the reform.

Parental Involvement

Parents play a significant role in implementing an assessment reform. They provide support to their children and feedback to schools. It is important that parents' understanding and expectations are aligned to the reforms' principles and aims (Ratnam-Lim & Tan, 2015). A strong partnership between schools and parents should be established to provide avenue for school leaders and teachers to effectively communicate with parents about their children's learning and discuss possible home-school collaboration activities to further support students. Teachers should work closely with parents/carers and the community to address their assessment information needs. Ensuring the alignment of their expectations with the school assessment culture will draw support from them. It has been shown that parents' expectations that are contrary to what teachers do in the classroom put pressure on teachers to revert to practices that meet parents' expectations.

Review of Contextual Factors

There are contextual factors that influence the adaptation of FA. These include large classes, rigid timetable, lack of resources and lack of PD opportunities. More importantly, workload allocations must be reviewed (Christoforidou & Kyriakides, 2021). Teachers' resistance to assessment reform usually comes from the fear of extra work associated with it (Hopfenbeck et al., 2015). When teachers perceive that meeting the expectations of the reform requires massive investment of their time, they will adopt a tick-the-box approach rather than ensuring meaningful learning and assessment experience for students.

Strong Focus on Building Students' Capacity to Engage in Assessment

Students are the key players of assessment reforms in the classroom. The Assessment Reform Group (ARG, 2002) positions students as the primary users of assessment data to monitor their learning and develop their subsequent learning goals. However, students' engagement in assessment is determined by their assessment literacy (Chan & Luo, 2021). Teachers should provide a range of opportunities for them to develop positive dispositions, knowledge and skills about assessment to ensure they can effectively navigate with any assessment tasks and processes (Hannigan et al., 2022).

Implementation of On-going Professional Development

The development of teachers' practical assessment knowledge depends on the quality of PD provided. The PD content should be carefully identified to address the knowledge and skills' needs of teachers (Christoforidou & Kyriakides, 2021). Any irrelevant content will discourage teachers and demotivate them to implement it in their classroom. In addition, teachers should have equitable access to an ongoing PD program (Arsyad Arrafii, 2021).

School leaders can develop a school-based PD program to ensure that teachers are well-supported in assessment knowledge acquisition and skills development.

Availability of Resources and Tools to Support Teachers and Students

Insufficient or inappropriate support and resources for teachers and students will negatively influence the implementation of an assessment reform (Arsyad Arrafii, 2021). The role of learning and teaching resources is inevitably important in ensuring effective learning and teaching. When new assessment activities are trialled by teachers, they might need to re-align their extant resources or develop or provide new resources. In addition, teachers and students should be provided with tools for self-reflection to improve their assessment literacy (Alonzo, 2016).

Implementation of Monitoring Scheme for Developmental Purposes

Teachers' implementation of assessment in their classroom should be part of performance monitoring (Arsyad Arrafii, 2021). However, the purpose of evaluation should not be accountability-driven but rather a strong focus on identifying their strengths and areas for further improvement. The critical feedback received by teachers will enable them to work closely with school leaders to find opportunities to address them. The implementation of monitoring scheme must be carefully designed and implemented to develop trust between teachers and school leaders. When the purpose of performance monitoring is not well understood by teachers, they will develop a negative perception about it, thereby undermining their motivation.

Safe Space for Teacher Experimentation

Due to the context-driven nature of assessment, a need for ongoing experimentation and adaption in approach and practice should be at the forefront of teacher practices. The development of automaticity of teachers' assessment skills requires time for trial-and-error in operationalising their theoretical knowledge and developing practical skills (Christoforidou & Kyriakides, 2021). When they are expected to deliver the outcomes at an unreasonable timeline, there is a higher tendency for them to revert to their previous practice. In addition, when the implementation of the reform is driven by accountability, they will become reluctant to try implementing a range of assessment strategies for the fear of failing. An assessment culture should recognise that teacher setbacks are part of their learning process.

Ensuring Trustworthiness of Assessment

Teachers' assessment practices are often critiqued due to their perceived low reliability and validity (Brown, 2019), and this critique negatively impacts teachers' confidence and actual assessment practices. Schools should ensure that their assessment culture is underpinned by concepts that promote the trustworthiness of assessment. These concepts that ensure the trustworthiness of teachers' assessment practices include theirs' and students' assessment literacy; implementing evidence-informed assessment practices and processes, assessment activities should be accessible, fair and equitable for students from culturally and linguistically diverse backgrounds, disadvantaged students and even gifted students (Alonzo & Teng, 2023). At the classroom level, the actual implementation of assessment should be differentiated to meet the needs of individual students (Alonzo & Loughland, 2022). As shown in Chapter 5, the one-size-fits-all approach to assessment is problematic because individual students have different prior knowledge, dispositions, ability level and backgrounds. Failure to account for students' diverse characteristics and needs and use them to inform the design and implementation of assessment activities would compromise their effectiveness.

Implications for Theory

The use of the phrase 'assessment to support learning and teaching' departs from the dichotomisation of assessment. As argued in Chapter 2, the conceptual distinction between FA and SA becomes irrelevant when assessment is conceptualised within a broader pedagogical model. This was earlier argued by Biggs (1998) and later extensively supported by Black and Wiliam (2018). If we continue to highlight the dichotomy of assessment, it will further limit the utility of SAs to further improve learning and teaching. Similarly, those labelled as FAs will not be used to contribute to assessment data to meet accountability requirements. Thus, teachers will continue to oscillate between these two assessment types, with a higher likelihood to favour SAs due to the accountability requirements imposed by the system. Rather than viewing assessments from two ends of the spectrum, the conceptualisation of Davison (2007) that assessment practices are a continuum of practice from in-class assessment to more formal SAs, including external high-stake tests, which results are used for formative purposes, should be the default understanding of assessment. By prioritising the learning and teaching functions of assessment, teachers draw on their agency and skills and use assessment data to adapt their teaching to meet students' needs. The timing, types and implementation might differ for every assessment, but the purpose hinges on improving learning and teaching. The accountability function of assessment comes secondary. Making the accountability function of assessment less prominent may limit the negative consequences of assessment. Teachers will not teach to the test or narrow the curriculum as there is no pressure to 'look good' in external examination results. Instead, teachers are engaged in providing assessment activities for students to elicit evidence of student learning to use it to further improve learning and teaching activities. Thus, we need to further advance the theorisation of the accountability function of assessment as a by-product of effective learning and teaching rather than a function of external high-stake examination.

More importantly, the conceptualisation of assessment must be viewed from broader educational theories, including curriculum theories and pedagogy. Owing to the principle of effective assessment practices, that assessment is an integral part of learning and teaching, its conceptual clarity and effectiveness lie on its clear intersections with learning and teaching against the backdrop of curriculum, policy and contextual factors. This approach to conceptualising assessment will answer the criticism of Baird et al. (2017) that assessment and learning are fields apart. Finding the nexus between learning and assessment requires more than establishing their intersections. Instead, all factors influencing them must be considered with a strong focus on policy and contextual factors. Failure to account for these factors will result in a problematic conceptualisation of the role of assessment in supporting learning and teaching.

Implications for Practice and Policy

Research in assessment has been very prolific in the last three decades, but evidence suggest minimal impacts on student learning. The backwash effects of assessment continue to proliferate due to inappropriate implementation of assessment and the competing demand for accountability.

If the school assessment culture is well defined and supported by system-level policy, and all other requisites (i.e. resources, PD, people and assessment knowledge, skills and dispositions) are available, the issue of implementing assessment can be resolved. These requisites will support teachers in implementing a student-centred pedagogically linked assessment practice. This practice requires effectively embedding assessment activities in the learning and teaching activities. Upon reflecting on their content knowledge and pedagogical content knowledge, teachers can identify the most impactful assessment strategy to help them engage students and provide them with meaningful insights about student learning. This assessment approach should also help students achieve the learning outcomes. Teachers should avoid the tokenistic approach to implementing a series of assessment activities without assessing their actual impact on student learning. The effective implementation of assessment to support learning and teaching does not rely on the numbers of assessment activities implemented but on careful planning and implementing a reasonable number of assessment activities that provide evidence of students' learning. Careful planning of the number of assessment activities is particularly important given the issue of teachers' workload and competing activities.

In addition, teachers should continuously engage in experimentation. The dynamic and context-based nature of assessment requires ongoing recalibration of practice as the one-size-fits-all approach is ineffective. Teachers should demonstrate the principle of assessment by recognising that mistakes are part of the learning process. The openness of teachers to experiment and reflect on the impact of their practice on learning and teaching will help them develop a plethora of practices that they can easily dispense when needed. Teachers who are afraid to implement new assessment activities may continue with their old practice. However, teachers must be supported to provide a safe psychological space for experimentation. Performance evaluation implemented by schools often constrains teachers' practice. The evaluative nature of monitoring teachers' performance deters teachers from implementing new assessment activities. Schools need to adopt a developmental approach to performance evaluation where the results are used to identify teachers' support and PD needs without the fear of being judged as effective or ineffective teachers.

The issue of accountability requires a systemic approach to addressing it. In an educational system with dominant external assessment, teachers orient their work to exam preparation. A large number of evidence internationally of what happens with high stakes supports this finding (Ball et al., 2012; Conway & Murphy, 2013; Datnow et al., 2019). To address this issue, there is a need to link system-level standardised assessments to school and classroom-level assessments and evaluations (O'Neill, 2013). This would ensure that assessment would positively benefit students and teachers while also raising the quality and equity of education outcomes in schools. Teachers operating in a system with a strong focus and emphasis on the accountability function of education do not value assessment work highly. Even though they talk much about external examinations, they do it to comply with systems' requirements. They will spend much time marking even external examination preparation and all associated data work. With this finding, there is a need to reinstate the primary role of teachers and schools in student assessment, and reporting will increase trust in teachers as professionals. They are particularly negative about data collection and their administrative duties. This relates to their broader work of intensification. Teachers value working with students. However, if assessment policies do not orient teachers to working with students at a personal level, they will not engage with them. Hence, assessment practices must build a stronger student-teacher relationship. This is supported by the findings that teachers disengage if the national assessment is not designed to be used by teachers.

Therefore, the role of teachers must be strengthened at all levels of assessment reforms. Teachers know what they need and what works in their classrooms, and to that extent, systems must place more trust in the professionalism of their teachers and school leaders. Teachers should be deeply involved in developing an assessment reform, particularly redesigning and articulating its purpose and testing new instruments in their work before they are implemented across the system. The primacy of one assessment brings risks. A lack of attention to a broader set of assessments in the policy will distort the nature of teachers' work and lead to negative attitudes. Many external examinations are presented and politically sold with overstated claims as to their potential (Gannon, 2012). Their implementation, including purpose and timing, does not usually suit the school assessment agenda. The so-called diagnostic capability was poor due to the broad scale of tests. More importantly, the tests were high stakes with discernible and observable negative impacts on teachers and students (Thompson, 2013; Thompson et al., 2018).

Thus, it is important that all assessments, including national assessment and reporting system, international assessments and classroom-based assessment, positively influence classroom practices, support collaborative professionalism in and between schools and remain efficient in administration. Therefore, all external assessment systems must link to school and classroom-level assessments and evaluations. This would ensure that the assessment would benefit students and teachers while raising the quality and equity of education outcomes in schools. The recent public and media discourse around external exams suggests that there is work to be done to restore teachers' confidence in the national student assessment system. Teachers as professionals should participate in a process that gives them a say in how well students do in school and how to improve their performance. Teachers are best positioned to keep student assessments safe from unintended consequences and policy changes that are not based on evidence or success elsewhere. Teachers expect education policies, including student assessment, to be consistent with effective assessment principles that support learning and teaching.

Implications for Future Research

We know much about the impact of assessment on learning and teaching, and many researchers have outlined best practices (Boud & Molloy, 2013; Cheung-Blunden & Khan, 2018; Militello et al., 2013), articulated guiding principles (Black & Wiliam, 2018; Brooks et al., 2019) and developed frameworks and tools (Alonzo, 2016; Hill & McNamara, 2012; Xu & Brown, 2016) to support the implementation of assessment, but some areas require further investigations. In particular, there is a paucity of literature demonstrating the dynamic nature of building a school assessment culture. Many studies documented that school assessment reforms are often teacher-centric, putting more responsibilities on teachers to change their practice within the same condition. Although there is a growing recognition of the impact of increasing the responsibilisation of all stakeholders, there is little evidence of how these responsibilities influence student outcomes. We need to establish the path of these influences to understand better if they are direct or indirect effects.

Reports in the literature are competing with some that reported a strong link, but other studies report otherwise.

There is a need to revisit how those key elements discussed above can be translated into assessment standards to guide teachers' assessment practices. In most assessment standards articulated in professional teaching standards, teachers' assessment roles in the assessment are articulated as a set of discrete knowledge and skills. This nature of standards treats teachers like technicians who need to perform those tasks without regard for their dispositions. The focus of further investigation would be on how to effectively develop those key elements into aspirational standards where teachers are given the agency to translate the elements into suites of practice operating within the assessment culture of their respective schools. These standards will allow teachers to recognise that and enact the context-driven nature of assessment. They will not be constrained by what is written in the standards at the risk of adopting a tokenistic approach to implementing them. Instead, they will draw from their agency and capability to develop their approach to using assessment to support learning and teaching.

Also, the conflicts among teacher beliefs, practices, school culture, policy and contextual factors, parental expectations and students' beliefs and engagement need further investigation. These conflicts are often cited in the literature, but there are limited studies on resolving them. This line of enquiry will provide critical insights on how schools could develop a strong assessment culture and how to support teachers to balance between what schools think assessment should be and what parents expect to see. Also, research on students' beliefs and engagement in assessment are mostly done in the higher education context and very limited in the schools' context. There are opportunities for researching students' assessment knowledge, skills and dispositions, especially in the primary school setting. Issues that are still unresolved include the timing (year level) of engaging students in assessment, the capabilities of younger students for self and peer assessment and nature of student participation in co-creating assessment, particularly rubrics.

Another important area for investigation is to evaluate the initial teacher education curriculum and the PD programmes for in-service teachers to explore how educational systems ensure the key elements of assessment to support learning and teaching are embedded in teacher education and development. The quality of teacher preparation is critically important to build pre-service teachers' assessment literacy (Oo et al., 2021). There is growing concern that graduate teachers enter the teaching profession with limited agency and capacity to design and implement assessment activities, elicit and give feedback, engage students in assessment and analyse assessment data to inform learning and teaching activities. There are reported gaps in the literature, including factors influencing pre-service teachers' acquisition of assessment literacy, the best approach to use and empirical support for the effectiveness of the current approaches (Oo et al., 2022). We also need longitudinal studies examining the impact of pre-service teachers' assessment training. By following teachers from their pre-service preparation into their early years of teaching, we can gain insights into the long-term effects of assessment training on their assessment practices, classroom decisions and student learning outcomes. In terms of in-service teachers' development, we need to evaluate how teachers are trained to develop and implement assessment for students from diverse backgrounds, accommodate individual differences and learning needs and ensure that assessments are fair and equitable for all students, regardless of their cultural, linguistic or socio-economic backgrounds. This is an important area of investigation that is often cited as teachers' needs but not fully explored in the literature. The paucity of literature on this topic reinforces the one-size-fits-all assessment practice. Also, we need a holistic framework to evaluate the effectiveness and efficiency of teacher training programmes implemented. PD programmes implemented at system and school levels must be treated as an evaluand, with evaluation activities across the program's life. Integrating evaluation activities at specific life stages of the program will ensure that insights are gathered to inform decisions about the progress and adaptation required to make the program more effective.

Conclusion

The key elements describe above challenge the existing conceptualisations and understanding of assessment to support learning and teaching. Building a strong assessment culture requires personal, social-emotional, conceptual, paradigmatic, practical, contextual, structural, organisational and policy changes. These changes are necessary elements to develop a holistic approach to building a strong assessment culture that effectively supports learning and teaching. The implications outlined above are also necessary requisites to ensure assessment is used to support learning and teaching. The theoretical reorientation, practical knowledge development and policy articulation will support schools, teachers and students to optimise the positive impacts of assessment on learning and teaching. Moreover, addressing the research gaps highlighted above will further provide insights on how to strategically lead and implement assessment reforms, articulate policies, develop assessment resources, implement preservice teacher training and in-service teachers' PD, change teachers' beliefs and practices and evaluate the assessment reforms.

References

Alonzo, D. (2016). *Development and application of a teacher assessment for learning (AfL) literacy tool.* University of New South Wales. http://unsworks.unsw.edu.au/fapi/datastream/unsworks:38345/SOURCE02?view=true

Alonzo, D. (2020). Teacher education and professional development in industry 4.0: The case for building a strong assessment literacy. In Ashadi, J. Priyana, Basikin, A.

Triastuti, & N. H. P. S. Putro (Eds.), *Teacher education and professional development in industry 4.0.* Taylor & Francis Group.

Alonzo, D., Labad, V., Bejano, J., & Guerra, F. (2021). The policy-driven dimensions of teacher beliefs about assessment. *Australian Journal of Teacher Education, 46*(3). https://ro.ecu.edu.au/cgi/viewcontent.cgi?article=4761&context=ajte

Alonzo, D., & Loughland, T. (2022). Variability of students' responses to assessment activities: The influence of achievement levels. *International Journal of Instruction, 15*(4), 1071–1090. https://doi.org/10.29333/iji.2022.15457a

Alonzo, D., & Teng, S. (2023). Trustworthiness of teacher assessment and decision-making: Reframing the consistency and accuracy measures. *International Journal of Instruction, 16*(3), 1075–1094.

Andrade, H. L., & Brookhart, S. M. (2020). Classroom assessment as the co-regulation of learning. *Assessment in Education: Principles, Policy & Practice, 27*(4), 350–372. https://doi.org/10.1080/0969594X.2019.1571992

ARG. (2002). *Assessment for learning: 10 principles.* https://www.storre.stir.ac.uk/bitstream/1893/32458/1/Assessment%20for%20learning%2010%20principles%202002.pdf

Arsyad Arrafii, M. (2021). Assessment reform in Indonesia: contextual barriers and opportunities for implementation. *Asia Pacific Journal of Education,* 1–16. https://doi.org/10.1080/02188791.2021.1898931

Baird, J.-A., Andrich, D., Hopfenbeck, T. N., & Stobart, G. (2017). Assessment and learning: Fields apart? *Assessment in Education: Principles, Policy & Practice, 24*(3), 317–350. https://doi.org/10.1080/0969594X.2017.1319337

Ball, S., Maguire, M., & Braun, A. (2012). *How schools do policy: Policy enactments in secondary schools.* Routledge.

Biggs, J. (1998). Assessment and classroom learning: A role for summative assessment? *Assessment and Evaluation, 5*(1), 103–110.

Black, P. (2017). Assessment in science education. In K. S. Taber & B. Akpan (Eds.), *Science Education: An International Course Companion* (pp. 295–309). SensePublishers. https://doi.org/10.1007/978-94-6300-749-8_22

Black, P., & Wiliam, D. (2018). Classroom assessment and pedagogy. *Assessment in Education: Principles, Policy & Practice, 25*(6), 551–575. https://doi.org/10.1080/0969594X.2018.1441807

Boud, D., & Molloy, E. (2013). Rethinking models of feedback for learning: The challenge of design. *Assessment & Evaluation in Higher Education, 38*(6), 698–712. https://doi.org/10.1080/02602938.2012.691462

Brooks, C., Carroll, A., Gillies, R. M., & Hattie, J. (2019). A matrix of feedback for learning. *Australian Journal of Teacher Education, 44*(4). https://ro.ecu.edu.au/ajte/vol44/iss4/2

Brown, G. T. L. (2019). Is assessment for learning really assessment?. *Frontiers in Education, 4*(64). https://doi.org/10.3389/feduc.2019.00064

Chan, C. K. Y., & Luo, J. (2021). A four-dimensional conceptual framework for student assessment literacy in holistic competency development. *Assessment & Evaluation in Higher Education, 46*(3), 451–466. https://doi.org/10.1080/02602938.2020.1777388

Cheung-Blunden, V., & Khan, S. R. (2018). A modified peer rating system to recognise rating skill as a learning outcome. *Assessment & Evaluation in Higher Education, 43*(1), 58–67. https://doi.org/10.1080/02602938.2017.1280721

Christoforidou, M., & Kyriakides, L. (2021). Developing teacher assessment skills: The impact of the dynamic approach to teacher professional development. *Studies in Educational Evaluation, 70*, 101051. https://doi.org/10.1016/j.stueduc.2021.101051

Clark, I. (2011). Formative assessment and motivation: Theories and themes. *Prime Research on Education, 1*(2), 26–36.

Conway, P. F., & Murphy, R. (2013). A rising tide meets a perfect storm: New accountabilities in teaching and teacher education in Ireland. *Irish Educational Studies, 32*(1), 11–36. https://doi.org/10.1080/03323315.2013.773227

Datnow, A., Lockton, M., & Weddle, H. (2019). Redefining or reinforcing accountability? An examination of meeting routines in schools. *Journal of Educational Change, 21*, 109–134. https://doi.org/10.1007/s10833-019-09349-z

Davison, C. (2007). Views from the chalkface: English Language school based assessment in Hong Kong. *Language Assessment Quarterly, 4*(1), 37–68. https://doi.org/10.1080/15434300701348359

Davison, C. (2013). Innovation in assessment: Common misconceptions and problems. In K. Hyland, & L. Wong (Eds.), *Innovation and change in English language education* (pp. 263–275). Routledge.

Davison, C. (2021). Enhancing teacher assessment literacy: One approach to improving teacher knowledge and skills in Australia. In X. Zhu & H. Song (Eds.), *Envisioning teaching and learning of teachers for excellence and equity in education* (pp. 33–43). Springer. https://doi.org/10.1007/978-981-16-2802-3_3

DeLuca, C., Pyle, A., Braund, H., & Faith, L. (2020). Leveraging assessment to promote kindergarten learners' independence and self-regulation within play-based classrooms. *Assessment in Education: Principles, Policy & Practice, 27*(4), 394–415. https://doi.org/10.1080/0969594X.2020.1719033

Fleer, M. (2015). Developing an assessment pedagogy: the tensions and struggles in re-theorising assessment from a cultural–historical perspective. *Assessment in Education: Principles, Policy & Practice, 22*(2), 224–246. https://doi.org/10.1080/0969594X.2015.1015403

Flórez Petour, M. T. (2015). Systems, ideologies and history: a three-dimensional absence in the study of assessment reform processes. *Assessment in Education: Principles, Policy & Practice, 22*(1), 3–26. https://doi.org/10.1080/0969594X.2014.943153

Gannon, S. (2012). My school re-dux: Re-storying schooling with the My School website. *Discourse: Studies in the Cultural Politics of Education, 34*(1), 17–30.

Hannigan, C., Alonzo, D., & Oo, C. Z. (2022). Student assessment literacy: Indicators and domains from the literature. *Assessment in Education: Principles, Policy & Practice*, 1–23. https://doi.org/10.1080/0969594X.2022.2121911

Hill, K., & McNamara, T. (2012). Developing a comprehensive, empirically based research framework for classroom-based assessment. *Language Testing, 29*(3), 395–420. https://doi.org/10.1177/0265532211428317

Hopfenbeck, T. N., Flórez Petour, M. T., & Tolo, A. (2015). Balancing tensions in educational policy reforms: Large-scale implementation of assessment for learning in Norway. *Assessment in Education: Principles, Policy & Practice, 22*(1), 44–60. https://doi.org/10.1080/0969594X.2014.996524

Hughes, C. (2014). Improving student engagement and development through assessment: theory and practice in higher education. *Higher Education Research & Development, 33*(1), 176–177. https://doi.org/10.1080/07294360.2013.783954

Lam, R. (2019). Teacher assessment literacy: Surveying knowledge, conceptions and practices of classroom-based writing assessment in Hong Kong. *System*, *81*, 78–89. https://doi.org/10.1016/j.system.2019.01.006

Leenknecht, M., Wijnia, L., Köhlen, M., Fryer, L., Rikers, R., & Loyens, S. (2021). Formative assessment as practice: the role of students' motivation. *Assessment & Evaluation in Higher Education*, *46*(2), 236–255. https://doi.org/10.1080/026 02938.2020.1765228

Loughland, T., & Alonzo, D. (2019). Teacher adaptive practices: A key factor in teachers' implementation of assessment for learning. *Australian Journal of Teacher Education*, *44*(7). https://doi.org/http://dx.doi.org/10.14221/ajte.2019v44n7.2

Militello, M., Bass, L., Jackson, K., & Wang, Y. (2013). How data are used and misused in schools: Perceptions from teachers and principals. *Education Sciences*, *3*(2), 98–120. https://doi.org/10.3390/educsci3020098

Nazari, M., & Molana, K. (2022). "Predators of emotions": The role of school assessment policies in English language teachers' emotion labor. *TESOL Quarterly*. https://doi.org/10.1002/tesq.3188

Nortvedt, G. A., Santos, L., & Pinto, J. (2016). Assessment for learning in Norway and Portugal: The case of primary school mathematics teaching. *Assessment in Education: Principles, Policy & Practice*, *23*(3), 377–395. https://doi.org/10.1080/09 69594X.2015.1108900

O'Neill, O. (2013). Intelligent accountability in education. *Oxford Review of Education*, *39*(1), 4–16. https://doi.org/10.1080/03054985.2013.764761

Oo, C. Z., Alonzo, D., & Davison, C. (2021). Pre-service teachers' decision-making and classroom assessment practices. *Frontiers in Education*, *6*(102). https://doi.org/10.3389/feduc.2021.628100

Oo, C. Z., Alonzo, D., & Asih, R. (2022). Acquisition of teacher assessment literacy by pre-service teachers: A review of practices and program designs. *Issues in Educational Research*, *32*(1), 352–373. https://search.informit.org/doi/10.3316/informit.475861785399488

Oo, C. Z., Alonzo, D., Asih, R., Pelobillo, G., Lim, R., San, N. M. H., & O'Neill, S. (2023). Implementing school-based assessment reforms to enhance student learning: a systematic review. *Educational Assessment, Evaluation and Accountability*. https://doi.org/10.1007/s11092-023-09420-7

Pastore, S., & Andrade, H. L. (2019). Teacher assessment literacy: A three-dimensional model. *Teaching and Teacher Education*, *84*, 128–138. https://doi.org/10.1016/j.tate.2019.05.003

Ratnam-Lim, C. T. L., & Tan, K. H. K. (2015). Large-scale implementation of formative assessment practices in an examination-oriented culture. *Assessment in Education: Principles, Policy & Practice*, *22*(1), 61–78. https://doi.org/10.1080/09695 94X.2014.1001319

Skedsmo, G., & Huber, S. G. (2019). Top-down and bottom-up approaches to improve educational quality: Their intended and unintended consequences. *Educational Assessment, Evaluation and Accountability*, *31*(1), 1–4. https://doi.org/10.1007/s11092-019-09294-8

Taylor, L. (2013). Communicating the theory, practice and principles of language testing to test stakeholders: Some reflections. *Language Testing*, *30*(3), 403–412. https://doi.org/10.1177/0265532213480338

Thompson, G. (2013). NAPLAN, MySchool and accountability: Teacher perceptions of the effects of testing. *International Education Journal: Comparative Perspectives, 12*(2), 62–84.

Thompson, G., Adie, L., & Klenowski, V. (2018). Validity and participation: Implications for school comparison of Australia's national assessment program. *Journal of Education Policy, 33*(6), 759–777. https://doi.org/10.1080/02680939.2017.1373407

van der Kleij, F. M., Cumming, J. J., & Looney, A. (2018). Policy expectations and support for teacher formative assessment in Australian education reform. *Assessment in Education: Principles, Policy & Practice, 25*(6), 620–637. https://doi.org/10.1080/0969594X.2017.1374924

Wiliam, D. (2013). Assessment: The bridge between teaching and learning. *Voices From The Middle:Urbana, 21*(2), 15–20.

Xu, Y., & Brown, G. T. L. (2016). Teacher assessment literacy in practice: A reconceptualization. *Teaching and Teacher Education, 58*(Supplement C), 149–162. https://doi.org/10.1016/j.tate.2016.05.010

Yan, Z., Chiu, M. M., & Ko, P. Y. (2020). Effects of self-assessment diaries on academic achievement, self-regulation, and motivation. *Assessment in Education: Principles, Policy & Practice, 27*(5), 562–583. https://doi.org/10.1080/0969594X.2020.1827221

Index

Note: Page numbers in *italics* and **bold** refer to figures and tables, respectively.

accountability-driven assessment practices 55–57, 63, 107, 152, 190–192, 216, 218

American Educational Research Association (AERA) 27

assessment *as* learning (AaL) 24, 61, 154, 156–157, 178

assessment culture 215, 217; curriculum structure 86–87; AfL practices 84–85; influence of leadership in 144–147; influence of teacher autonomy 84, 86–87; national professional development programs 85–87; principles of effective assessment 85; role of school leaders and teachers' agency 213; *see also* changes for improving assessment culture

assessment *for* learning (AfL) 24, 27, **28**, 29–31, 61, 107–108, 110, 171, 178, 181, 206; in Australia 33; in Brunei 35; definition 30; in high-stakes test environment 33; in Hong Kong 34; implementation of 33, 35; in Norway 190; in Norway and Portugal primary schools 84–86, 190–194; principles 28; reconceptualisation of 35; reforms 88–89; role and nature of teacher professional development 34; in Singapore 34; teacher understanding of 191

assessment literacy framework 169; descriptive frameworks and models 170–171; policy and contextual factors 169; prescriptive frameworks and models 171–172; research-based model 172–173

Assessment Literacy Inventory 11

assessment *of* learning (AoL) 24, 61, 178

assessment pedagogy, reconceptualising 50–54, 64–65; implications 53–54; problems and factors influencing problems 51–52; tensions and struggles of teachers 50–51

Assessment Reform Group (ARG) 26–27, 165, 190, 206, 214; definition of AfL 28; principles of AfL 28

assessment reforms 135, 137, 188; accountability approach to 190–192; balancing tensions in 190–194; bottom-up approach to 190–191, 193; case of AfL 88–89; complexities of implementing 92; contextual barriers for 198–201, 214; credibility of programme implementers and 192; cultural adaptation 93–94, 213; curriculum content and structure 212; design and implementation of 92–95; economic and productive sectors, involvement of 89; family social classes and 90–91; foreign expert's views 90; governance tradition and 89; historical dimension 87, 92; ideological dimension

87–88, 92; implications 193–194; linguistic adaptation 93, 213; parental involvement 213–214; pedagogical/ practical adaptation 94; political power and ideologies, role of 88; polysystems theory and critical discourse analysis 88; public opinion and 91; quality of teacher education, influence of 91; realigning of practices, expertise and policies 212; responsibilisation of stakeholders 211–212; role of school leaders in 144–147; stakeholders' understanding of 189; structural, organisational, social and behavioural factors 194–197; systemic dimension 87, 92; teacher assessment literacy adaptation 94–95; teachers' autonomy in implementing 192–193; teachers' resistance to 191–192; top-down approach to 188–189, 191

assessment strategies 1, 42; accountability-based 55–57; benefits of 54–55; effect of cultural, political and economic factors 9–10, 63, 131; future research 219–221; interactive nature of 45; nature of curriculum and 46; student outcomes, impact on 46, 80; students' involvement in 64; as teaching strategies 44–47

backwash effects of assessment 152
barometers of influence 2
Board of Studies Teaching and Educational Standards (BOSTES), Australia 33
Brunei Common Assessment Tasks (BCATs) 35

calibrated peer review (CPR) process 44
changes for improving assessment culture: conceptual 207–208; curriculum 208; knowledge and skills 209; paradigmatic

208; personal 206–207; policy 210–211; practical 209–210; shared organisational 211; social 207; structural and organisational 210

classroom assessments 12; accountability requirements 72; autonomy of teachers, importance of 73; bottom-up teacher-centred approach 72; collaborative approach to data use 73; context-driven nature of 75; data literacy skills and 70; description 69; factors influencing 70–71; goal-setting process 74; high-stake accountability mandates 70, 73; normative conditions 71; organisational and structural changes 75; relationships between content, pedagogy and 74; school data culture 72; self-reflection and adjustment process 72; state policies and frameworks, influence of 71; structural conditions 71; teacher-centred approach to data use 73; teachers' perception 70, 74–75

conceptualisation of assessment 217; Black and Wiliam's conception 26–27, 30–31; dichotomy between SA and FA 25–26, 37; factors influencing 63–64

conferencing 45
context-driven nature of assessment 75, 80, 198, 215, 218, 220
Core Skills Test 33
cultural adaptation of assessment 93–94, 213

dialogic feedback 50, 93–94
differentiated assessment 83

educational accountability 51
Educational Assessment of Students 11
effect size of an intervention 2–3
embedding assessment in learning and teaching, case study 47–50; assessment discourses in classrooms 49; classroom observations and fieldwork 48;

228 Index

data analysis 48; feedback content and processes 49; implications 50; importance of teacher feedback 48; overview of Swedish primary school 47–48
English as an additional language or dialect (EAL/D) learners 79
English language education, assessment for 34

fairness of assessment 126–129; ambiguous communication and 128; demographics' influence on 128; factors influencing 126–128; grade adjustment and 128; reliable or dependable data 127–128; students' emotional state and 128; students' perception 126; teachers' incorrect interpretation and application of grades and 126–127; teachers' use of personal rules and 127
feedback 25–26, **28**, 30, 42, 45, 83; actionable 43; content 49; dialogic 50, 93–94; importance of 48; individual 93; in peer assessment 103–104; processes 49; school students' conception of 49–50; as a strategy to improve students' motivation 43
formative assessment (FA) 24, 61, 120, 171, 216; application in specific key learning areas 64; of Australian Curriculum 142; Black and Wiliam's conception 26–27, 30–32, 61; definition 25, 27, 29–30; distinction between summative assessment (SA) and 25–26, 37, 61–62; effects in learning and teaching 26; importance of feedback 26; interconnectedness of SA and 30; problems with term 27
functions of classroom assessments, case study: description 62; factors influencing 63–64; integrated conceptualisation of FA and SA 62–63

holistic assessment system 137–138

Inside the Black Box 30

kindergarten education 153–157; appropriate assessment practices 156–157; priorities of 154–155; self-regulated learning and assessment 154–158; students' academic achievement 154–155; tension between FA and SA 155–158

leadership in assessment culture change 148; clear communication 146; context of national assessment accountabilities and community expectations 144–145; role of school leaders 145–147
learning from assessment, case study 44–47
linguistic adaptation of assessment 93, 213

monitoring: of student learning progress 5, 9, 28, 55, 100–101, 109, 113; of teachers' assessment practices 33, 82, 169, 193, 200; of teachers' implementation of assessment 203, 215, 218

National Assessment of Educational Progress 55
National Curriculum Task Group on Assessment and Teaching 27
needs-based professional development 181–185; competency-based approach (CBA) 181–182, 184; design 183; dynamic approach (DA) 181–182, 184; implications 183–184; role of school leaders 183
Norway's educational system 190

outcomes of assessment 164–166; learner motivation 164–165; 'other' outcomes 153, 165; social-emotional and behavioural outcomes 164–166; student academic achievement and self-efficacy as 161–164; student positive perception of learning

158–161; students' independence and self-regulation 153–154

parents' beliefs about assessment 137–138; 'bite-sized' assessments 140; implication for parental assessment literacy 140–141; policy of holistic assessment 138–139; use of high-stake tests 139–140
pedagogically-linked approach to assessment 94
pedagogical/practical adaptation of assessment 94
pedagogy experts 13, 42
peer assessment 2, 45; at Cyprus secondary school 101–105; engagement in 103; feedback 103–104; feedback provision 46–47; impact of inadequate training 103; impact on student learning 45; need for peer assessor training 104–105; risk of inaccurate assessment 104; students' understanding of assessment criteria and content 102–103; teacher support in 103; as a teaching strategy 46; validity and reliability of 102, 104; variability in marks 102
performance evaluation 169, 185, 218
professional development (PD) programmes 3, 8, 13, 15, 33–34, 142, 149, 157, 169–170, 172, 180, 183–185, 202, 206, 221; competency-based approach (CBA) 181–182, 184; design 183; dynamic approach (DA) 181–182, 184; impact on teacher assessment practices 87; implementation of ongoing 202, 214–215; in-service teachers' 181, 220–221; national 84–86; *see also* needs-based professional development
programmatic assessment 119
psychometrics 120, 131

questioning technique design and implementation 106; assessment literacy and 109–110; in Malaysian primary schools

107–110; monitoring of student responses 113; teachers' philosophical orientation 109

reliability and validity of teacher assessment 118–119, 129, 131; classroometric principles 118–120, 130

safe space for teacher experimentation 215
school-based assessment for learning (SBAfL) 35
school leaders 145–148; accountability requirements 147; communication skill 146; instructional leadership 146; intent 146; role in assessment reforms 144, 147; understanding of assessment 144–145; working with parents 146
self-regulated learning and assessment 2, 36, 153–158; design 163; knowledge tradition, influence of 163; levels of motivation 163; motivational and affective factors 163–164; self-assessment diaries 161–162; students' knowledge of 163; teacher preparation and effort 163; time for engaging in 162–163
space for teacher-student interactions 105–107, 215
stakeholder assessment literacy 136, 149
Standards for Teacher Competence in the Educational Assessment of Students 11
student achievement 1, 42, 152–153; effects of interventions on 2; feedback about students' performance 25; 'other' outcomes 153, 165; *see also* outcomes of assessment
student agency in assessment 106
student assessment literacy 98–101, 106, *112*, 148; affective or non-cognitive skills 113; identification, reporting, analysis and interpretation of feedback 113; influence of teacher assessment literacy on 107–110; involvement

230 Index

and participation in formative and summative assessments 112–113; monitoring of student responses 113; principles, processes and practices of assessment 111; reflective practices 113; valid and reliable strategies and decision-making skills 112

student learning 2, 4, 9, 11, 13, 62; autonomy 6; formative assessment (FA), impact of 79; peer assessments, impact of 45; students' language background and proficiency 93; summative assessment, impact of 29–30, 32, 36–37; teacher assessment literacy and 13–16; teacher interactions, effects of 9, 33; teacher judgement of 122–125; utilisation of assessment for 16–17, 25–27, 29, 31, 55

Students as Partners 101

students' attitudes towards FA and SA: affective and instrumental attitudes 66, 68; factors influencing 67–68; implications 68; meaningful purpose of assessment 66–67; personal factors 67; stage of schooling and 67; in terms of use 68

students' engagement in assessment 98; assessment literacy and 109–110; questioning-based discourse analytical framework 105; space for 105–107; teachers' philosophical orientation 109; see also peer assessment

students' perceptions of assessment practices: achievement levels 81–82; average-performing students 81; effectiveness of teacher's assessment 82; high-performing students 81; impact of differentiated assessment 83; preferences of assessment activity 82; of secondary English students 80–81; teacher monitoring of student responses 82; teacher's intention and 82–83

summative assessment (SA) 24, 61, 86, 118, 120, 145, 153, 171, 216; Biggs' critique 29–30, 61; definition 25; distinction between formative assessment (FA) and 25–26; effects on students' learning 29–30, 32, 36–37; interconnectedness of FA and 30

teacher assessment literacy 4, 64, 101, 106–110, 149, 169; adaptation 94–95; Brookhart's model 171; competencies 11; conceptual, praxeological and socio-emotional dimensions of 173–177; as a context-driven construct 169, 173, 178–181; in context of supporting student learning 13–16; Cowie and Bell's model 170; critical views of 11; Davison's model 170, 172; definition 16, 136; dimensions 11–13; discrepancy between teachers' perceived levels of literacy 179–181; factors shaping changes 10; framework *14*, 184–185; Harlen's model 170–171; Hill and McNamara's model 172; holistic view of 10; interpretation of assessment 10–11; key characteristics 16–18; as part of pedagogical content knowledge 181; Pastore and Andrade's model 176; professional development 170; relevance to classroom activities 15; understanding and expectations of stakeholders 11, 17–18; Wiliam and Thompson's model 171

teacher-based language assessment 120–121; 'best fit' appraisal 122; 'on balance' judgements 122; race and gender differences 121–122; of students' performance 122; task-based assessment criteria 122; teacher judgements 122–123; teacher reflexivity and meta-reflection 122; use of holistic and analytical thinking 121

Index   231

teacher implementation of assessment practices 201–203; appropriate articulation of policy 143; building students' capacity 203, 214; development of shared organisational assessment culture 202; formative assessment practices 141–142; implementation of ongoing PD 202, 214–215; monitoring scheme 203; policy-makers support 142–144; resources and tools for 202–203, 215; school influences 199–200

teacher judgement of students' learning 56, 122–125; classroom characteristics and 125; in high-SES classrooms 125; inaccurate judgement, effects of 124; reference-group effect 125; student characteristics and 124–125; of students' academic achievement 122–125

teachers' beliefs: about assessment to support learning and teaching 5–6; about learning 4–5; about student roles in assessment 6–7; as assessors 13; impact of contextual, cultural and personal factors 9–10, 63, 131; involvement in a Community of Practice 8–9; as motivators 13; as pedagogy experts 13, 42; role as assessors 8; as stakeholder partners 13; as student partners 13; students' performance 8; students' zone of proximal development (ZPD) 8; as teacher learners 13; teacher–student relationship in assessment 7–8

teacher time in assessment 107

theoretical and empirical support for using assessment 1–10; effect size of an intervention 2–3; importance of social interactions, cultural contexts and belief systems 4; influence on learning 4; in professional development 3; as a tool 4

Tools to Enhance Assessment Literacy for Teachers of English as an Additional Language 120

trustworthiness of assessment and assessment decisions 130–131, 216; assessment processes 131; capability and integrity of people 130; data management system 131; decision-making processes 131; impact of contextual, cultural and personal factors 131; influences of assessment policies 131; quality of assessment design, tools and strategies 130–131; see also fairness of assessment; teacher judgement of students' learning

zone of desired effects 2

zone of proximal development (ZPD) 8, 50–51

Printed in the United States
by Baker & Taylor Publisher Services